AF774075

Guerrilla Dancer

Guerrilla Dancer

Joan Stone

Anamcara Press LLC

Published in 2026 by Anamcara Press LLC

Photography by Dave Dickson, Virginia Blaisdell, Suzanne Burdick, and Terry Evans.
Editor Amber Fraley
Cover design by Amber Fraley
Book design by Maureen Carroll & Amber Fraley
Garamond, Gadugi, and DINosauar
Printed in the United States of America.

Book Description: Guerrilla Dancer is a vivid memoir of movement, protest, and personal awakening set against the turbulent social revolutions of the 1960s and 70s. Joan Stone traces how a lifelong devotion to dance fused with a growing political consciousness to create a new artistic path—one that leapt off the stage and into the streets.

ANAMCARA PRESS LLC
P.O. Box 442072, Lawrence, KS 66044
https://anamcara-press.com/

Ordering Information:
Quantity sales. Special discounts are available on quantity purchases by corporations, associations, and others. For details, contact the publisher at the address above.
Orders by U.S. trade bookstores and wholesalers. Please contact Ingram Distribution.

Brin, Joan Stone, Author
Guerrilla Dancer

SOC072000: SOCIAL SCIENCE / Activism & Social Justice (Primary category for general activism)
PER003040 PERFORMING ARTS / Dance / Modern
BIO001000: Biography & Autobiography / Artists, Architects, Photographers
ART015000: Art / Women Artists (or Women in Art)

ISBN-13: 978-1-960462-81-7 (Paperback)
Library of Congress Control Number: 2026935874

Contents

Dedicated To The University Of Kansas Dance Department

Photographs

Figure 01. Joan and Harris Stone (foreground) at a rally protesting the Vietnam War, Washington D.C., Spring 1965. Photographer unknown.

Introduction

It was the revolutionary moment of the late 1960s and early 1970s that turned me into a guerrilla dancer. I never would have suspected that my passion for dance and growing social consciousness since childhood would come together and set me on a journey which has continued for more than fifty years.

It was the moment of marches and meetings, meetings and marches
for civil rights
for an end to war
for women's rights
for saving central cities from corporate bulldozers.
It was the moment of rallying cries:
I have a dream!
Power to the people!
Hell no, we won't go!
Out from under women unite!
We shall overcome!

In that moment, dance assumed its ancient role as vital to culture. The doors of the theater opened, and dance moved back and forth between the stage and the street, with the street the more important venue. We suddenly found dance in our midst in the form of marches, parties, and happenings. Circles of people formed to hold hands, sway, and sing, "We shall overcome." People on streets and in parks, dressed in anything but business suits, rediscovered their torsos and limbs, abandoned their inhibitions, and danced the body electric.

In that moment dancers crossed the boundaries between ballet, modern, jazz, tap, ballroom, folk, and world dance forms. Some choreographers turned their backs on formal dance vocabularies and worked exclusively with gestures from everyday life, such as walking and stopping, running, sitting on chairs, dragging boxes and mattresses, and dressing and undressing. Non-dancers joined dancers in structured events. The movement-happenings of the moment were being shaped into dances, as the gestures of the court had been shaped into ballet dances, the rhythms of the countryside into folk dances, and the patterns of earth and sky into tribal dances.

I had danced since childhood in my hometown of New Haven, Connecticut. My first teachers were retired vaudeville performers, who taught a little tap, a little ballroom, and just enough ballet for me to move on to a great teacher. Jack Quinn had danced with the Metropolitan Opera Ballet in the 1930s, when the legendary Michel Fokine was the director. I performed in Mr. Quinn's versions of Mikhail Fokine's *Les Sylphides* and *Peter and the Wolf*. While dancing the role of Peter, I memorized all the other parts, so I could direct students in my junior high school for a production at our annual talent show. The following year, having learned excerpts from *Coppélia*, I recruited students for my own version of the whole ballet.

Yale also played a role in my development as a dancer and performer. In fifth grade, I was chosen to be one of the children in a Yale Drama School production of Georg Buchner's *Wozzeck*. In high school, Yale being all-male at the time, I was recruited to dance in musical versions of *The Great Gatsby* by F. Scott Fitzgerald and *Women of Trachis* by Ezra Pound. I knew that all three literary works were important, but it wasn't until college that I read and understood them.

At the age of eighteen, I was unsure about pursuing a professional career in ballet. As an all A's student from the inner city, I was awarded a big scholarship to attend Sarah Lawrence College, at the time, a liberal arts college for women in Bronxville, New York where only modern dance was taught. Ballet had to be pushed into the background, as I was introduced to the approaches of major figures in modern dance, including Martha Graham, José Limón, Lester Horton, Alwin Nikolais, and Murray Louis. Most important were the composition classes with Bessie Schönberg, where I began to discover my own voice as a choreographer and performer. I also started writing about dance in depth in a tutorial on *Psychology of Dance* with Rudolf Arnheim.

At the American Dance Festival in 1959, along with being Bessie's assistant, I studied with Merce Cunningham, Helen Tamiris, Daniel Nagrin, and composition with Louis Horst. These experiences gave me lots of ideas to draw upon when I began my own career as a choreographer, performer, teacher, and writer.

During the years of growing as a dancer, I was also developing a deep social consciousness. Born in 1939, I still have memories of World War II: the air raid warnings, the rationing, the parades, the big victory celebration in 1945. Soon after that war, which I thought would end wars, the United States entered another conflict in Korea, which started my questioning of war as a solution to world problems.

My anti-war thinking was also fostered by the experiences of my mother and father. Both of them were immigrants. My mother, Frances Chasnoff, left Ukraine in 1910 at age four. She came to the U.S. with an older sister, her parents, and her father's parents. My great grandmother was a shopkeeper, and during the pogroms, her shop was always targeted, and the family had to hide for their lives. My father, George Phillips (changed from Faiweuscewitz at Ellis Island) left Poland in 1921 at age sixteen. The town where he was born was totally destroyed during World War I. His parents died when he was young, and he moved with his oldest sister and her family to another town. The Holocaust came close to home, when her daughter arrived in New Haven with numbers on her arm from her imprisonment in Auschwitz, and told the story of how her mother and father were taken away one day; she never saw them again.

The late 1940s ushered in the Cold War with the Soviet Union and its infamous concomitant, the McCarthy period. The passage of the Smith and McCarron Acts had a devastating effect on the inner-city neighborhood, where I grew up. These two laws created broad and severe restrictions on civil liberties, causing fear while implicating anti-war activists. Families who had lived there for years disappeared overnight because of their left-leaning political views and activism. I returned from school one day and found my father at home because of a migraine. His face was ghostly white, not from the headache, but from what he was watching on television: the hearings of the House Un-American Activities Committee with Joseph McCarthy presiding.

This is the Inquisition," he said, "I never thought to see this in the United States."

Central to building my political consciousness was the rabbi from the reform temple where I went to Sabbath school. He was the first member of the clergy in Connecticut to speak out against McCarthy. In 1954-55, when I was a student in his confirmation class, we focused on the right to protest against authority, if in good conscience, we believed it to be oppressive and unjust. We read excerpts from the prophets, especially Jeremiah. We saw the film version of *The Cain Mutiny* by Herman Wouk and I heard about a Yale production of Billy Bud by Herman Melville and went to see it. I absorbed all of this history and politics without knowing where it was leading.

Three incidents come to mind that indicate the conflicting politics of my years at Sarah Lawrence: 1957-1961. On the one hand, the continuation of the McCarthy period: The folk singer Pete Seeger, known for protesting injustice, gave a concert at the college, which was picketed by the Connecticut Anti-Communist Crusade. He was told he could sing, but not speak. On the other hand, a thaw in McCarthy's witch hunt: My three suite mates and I went to the Figaro Café in New York City to see the films of Charlie Chaplin, which had been banned for ten years because of his association with Communism. And finally, a sign that the times were changing: In my senior year, I knew students who participated in the first sit-ins for the rights of African Americans that were taking place at a Howard Johnson's in a nearby shopping center.

At Sarah Lawrence, the non-dance courses broadened my perspective on world politics. In International Relations, one semester was devoted to the history of the Arab world, and I studied Israel's embattled position in the Middle East. In Anthropology, I wrote papers on how colonialism affected the Australian Aborigines and on creation myths of tribal societies in three different parts of the world, linking them with place and work. For a Shakespeare course, I researched the real Macbeth and found he was a good king, which taught me how history can be altered to fit the political agenda of a powerful leader.

While I was developing intellectually, my internal struggle is reflected in my decision to drop out of dance during my junior and senior year. Beginning in my sophomore year at Sarah Lawrence I knew something was wrong, but I didn't know what it was. I weighed 72 pounds; I wasn't anemic, because I studied the relationship of foods and nourishment. In the summer after my junior year, my brother, Alan who was in Yale Medical School, sent me to an internist with a psychological bent who gave a name to my problem. I learned that I had anorexia nervosa. Junior year of college, spring semester, I wanted to quit.

"You're so close to finishing, Josie. If you quit now, you'll regret it," said Alan. "When you graduate, you can travel, you can do what you want. But finish college first."

It helped to have discussions with Alan about things in our family history that contributed to the illness. We determined over many conversations that the root of my problem was that my father loved my mother, but she didn't love him. My father kept saying to me: "You should marry someone that you love. You both should love each other."

I wanted to LOVE. I began my recovery in my junior year, and got through it without being institutionalized, which would have killed me. Two years after college, I met Harris Stone. I taught second grade for a year, after college. Although I was very good at bringing out the creativity in my students in the form of dances, stories, and poems, I realized elementary school teaching was not for me. My salary gave me the funds to go to graduate school in anthropology at Columbia for a year. During that time, I met my future husband, Harris, who was an architect. We knew from the first date we were going to marry—we had each met our soul mate!

Our wedding took place on a momentous day in American history: August 28, 1963—the day of Martin Luther King's "I have a dream" speech. The rabbi, who sparked my awareness of protest politics, had gone to jail in Selma, Alabama, with King. Having developed a friendship with Harris and known me fondly for many years, he said: "Only for the two of you would I miss that march!"

Although I considered continuing my studies in anthropology, Harris asked, "What will I do when you go off to the Amazon to do field work?" I didn't want to be away from him and wasn't enough of a feminist to say, "You'll come with me." Instead I decided to learn more about Harris's field, architecture. New Haven was a Model City nationally for the Urban Renewal Program, which opened up new opportunities for architects, as old buildings were torn down and new ones constructed in their place. Prepared by my background in the social sciences, I took a research job in the New Haven City Plan Department. After a year of working, I wanted to find out more about urban planning and went through a master's program at Yale. Meanwhile Harris's private architectural practice was floundering, and he was hired by the Redevelopment Agency, the hub of Urban Renewal activity.

All this time, my compelling need to dance was as strong as ever, but how, what, where, why? I would not have thought that becoming a political activist would bring me back to dance, but that's what happened. The separate paths of dance and politics since childhood came together in 1966, when I joined the American Independent Movement (AIM), which grew out of Students for a Democratic Society (SDS) as a counter-voice to mainstream politics on issues such as equal rights, the Vietnam War, education, and urban renewal. As insiders who became disillusioned with the urban renewal program, Harris and I were particularly qualified to lead the fight against it. Suddenly, there were things to dance about and people to dance for. I realized dance could be a social as well as a personal quest, a reach outward to history and nature, as well as inward to self and personal experience. It wasn't necessary to dance on the stage of a theater or master anyone's technique except my own. I could dance wherever there was a space and whenever there was a significant reason. Clear a space and I'll dance!

Once my dual concerns—dance and politics—started to merge and develop, solo and group mobile theater works emerged one after the other. I also began a journal, which I've kept from 1967 to the present. The entries are not daily, but frequent enough to follow my struggles as a dancer and thinker in an ever-changing historic context. In addition to the journal, I've kept an archive of choreographic notes and a record of my performances with date, place, program, and commentary. The raw notes have the liveliness of a new and daunting exploration, which I've tried to preserve in a more readable form for this book. The chapters deal with the dances of my activist period (1967 to 1972) in the order in which I composed them. Each account begins with the process of choreographing the dance. I move on to how it played out in performance. And then, the audience reaction, which was usually extensive, because I was performing up close to people about issues that were affecting their lives.

A dancer's life is about dancing, but our movements are so difficult to translate into words that writers tend to minimize the descriptions. As a dancer and writer, I have worked to weave the moves into the narrative of events in such a way that the reader can visualize the gestures, follow the spatial configurations, feel the rhythms, and even sense the emotion: the difference between a sharp kick and a slow kneel to the floor. I've used as few strictly dance terms as possible, choosing instead movement words that we all know. One reader of a draft wondered if he should try to do the moves, and I answered with a fervent yes! That would be a way of adding experiential understanding to both the dance and the social issues I was embodying.

Time and again, I have asked myself why the actions of the human body can't be as interesting to read about as the actions of grasses, clouds, and rivers. Since choreographing my first pieces, gesture has been my focus, often turning to literature and the visual arts for ideas. For me, gesture brings together the movement and the word. I have experimented with gestural writing for decades and hope the results in Guerrilla Dancer will lead to a verbal, visual, and visceral experience for readers.

By 1976 when Harris was teaching at Hampshire College in Amherst, Massachusetts, and we moved to Northampton, MA, the revolutionary moment of marches, meetings, and rallying cries had passed, and the portal between theater and street had closed. But the ideals of that period have continued to sustain me. Each time I make and perform a dance and lead people in the lines and circles of a farandole, a dance that probably goes back thousands of years to the first time people joined hands and discovered the power of moving together, echoes of that moment surge up and keep me dancing and encouraging others to clear a space and dance.

Figure 02. Joan Stone, Guerilla Dancer

Chapter One: Dances Against Comfort

1967 Marches and Meetings

During the marching and meeting days, Harris went to all the counter-culture events with me, and they changed both our lives. While I was searching for a pathway as a dancer, he was finding his way as an architect. We attended happenings, plays, films, and art shows within driving distance from New Haven. We saw performances of dances by Merce Cunningham, Anna Halprin, and Yvonne Rainer, on which Harris commented in fascinating and insightful ways, especially about the use of space and the structure of the works. We walked the streets talking about architecture and city planning, and he enjoyed my gestural and rhythmic responses, saying they brought the buildings and spaces to life. I was reading Bertolt Brecht's poems, plays, and writings on theater, searching for guidelines on art and politics, and would read sections out loud to Harris. We had long discussions about everything we were seeing, reading, and doing. When I found rehearsal space in the basement of an arts center, I persuaded Harris to work with me on a duet for dancer and architect, my first venture into choreography of the moment.

1967 Duet for Dancer and Architect

The arts center space served as an auditorium as well as a classroom for art students. There was a small raised stage at one end and a large open space below where chairs could be set up for an audience. Following the experiments of the time, Harris and I immediately decided to put the chairs and audience on the small stage and use the large open space for our performance area, allowing its layout to influence the choreography. Objects for the art classes—a model's platform, tripod, easels, paintings, stools, and tables—became the set and props for the piece. Whatever lights were in the room served as theatrical lights, which we changed in full view of the onlookers.

Harris had no dance training, though at one time he had thought of becoming an actor. He moved with confidence and concentration, had a buoyant walk, had worked construction, and was a strong, graceful swimmer, all of which could be turned into movement sequences. To guide the choreography I worked with the piano version of *Pictures at an Exhibition* by Modest Mussorgsky, which seemed fitting for a dance created and performed in the midst of a space used for art classes. The music is structured as a rondo with a haunting theme that begins and ends the piece and links the episodes of different moods, textures, and tempos. Mussorgsky designed the score programmatically to evoke a person walking, pausing to look at a picture, walking and pausing, walking and looking. I decided to use the recurring theme for everyday actions or tasks, such as changing costumes, props, and set, and the episodes or pictures for more formalized dance sections.

For two months, Harris took as much time as he could from his architectural job to rehearse, and when he couldn't join me I worked alone, reviving old studies and creating new ones. We used a recording of *Pictures* for rehearsals, but by a happy coincidence had a live pianist for our performances. When I went to the Yale Music Library to look at the score of *Pictures*, I walked by a rehearsal studio where to my amazement someone was playing the piece. I knocked and went in, and it didn't take much persuasion to convince the graduate student to play for us. He liked the concept of the dance and turned out to be an excellent accompanist.

Harris and I talked, laughed, argued, and practiced things again and again, and finally *Pictures* was ready for an audience. I scheduled two performances, the first for friends in AIM and the second for the board and faculty of the arts center where we had been rehearsing. The heating system had broken down several times, and sure enough, on the day of the first performance—a frigid Sunday in February—when we went to the building for a last run-through, there was no heat. I had to telephone all the friends we had invited and ask them to come the following Sunday. Some decided to come on Tuesday to the second performance, which went on as planned. Very few of those invited from the arts group appeared. One board member said I had picked a bad time: everyone was away skiing. Unknown to me there was an art class scheduled to meet that night in a corner of the auditorium. I enlarged the audience to about thirty by persuading the class to watch the performance and to work before and after it.

Premiere of Pictures at An Exhibition: Duet for Dancer and Architect

As the pianist played the grand opening theme of Mussorgsky's music, I made a grand entrance standing on a model's platform, wheeled by Harris. (The audience tittered as we approached the stage.)

I stepped off the platform and skittered in and out of flat, two-dimensional moves, accented by sharp turns of the head, like a figure escaped from an ancient frieze. (More tittering came from the audience at the sharp movements.)

While I changed accessories to a basic costume of black tights and top, Harris, also dressed in black, set up a tripod and then acted as a mock photographer for a circle dance—arms, legs, torso, the whole body circling on axis and through space to create a moving landscape.

I watched as Harris changed clothes and then danced a solo of effort and play, based on swimming motions.

A contrapuntal duet followed. Harris walked three distinct spatial pathways at different tempi, while I lunged, crawled, and marched along intersecting pathways, suggesting people on the New Haven green.

Harris set up a table with a light over it. I climbed up on the table and put on a yellow chiffon sack, tied at the top and open at the bottom, which covered me from head to toe. Like a chick emerging from its shell, I kicked, wiggled, punched, bent this way and that, shrugged, and shook, and finally freed myself from the sack.

A story duet followed with me acting as the servant, placing stools one after the other for Harris as the master to step on, until the servant rebelled by climbing up on a stool and confronting the master eye to eye.

Harris and I changed costumes, props, and lighting and performed a task duet—a frantic race to find easels, line them up, and put paintings on them. The trick was to place the last painting on an easel exactly on the last chord of the music. We did it! (And the audience applauded.)

Illuminated by only one light held by Harris, I moved along the floor as if stuck in a cave—hands always tied to feet, body extending and retracting, rolling and writhing, culminating in a sustained tied and twisted pose, and then a release.

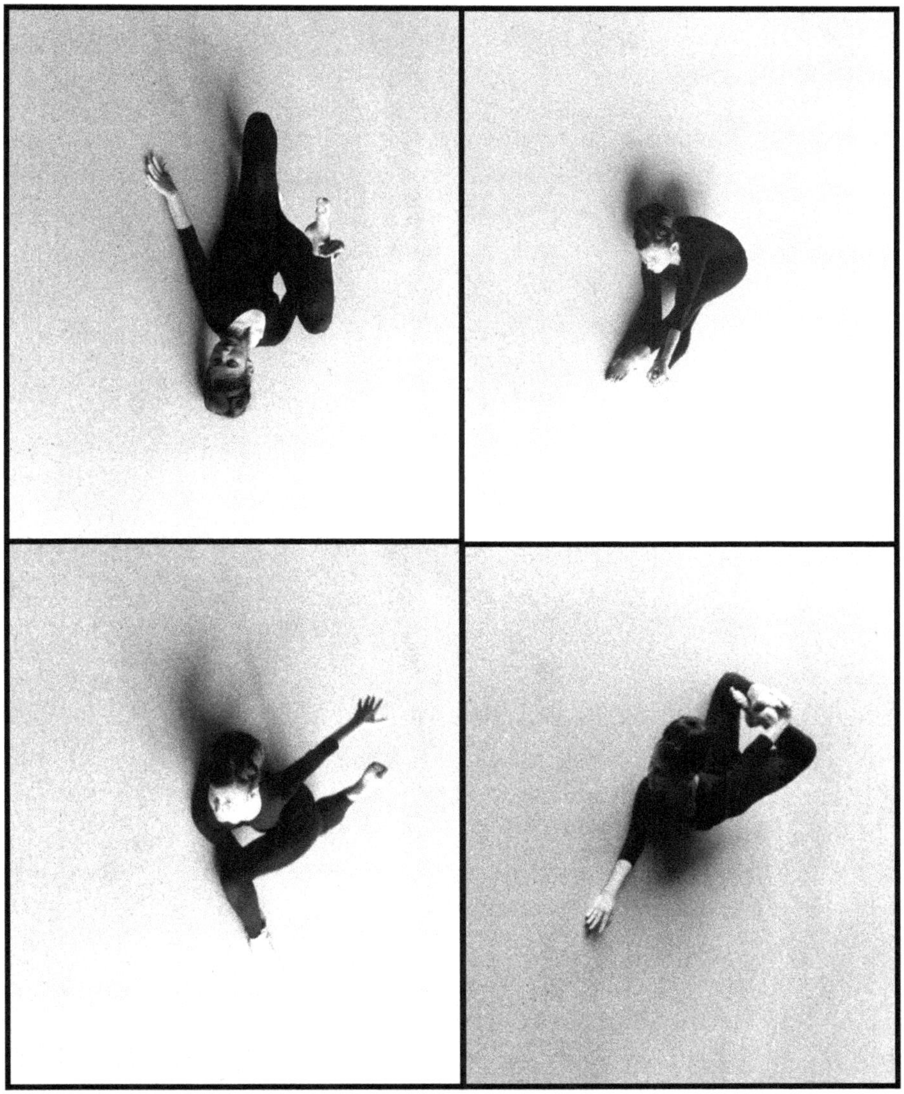

Figure 03. "Hands Grasping Feet."
Read from top right—counter clockwise—to bottom right.

Harris put the light down and stretched out on the floor. To demonic-sounding music, inspired by the witch Baba Yaga, I approached with bold hitch-kicks and struts, walked on the prone body, leaped over and around it, and strutted away.

For the finale, as Mussorgsky's theme built to a monumental climax, Harris swept the performance space with a broom and then piled tables and chairs on top of each other to make a high platform. I put on ballet slippers, a sash, and a crown of flowers and ascended to the top, assuming more and more triumphant poses, as Harris switched all the available lights on and off, on and off, on and off.

A GOOD BEGINNING I wrote in all capital letters in my journal. Harris was at ease and delightful from beginning to end of the premiere. I was nervous about dancing after a long hiatus, but made it through everything and was overwhelmed to receive a red rose from a spectator. A few nights later, I performed more confidently for the larger audience of friends, who laughed and applauded at all the right moments and gathered around us at the end.

One friend observed: "The gestures were literal and yet not—literal and abstract at the same time." Another commented: "I liked the political implications of the smaller person finding ways to challenge and even overcome the bigger one." Two of our friends had a disagreement. One said, "You've made us laugh. Can you make us cry?" The other countered, "Comedy is more difficult, especially in dance. Stay with comedy."

Duet for Dancer and Architect had only one more performance at a nearby state college about a year later, but it laid the groundwork for much of what came after. Harris returned to architecture, and I took on the challenge of creating and organizing a mobile theater event as part of local activities prior to a national mobilization against the war in Vietnam.

1967 Mobile Theater: Anti-War Collage

Eight members of AIM, including Bob Cook, the candidate we were running for U.S. Congress in Connecticut's third district, agreed to perform in a fifteen-minute collage of anti-war songs, poems, dances, and short speeches by famous and anonymous people. After many trips to the police department and the Department of Traffic and Parking, we finally secured permits to appear on the downtown Green, in a parking lot way behind a high school, in two parks frequented only by insects and birds, and on the campus of Yale University.

We tried to rent a flatbed truck for our performances, but the rental agency said there was no truck available, until Bob Cook called the manager, who immediately found a vehicle for us. Then the Department of Traffic and Parking told us we couldn't park the truck anywhere, because every street in New Haven is a highway. We could have challenged that declaration, but came up with an alternative, which was less trouble, cheaper, and turned out to be better. We collected twenty-four large coffee cans, painted them bright red, filled them with rocks, and set them up to define a rectangular playing area wherever we went. From the first performance we realized that being on the same level and up close to spectators had the decided advantage of encouraging more interaction.

Bob Cook began the happening by going right up to the audience and saying:

Don't be afraid of asking, friends!
Don't be won over, see for yourselves.
What we don't know ourselves, we don't know.[1]

As Bob played the guitar, the rest of the cast marched in, dragging one leg and one arm and singing:

Where are the legs that used to run,
When first you learned to carry a gun?
I fear your dancing days are done ...[2]

A speaker broke away to quote a poet of far away and long ago, as the rest of the group slowly kneeled down:

The city in utter confusion ...
And I turned into a refugee ...
Everywhere the bones of the dead were scattered,
And on the roads were starving women,
Putting the children they could not feed
Into the grass to die.[3]

'War,' 'war,' 'war,' 'war,' 'war,' 'war,' 'war,' 'war'—eight different voices, one at a time.

Half of the performers stood up and spoke: a *massacre of people who do not know each other ... The other half stood up and spoke: for the profit of people who know each other but do not massacre each other.*[4]

Kill for peace ... kill, kill, kill for peace ... the guitar player sang out in irony, quoting politicians who spoke the same words in earnest.[5]

Bob stepped to the center of the performing area to read a presidential statement: *There are those that say I ought to drop bombs to wipe out enemy supply lines, but we don't want to get tied down in a land war ...*[6]

The performers divided into two groups to recite responsively:

Group one—*When the leaders speak of peace*
Group two—*The common folk know that war is coming.*
Group one—*When the leaders curse war*
Group two—*The mobilization order is already written out.*[7]

Did anyone in any of the Mobile Theater audiences recognize the words of a Vietnam veteran and local political activist before joining the Black Panthers, who survived the war, only to die at home protesting racial injustice?

I *was on an aircraft carrier. We never had any feeling about killing people. Even the pilots, most of them just went ahead with orders ... They would bomb roads in the day, and at night hundreds of old people and children would work filling up the craters with sand. So the planes would drop flares and come in low and strafe them. That was the big joke of the fleet. Here were those poor people trying to fill the roads by hand and we with our machines could mow them down. I guess it showed the supremacy of imperialist technology or something ... The people we bombed couldn't fight back.*[8]

And how many deaths must there be till we know / That too many people have died? sang the group. *The answer is blowin' in the wind ...*[9] I danced to that song—swings, runs, falls, and reaches from modern dance, an art form that grew out of protest and thrives in periods of unrest.

A tribal peace chant followed the dance. The performers in a cluster reached up with one arm and said: *The clear sky is good.* They crouched, slapped their hands down, and said: *The green fruitful earth is good.* They rose, faced each other, and said: *But peace among people is better.* They turned, faced outward to the audience, and said: *But peace among people is better.*[10]

Then I began a simple polka step in silence around the perimeter defined by the red coffee cans. The guitarist picked up on the rhythm and started to sing: *We ain't gonna study war no more ...*[11] One by one the group joined in the song and dance, ending in a circle with each person's right arm on the shoulder of the next person.

Speaking in unison: *We call for the enlistment of people and resources in a fight against our real enemies ...*

Speaking successively: *'hunger,' 'disease,' 'ignorance,' 'hate,' 'fear,' 'hopelessness,' 'apathy,' 'discrimination,' 'inequality.'*

The group dispersed to distribute leaflets about the upcoming mobilization, leaving the final words to the candidate:

Add up the reckoning,
It's we who must pay it.
Put your finger on each item,
Ask: how did this get here?
We must take over the leadership.[12]

The most successful presentations were on the Yale campus, where lots of people gathered, watched, and responded. A pretty good crowd collected in front of the headquarters of the Hill Parents Association (HPA), an inner-city civil rights group that had a close connection with AIM. But only a few people stayed from beginning to end. The rest came and went, and the cast and I realized that our effectiveness with this important audience was limited. At a high school, only a few previously informed supporters and a group of hecklers made their way to a distant parking lot. The performance was difficult, but the political exchange following it was valuable for performers and audience.

On the Downtown Green there was one good presentation for political supporters. At the other one, we thought we had collected a real grassroots audience only to discover that most of the grassroots were local, state, or federal agents on a training mission. When I tried to track down a photograph of the performance that appeared in the *New Haven Register*, the photographer said: "I don't have it. I gave it to the F ... B ... Oops!"

"The F.B.I.?" I asked. "I'll get it from them."

A member of the cast accompanied me to the local F.B.I. office. There were two agents shuffling papers and moving about their desks as we entered. They stopped and stared at us. I asked for the photograph of our theater event that had appeared in the *Register* to use for an article in our newsletter. After looking at each other and hesitating, one of the agents went to another room, returned almost immediately with the photograph, and handed it to me. Not another word was spoken. The agents remained standing and staring, as the cast member and I went out the door.

There was one presentation of the anti-war collage in a renewed inner-city neighborhood where lots of singing, dancing, and knocking on doors finally managed to attract six children, three dogs, one parent, and a motorcycle cop. Low densities, which prevailed throughout the city, especially since urban renewal, posed an enormous problem for street theater.

"How about shopping centers?" someone suggested.

Calls to them resulted in predictable responses: "Shopping centers are strictly for shoppers and shopping."

A lawyer said that could be challenged, but I realized that Mobile Theater didn't have flamboyant enough theatrical techniques to make itself audible and visible, and members of the cast had other commitments that limited their time for rehearsing and performing. All in all, the difficulties of street theater seemed to outweigh the advantages, and I decided, at least for the time being, to concentrate on dancing as a soloist.

1967

WHEN THE LANDLORD LEFT, I DID THE ONLY THING A POOR SOUL CAN DO, I WALKED AROUND THE ROOM AND SCRATCHED MY HEAD

At an AIM meeting, in which we were discussing the effects of urban renewal on inner-city neighborhoods, a tenant from the last neighborhood slated for the bulldozer claimed the floor:

"I was at home needing rest because I hurt my leg at work. A social worker came to check up on me. A cop barged in with questions. A Yale student wanted information for the university newspaper. Somebody from a concerned citizens group came for an interview. A housing inspector walked in to look around. At the end of the day, the landlord knocked on the door and said: 'This building has been sold. You'll have to move.' The fifth move due to urban renewal! When the landlord left, I did the only thing a poor soul can do, I walked around the room and scratched my head."

That last line immediately triggered movement ideas and ultimately became the title of a new dance. Having worked for the New Haven Redevelopment Agency, studied city planning at Yale, and written my master's thesis on relocation caused by urban renewal, I was familiar with each character and event in the tenant's story. It was more revealing of urban renewal and its impact on the people least able to fight it than any official or academic document. The problem was how to make the story into a dance.

I began by establishing movement motifs for each character:
a slow limping walk for **Inner-city Tenant;**
a toe-heel, legs apart, body leaning back, hands-tucked-under-the-chin step for **Landlord;**
a striding and stamping pattern for **Police Officer;**
quick little steps on the toes to move around and tap dance steps at stopping points for **Social Worker;**
scrapes of the feet along the floor, rocks backward, and bends forward for **Housing Inspector;**
runs alternating with falls to the floor and a syncopated nonchalant walk for **Student;**
a brisk march, abrupt stops, and grooming motions for **Concerned Citizen;**
deep glides, slow turns, and slashes of the arms with hands clasped for **Bulldozer**.

A chair became a central storytelling ingredient.
Inner-city Tenant carried it in,
Landlord sat on it,

Police Officer knocked it down,
Social Worker danced around the fallen chair,
Housing Inspector examined it,
Student picked it up,
Concerned Citizen moved it around only to put it back where it was at the start,
Bulldozer removed it.

After developing the movement motifs into two- or three-minute character sketches with the chair as a pivotal prop, I despaired of getting the sketches to coalesce into a piece. I asked Harris to come and see what I had done so far. He watched with his usual palpable intensity and at the end nodded his head in approval. Then without saying a word, he started collecting all the chairs in the room and moving them around. When he finished they formed a room-like arrangement for the audience to sit on. There were two short lines of chairs facing each other that became a corridor for entrances and exits. There was a long line and a curved line of chairs that formed a wall with a bay window. There was a broken line of chairs that pointed toward a freestanding corner of chairs. Each character could move in and out, around and through the unusual lines and spaces in a different way.

The central chair, within an arrangement of chairs on which the audience sat, within the larger space in which the performance occurred, allowed me to dance eight different characters in relation to self, immediate audience, and larger world. Moreover Harris's chair arrangement set off an ongoing exploration of space as a narrative ingredient of choreography. After the first few performances—and especially after—I added more dances to my repertory and I no longer had to set up the chair arrangement. The spatial patterns were built into the dance, and I could perform it in any large space or even on a stage, though it had more impact up close to the audience.

I danced *When the Landlord Left…* in many different spaces in the neighborhoods of New Haven from 1967 to 1972. People, who opposed tearing up inner-city neighborhoods and removing residents to make way for highways, corporate headquarters, and other uses desired by the ruling elite, nodded in agreement, laughed, clapped, and sometimes asked for an encore. People, who lived further from the urban upheaval or expected more traditional dance or disagreed with the point of view on politics and/or aesthetics, frowned, crumpled their programs, refused to watch, turned their backs, and even walked out.

At a Senior Center a loud argument broke out when **Police Officer** attacked the chair. I could hear the contending voices as I continued dancing.

First voice: "It's not like that."

Second voice: "Yes, it is."

First voice: "No, it's not. The dance and you are both wrong."

Second voice: "Have you seen what's happening in this neighborhood?"

New voice: "Come on, we have to get out of here."

For a few performances, I used lighting to underline the behavior of the characters. At a social action meeting of a religious group, the audience shrunk by a quarter when **Concerned Citizen** entered the performing space with the lights turned off, and proceeded to drag and bump the chair around in the dark.

At first I didn't mind when someone walked out in anger, reasoning that it was better to provoke a strong reaction in people than to have them sitting passively, going to sleep, or leaving out of boredom. For some, the discomfort did what I hoped it would do. One person commented:

"We don't understand the characters you're portraying. That's our fault, not yours."

Another person called a week after a performance and said:

"I can't stop thinking about the dance. Thank you for presenting things I've never thought about before."

For others, the experience was too much—totally negative.

After more thinking and talking with Harris and our AIM friends, I concluded that the challenge of dancing on the same level and right up close to viewers was not to drive them out, but to try and set off a significant dialogue. I would dance, spectators would react, and we would discuss my dance and their reactions. I would change, some of them would change, and my dances would change. In this way, the making of dance would become a social as well as an individual process.

I began to test the process with political co-workers. After a performance of *When the Landlord Left...* one of them commented that my portrayal of the landlord was too one-dimensional. He was developing a good relationship with a landlord, who listened to different views of the issues, sympathized with the plight of tenants, and saw the urban renewal program as making inner-city problems worse. I experimented with the timing and sequence of the landlord's gestures, introducing moments of slowing down, looking up, and stopping, interspersed with the more aggressive toe-heels, grabs, and claps. A more general question came into my mind: How does one indicate in dance terms a character's potential for change?

Another political co-worker, remembering an article on the police in the AIM Newsletter that brought a request from the local force for thirty copies, questioned the portrayal of the police officer as the embodiment of brutality. I took a few ideas from the article—added grunts and clearings of the throat, a humorous gesture of pulling up my trousers, and a friendly salute—and began to receive a positive response from those, who would have been angered by the earlier version.

Columbia Liberation School

I don't remember who invited Harris and me to give a presentation at the Columbia Liberation School in New York City about AIM's anti-urban renewal activities. My journal includes very scanty notes, not even the exact date, just July 1968. I do remember the thrill of seeing the red flag flying at the entrance to the School, which took over a fraternity house at Columbia University, where I was a graduate student in anthropology from 1962 to 1963. I also remember the small narrow living room, where I performed, trying not to trip over the furniture, and the audience of about twenty people, hardy and committed enough to come to an urban problems seminar on one of the hottest days of the summer.

About the reaction to *When the Landlord Left...*, my only remembrance is a disagreement between two audience members about the characterization of the social worker.

One said: "I'm a social worker"—big grin—"and your character is so clear, so right, I wish the whole Welfare Department could see your piece."

The other person said: "I don't agree with your characterization. I have friends who are social workers. They're trying—they're doing the best they can."

I didn't change the movements of the social worker, though the exchange made me think about the difference between caricature and character.

Performances in New Haven Area Schools

High School

At a suburban high school, when I appeared for a second performance—at the first there were about twenty-five students and at the second, more than eighty—an administrator asked me if I ever presented the positive view of urban renewal.

"No," I said, "The *New Haven Register* does a good job of that."

The questioning continued: "Are there other dancers, who present that view?"

"I don't know of any," I replied, "most dancers stay away from politics."

The administrator was clearly agitated about the political club in the high school that had organized the performances. That group wanted more of their peers to think and talk about social issues and take action.

The students proved to be acute observers. They questioned and commented on both the politics and aesthetics of *When the Landlord Left...*

"There were no words, but there were sounds. The police officer's rap was sharp and short, whereas the social worker went on and on."

"Why did the police officer keep turning away from the audience?"

"Why did the student pick up the chair and not another character?"

"Why did the housing inspector turn out the lights?"

"I wanted you to show the inner-city tenant's reaction to each character."

"That would make an interesting duet," I replied.

"How would you portray a radical?"

"That's a portrait I have yet to make," was my response.

A week after the performance one of the students came to an AIM meeting and spoke to me afterwards. "I'm writing a play about war. A whole bunch of characters confront a soldier. It's kind of like your dance."

Alternate Public School

The teacher, who invited me to perform for a group of inner-city students in an alternate public school program, was a little apprehensive. They had walked out on several speakers. How would they react to a solo dance in silence? *When the Landlord Left...* was based on the story of an inner-city person, who had been my imagined audience all through the time I was composing the dance. The students not only responded to each character during the performance, but also stayed and talked.

"That person on the chair ... just like my uncle ... nothing to do but sit and look at his hands."

"Your foot taps are very good. Could you teach 'em to me?"

"My friend..."

"My cousin..."

"My family got moved out by urban renewal."

Elementary School

A local support group for dance activities asked me to give a lecture-demonstration in an elementary school, prior to a children's concert by a New York modern dance company. Although angry that the support group put all its energy and money into promoting New York dancers and gave no help to local ones, I agreed to make a presentation.

All the fifth- and sixth graders were marched into the gymnasium and herded with shouts and whistle-blowing into bleachers against the walls on three sides. The teachers left, shutting the gym doors behind them, and the battle began. I tried to speak about the upcoming concert. It was hopeless against the incessant talking and laughing. Maybe dancing *When the Landlord Left...* would work. I carried a heavy chair into the center of the space and crashed it down on the floor. There was momentary silence, which allowed me to say:

"This is a dance about a person from your neighborhood, who was pushed around by urban renewal."

I plunged into the various characters, trying to ignore the noise that built to a crescendo, died down, and revved up again. The students found sexual innuendos in every motion. Raising the chair overhead as I danced Bulldozer, I was tempted to crash it down on a few heads. The threatening gesture quieted the crowd, and soon after, the dance, or rather the ordeal, was over.

A trio of students broke away from their class and came to where I was changing shoes and preparing to leave.

"How much did you get paid for doing this?" one of them asked.

"Nothing!" I said.

"Why did you do it?" another one asked.

"Good question. Because I believe in the art of dance."

"Oh," they said.

The trio accompanied me down the hall to the exit doors. A teacher came out of a classroom and said,

"I looked in. The kids were talking, but they were in their seats, not hitting each other or throwing things. Thanks for coming."

The trio continued to walk down the hall with me. I became aware that one of them was imitating the housing inspector's scraping and rocking gestures. When we reached the exit doors he waved good-by right on pulse. I waved back.

Parochial School

For an arts festival at an all-girls parochial school, I was asked to speak as well as dance. I had been reading a lot about art and politics, and my ideas came together in response to an article in *Time Magazine* (March 15, 1968), titled *Dance: The Great Leap Forward.* After performing *When the Landlord Left...* I gave the following speech:

Dance and Politics

In the national magazine article I'm holding in my hand, dance is pictured as
a world of youth, beauty, and unlimited money;
a world of clean, dazzling technology well under control;
a world of fantasy, escape, and abstraction.

In sharp contrast is the scene on the streets of our cities and towns, where most people are not in their teens and twenties, are not beautiful as defined by magazines, and don't have unlimited money. Most couldn't afford to go to the dance concerts discussed in the article.

There are lights on the streets of our towns, but not strobe or spotlights; colors and technology, but not under control. From automobiles, the most prevalent technological sign, exhaust emanates that dulls all lights and colors. The daily scene is technology out of control—take a deep breath or a sip of tap water, and you'll know what I mean.

On stage: fantasy, escape, and abstraction. Just outside the theater: a person vomiting in a doorway, an armed police officer on the run, two children screaming and pulling on an adult loaded down with bundles waiting for a bus, a person in ragged clothes picking through a trash can, and an old person on a bench.

All of a sudden something is wrong with the picture of the dance world—just as something is wrong with the ad in the same magazine for a gold Cadillac with a chauffeur and young couples in evening dress in front of a luxury hotel. What's wrong is that it's a picture that excludes most of the people of this nation (let alone the rest of the globe), and a picture that excludes most of the issues of the real world. It's those people and those issues that a dancer like myself tries to address.

Youth and beauty

In well-known dance companies, performers tend to be in their late teens or twenties—younger in ballet and musical theater than in modern. Have a look at audition notices for ballet companies: dancers between the ages of fourteen and twenty only!

'How do we choose? We take the most beautiful,' boasts a ballet adjudicator.

The few, who are accepted from a line of hopefuls stretching around a city block, 'are properly proud and a little haughty,' says the magazine article, which goes on to quote a seventeen-year-old: 'We saw an old film of international ballet stars, and I can tell you that they were pretty bad. I don't think they would get accepted here today. They just weren't good enough.'

If you are over twenty and not better than the ballet stars of the past, forget it—or become a different kind of dancer! Hardly anyone in the chorus of a ballet company is over thirty. Stars can age a little, but few dancers last to forty, let alone fifty or seventy.

Spectacular dance is a cult of youth and beauty. Its history is a history of increasing specialization, athletic virtuosity, and therefore exclusiveness in terms of age and appearance. Yet many of us dance even if we have a flaw or two, and some of us are not stopped by aging. We imperfect and long-distance ones seek out unusual gestures, rhythms, and spatial designs. Sometimes we dance in very interesting ways that inspire audience members to think, talk, laugh, weep, and best of all, dance themselves.

Unlimited money

It costs a lot to achieve a look of unlimited money. The prominent dance groups that look in the national magazine article and on stage as if they have unlimited money do not, of course. Costs are prohibitive. Fund-raising is a major activity. Although ticket prices are high, intake at the box office does not begin to cover expenses. Programs must please those who can afford to come and see and finance them. Controversial ballets even by renowned choreographers quietly disappear from a repertory. Big budget groups can do only things that are 'no risk.'

For dancers who aspire to be 'peerless pros,' costs are also prohibitive: lessons with star-making teachers, shoes and other appearance-related paraphernalia, transportation to-and-from or a place to live in a big city. Who can afford to be such a dancer? Very few of us. What happens to those who are not chosen?

If it cost a lot of money to perform my dances, I couldn't be here today, and that would be a loss. If I needed a lot of money to make my dances, I couldn't dance, and that would be tragic. Without experimentation dance dies. More of us need to take advantage of the freedom to try out our ideas, to make mistakes, to have small successes, to be hated by some and loved by others.

Technology under control

Beginning with the cover, the photographs in the article under discussion document striking productions, 'riots of sight and sound.' Does the lighting dazzle without illuminating? Do the projections and sound-assaults conceal rather than reveal? Does technology come across as magic or a usable tool? We may choose to follow the lead of the old avant-garde, who believed in showing control over production technology in full view of the audience—or we may choose to ask if face-to-face communication still has any meaning. Dance, dancer, audience: is there a need for anything more?

Fantasy, escape, abstraction

The magazine writer devotes only a few sentences of a ten-page article to what dances say and how they say it. Works with social and psychological content are mentioned for bleak diversion from the tribute to 'glitter and grin.' The emphasis in the writing as in the dance world described is on 'show' and 'business,' both of which favor a theater of fantasy, escape, and abstraction as an end in itself to a theater of realism, questioning, and abstraction as a way of processing raw material. Members of the audience have to leave their seats wanting to buy more tickets and products, not wanting to make their own dances, that is, their own lives.

The picture of dance in the national magazine leads to a lot of daydreaming, but not action. If you have to dance no matter what, read the article but then throw it away or argue with it. The odds are against your having the looks, talent, training, money, and luck to be one of the few photographed there. You are more likely to be just one of the many who want to dance, in which case the task is to figure out what a person can do with an idea, a desire to communicate it through movement, and a lot of hard work.

A few mothers and daughters remained to offer comments.

Figure 04. Speaking to students at a parochial school after performing *When the Landlord Left* . . . (1968). Photographer unknown.

One mother said, "I can't afford to send my daughter to New York for ballet lessons. Now I feel encouraged about alternatives." Heads nodded in agreement.

Another mother remarked, "I was excited to see you dancing about social issues and hope my daughter will pick up on that."

One of the students said, "I think it would be easier to dance in a ballet company or a musical than to do what you do."

That comment surprised me and gave me pause.

Yale Architecture Students

On the spur of the moment I had the opportunity to perform *When the Landlord Left...* for a group of architecture students. They had walked out of a regional architects' convention and set up their own counter-convention. Harris, who had been invited to speak and lead one of the seminars at the main convention, left with the students. My dance turned out to be a good starting point for an extended critique of what was happening to the physical environment, and a couple of students decided to join the AIM campaign against current urban renewal policies.

Dancing at the Strand

Another spur-of-the-moment performance of *When the Landlord Left...* remains with me as one of the most memorable. I wrote extensive notes in my journal on the spectators and their stories with the idea of turning the material into a dance. No new dance developed, but from my notes I can return to that remarkable night of dancing at the Strand.

It was the last affordable downtown residence hotel, and it was scheduled for demolition to make way for more city government buildings. The residents, who were all older people, living alone and dealing with various infirmities, had formed themselves into a supportive community and wanted to stay together. An AIM worker, who lived near the hotel, had come to know the residents and was trying to help them pressure the relocation authority into moving them as a group.

Harris and I were having lunch in a downtown restaurant, when the AIM worker walked in and sat down with us. She and the residents had planned a series of meetings, including one scheduled for that night, to talk about the Strand situation and how to let the public know what was happening. She asked if Harris would lead the discussion about fighting urban renewal and if I would dance *When the Landlord Left...* Harris agreed immediately, and I said I would be glad to dance if there was a space suitable for a performance. She suggested we come to the hotel to look at the spaces, and she would run the idea of a performance by the residents. When we arrived in the lobby, four of the most vocal members of the Strand community were there. The AIM worker introduced us to Donovan, a World War II veteran and retired police officer; Elinor, a retired factory worker and long-divorced mother of four; Jo Jo, who had been a clown with Barnum & Bailey Circus; and Rosie, a former carnival worker, who still liked to tell fortunes.

The four of them led the way to an empty store on the ground floor, where they thought I could perform. The walls were covered with mirrors and psychedelic murals, painted in swirls of neon orange, chartreuse, hot pink, yellow, and turquoise, set off by thin black lines, some in the shape of eyes.

"One day the two of them just disappeared," explained Elinor. "They never had much to sell—beads, scarves in crazy colors, incense, and weird-looking pipes. They wouldn't talk about their backgrounds. When they first moved in, I went up to them and made the V-sign and said, 'I'm a friend,' and then we sat down on cushions and listened to music."

I moved around the space and concluded it was large enough, not too dusty and grimy, bright enough from the overhead globes and wall sconces, and all in all an interesting setting for the dance because of the mirrors and murals.

"We can bring chairs from the hotel," said Donovan, who was clearly the leader of the group, "and we can clean the floor. How would you like the chairs arranged?"

I said they should be in a U-shape, set back a little from the walls, and I would perform in the middle. Harris, who knew where there should be openings in the line-up of chairs for entrances and exits and sequences that played off the walls, offered to help.

When Harris and I returned that evening, the store had been thoroughly cleaned and the chairs arranged as I asked. At about seven-fifteen the residents started to assemble for the seven-thirty get-together. I paced back and forth and around the space, stopping to greet Donovan, Jo Jo, and Rosie. Elinor looked in and went out several times before deciding to stand behind a chair near an exit door. She didn't sit down until more than halfway through the performance.

After an announcement by Donovan that a discussion would take place after the dance, I introduced myself and briefly told the story of the person facing relocation for the fifth time, who had inspired the piece. Heads nodded in recognition as I recited the quote that became the title: "When the landlord left, I did the only thing a poor soul can do—I walked around the room and scratched my head. I said I would announce the name of each character and walked to the edge of the space."

Inner-city Tenant picked up a folding chair, limped to the center, set it up, and sat down. The audience became silent and remained so throughout the anguished sitting, gesturing, and walking—not a cough, scuff of a chair, or rustling of fabric—until **Inner-city Tenant** limped out.

Landlord leaned back and toe-heeled in. Laughter erupted and kept erupting at the claps, shrugs, slides, and stops with hands clasped in prayer or held out palms up, as if demanding payment.

Police Officer entered with a forceful stride, gesticulated, stamped, moved about, knocked the chair down, and exited. Neither Donovan, who had spent years on the police force, nor anyone else showed signs of being offended.

Social Worker tiptoed in, tap danced in front of and all around the fallen chair, and tiptoed out. Jo Jo wiggled to the edge of his seat and leaned so far forward, he looked ready to fall off or pop up and start dancing.

Housing Inspector shuffled in and looked around. Stamps on the creaky uneven floor set off a guffaw and then a loud whisper, "roaches," that was picked up and passed around the room—"roaches"… "roaches"…"roaches"... No audience before or after added so much input. The whispering didn't stop until **Housing Inspector** shuffled out.

Student ran, bounced off the walls, dropped to the floor, walked nonchalantly to the fallen chair, picked it up, and set it on its feet. Elinor finally took a seat. Was she remembering the two, who ran the psychedelic shop? Upon sauntering out, student flipped the switch to turn off the lights.

Concerned Citizen entered the dark space and began relocating the chair from spot to spot. In the indirect light from the street, the room took over. The loopy designs on the walls and broken reflections of the audience in the mirrors became eerie players in the action that ended with the chair back at the starting point.

Bulldozer turned the lights back on for a barrage of destructive moves all too real and threatening to the hotel community.

When the dance ended, Donovan stood up immediately. "We have to have refreshments after such a good show." Rosie headed for the door. With her painfully slow walk in worn-out espadrilles, she had designated herself to fetch coffee and doughnuts. Jo Jo and a few others brought in a large table from the hotel. Some of the residents left, but the rest pulled up their chairs and became performers, while Harris and I sat back and became their audience.

Donovan led off: "The people in your dance are accurate, including the police officer."

"Thank you," I said.

"I was worried about how you would react to that character."

"You tell the truth about the police, but only a corner of it."

Donovan made everyone laugh with his stories about Miss Tucker and the Children's Center, a doctor who was always running stop signs, and how Clam Town and Goatsville got their names. Then came the story he really wanted to tell.

"In twenty years on the force, I never arrested a drunk. One time when I was a rookie cop, I came upon a little guy fighting a telephone pole. He was revving up to swing—swearing and cussing out that pole. A swing and a miss—another swing, and he missed with his hand, but not with his head. Smash! The pole won the match.

"I stood the guy on his feet and asked for an address. He pointed to a three-family house up the street. I half-carried him along the sidewalk, up the steps, and let him sink down on the porch. Then I rang all three bells, ran across the street, and hid behind a bush to see what would happen. Pretty soon the front door opened, and a large woman in a long robe came out. She hoisted the body up like a sack of potatoes and flung it through the doorway." Donovan thought no one had observed the incident until years later, when he met Nora, now a maid at the Strand, who had watched the whole thing from a window in the house next door.

While Donovan's stories came from his work, Elinor's came from her life. "Every time I go to the hospital they destroy me a little more. My marriage broke up after my first breakdown. I never see my kids. One of them works at the factory where I worked. Another is applying for a job at the newspaper. While I was in the hospital, the best of the bunch kept house—dishes, beds, washing, ironing, cleaning, cooking—and made straight A's at the same time. She got into the national honor society and won a four-year scholarship to Syracuse University. I'm so proud of her!

"My family was never proud of me. They laughed whenever I talked about being on the stage or dressed up in a costume or tried to do a dance. They told me to stop primping and showing off. I'd never make it. I was too ugly." She stood up to hum and dance a few bars of "East Side, West Side." Everyone around the table smiled and applauded.

Elinor almost didn't come to my performance. "I was afraid it would be like a recital. I saw enough of those at the hospital. Teachers would bring little girls, all dolled up in glittery costumes and too much makeup, to practice their steps for the crazy people. I was glad to see that you were wearing a dark green outfit, no makeup, and dancing about everyday life. I decided I could stay. You know what I always wanted? A clown suit so I could go around and make people laugh."

If Elinor had been a playwright, she couldn't have written a better entrance cue for Jo Jo. Short, wiry, and bouncy, he had slicked his hair down and dressed up for the performance in a white shirt, navy trousers, red suspenders, and a red bowtie. He popped up and gestured with his head and hands as he spoke: "Barnum & Bailey... traveled around the world... pretty good clown act... stories with no words... like your dances... you should dance around the world." Jo Jo sat down with a bounce. "I would love to do that," I said.

Donovan entered the conversation. "Do you know how I first met Jo Jo? He was doing motorcycle tricks in a factory parking lot. It was nighttime and quiet, but a shift was about to break."

"Do you know what you're doing?" I asked.

"Used to be a clown in the circus," he replied.

"Do you have a license to ride a motorcycle?"

"Not sure. Let me see." Jo Jo turned all the pockets of his pants, jacket, vest, and shirt inside out. "No license ... but my pal has one."

"Better drive the motorcycle back to your pal, then," I said.

Jo Jo grinned in remembrance. In mock trials at the hotel with Donovan as judge, he and Rosie were constantly in contempt of court. It wasn't surprising that Rosie with her slow little steps took quite a while to procure the refreshments. When she returned, she insisted on going around the table and serving each person.

"Angelo, have a doughnut." He had owned a trucking firm where Jo Jo once worked.

"Cornwall, have some coffee." He was a heavyset, retired businessman and often the spokesperson to the press about the Strand. He was light on his feet, according to Mary, a former dancer, though I never learned what kind of dancing she had done. Rosie didn't say anything to Mary. Were they rivals for the attention of the men?

"Sam, here's some coffee. You need it." He had faded in and out throughout the evening, only coming to life when Jo Jo mentioned dancing around the world. He said he had seen Geishas, Indians, and Africans dance, and my act was good, but I needed to learn the dances of other peoples.

"A doughnut and coffee for you, Father, maybe two doughnuts." Among the Strand community was a retired priest, who had been going around giving out cash and food coupons ever since his alcoholic brother died and left him a little money.

We all urged Rosie to stop serving and sit down, and finally she did. "I worked at the amusement park until they tore it down. Fortune telling is what I like. Fate: my fate, everybody's fate. I had a bad life... bad dreams... This hotel is haunted, you know. It has ghosts that walk with me at night. Come back for a séance. 'Ring around the Rosie.' Now there's an idea for a dance."

Somehow, eating and drinking stimulated the Strand residents to offer suggestions for dances I should make. Elinor thought I should make one about big business and Yale gobbling up the city—and one about urban renewal building a coliseum instead of what people really need.

"A dance about a coliseum would be easy," said Jo Jo, who had popped up and was making circling gestures with one hand. "All you'd have to do is run around in circles."

Donovan suggested I do a piece about the courts and proceeded to make faces, slouch, tap and pound the table, growl and squeak in imitation of the various judges. "A cop on the beat would also make a good subject," he added.

As the gathering broke up, he and Elinor accompanied Harris and me to the door. "I can see why you want to stay together as a group," said Harris.

"We're trying," said Donovan. "The relocation people say they can't find a place big enough for all of us."

About a year later, I received a note from Elinor:

"I'm keeping my promise to tell you the news, though you may not want to hear it. We're scattered all over. No more hotel community. No more hotel. Relocation found places for the three, who made trouble and were interviewed by the newspaper. Donovan died soon after you danced for us. Your friend from AIM found me a room in a house. When is your next performance? Maybe I can come."

I made a point of sending Elinor a flier, but she didn't appear.

1968 Newspapers

A chance to perform for protesting neighborhood residents or rebellious students or any other kind of audience didn't come every day, every week, or even every month. While continuing to work on AIM causes, I spent most of my time trying to compose good dances and become a good dancer. More and more I saw dance as my political work. The piece *Newspapers* came fairly quickly because of a theme and variations for harpsichord that provided the structure and a palette of different speeds, textures, and moods.

Les Folies Françoises ou Les Dominos by François Couperin intrigued me. The score has twelve sections, each sixteen measures long in three-quarter time (three beats to a measure), each designated by a folly, such as innocence or gallantry, and the color of a domino or costume that might have been worn at a masked ball to bring out the nature of the folly. The music intrigued me at least partly because I had studied the use of historic musical forms to structure contemporary dance works.

At first I thought of setting off the follies by using towels in different colors, and even went out and bought them. But I was reading about "poor theater" at the time, which I immediately translated into "poor dance"—poor in commodities but rich in ideas. The purchase of towels was definitely out of keeping with "poor dance," so they went back to the department store, and newspapers took their place, which immediately increased the potential for meaningful comedy. I maintained Couperin's names for the follies and recited the name of each folly before performing the actions.

Liz and Harry Henderson, political co-workers with theatrical experience, joined Harris for a preview of *Newspapers* in the multi-purpose room of the suburban synagogue where I was currently rehearsing. Their laughter through many of the sections indicated I was on the right track.

Innocence—walk down the center of the space, opening the folded newspaper and scattering the ten pages on the floor one by one.

Modesty—fold a page into a small square and hold it up to hide the face—back up, unfolding the paper to shield more and more of the body—open the page to full size and crouch down into a small knot behind it.

Passion—kneel down and fold a page carefully and precisely into a narrow strip, raise it slowly above the head as if it were a heavy dumbbell, lower it to one side, letting it open into a fan, and use it to fan the face and body.

Loyalty—move the right hand from down at the side up to the heart—pledge allegiance! up to the forehead—salute! out to high forward, arm straight—Heil! down to the right hip—thrust the buttock out and rub.

Perseverance—put one sheet of paper down after another and crawl across them on hands and knees like a worker cleaning a floor.

Hope—bunch a page into a bouquet, alternate down-up-up steps across the space and back with deeper and deeper bows to viewers—end by lying down and placing the bouquet in front of a viewer.

Laziness—scuff along, dragging a sheet of paper behind by one corner—stop, spread the paper on the floor, straighten it out, lie down, and roll up in it like a homeless person.

Flirtatiousness—skip, run, and gallop from page to page—throw one page in the air, let another sail out behind, swirl one over a viewer's head, leap over another, curl one up the body, throw it down, and stamp on it.

Gallantry—march in a square, alternating goose-step-like kicks, body erect, paper held aloft like a canopy, with a scraping walk, body bent lower and lower, paper saddling the back.

Foolishness—run around, gather up all the papers, smooth them out, and pile them in one spot, finishing with the last note of the music.

Jealousy—take a sheet of paper, open it out, cross the feet and turn slowly, moving the fingers along the edges—re-cross the feet and turn the other way, wrapping the sheet around the body like a shawl—grab the paper by one corner and begin to crumple it, while spiraling downward—crumple and spiral, crumple and spiral, until sitting on the floor, hunched over, hugging the ball of crumpled paper.

Despair—roll the pile of papers into a weapon and swat outward, bat round and round, garrot the neck, stab the belly, slash the wrists, guillotine the neck, pierce the heart, and finally lie down and unroll the papers like a shroud. From the fallen position, rip the shroud in two and slam the pieces down on either side of the body.

Liz and Harry applauded and made encouraging and helpful comments. Harry suggested that I have a member of the audience hold a page of a newspaper during the "loyalty" section. I tried out his idea at the premiere for an AIM audience. It worked, made the "loyalty" section and the whole dance stronger, and launched an ongoing exploration of audience participation.

When Liz saw my early dances, she immediately connected my approach to gesture with Meyerhold's biomechanics. She realized I had found my way to his conviction that if the physical gesture is right, the meaning follows. She was working on a doctorate in Russian Studies at Yale with a focus on Meyerhold, Mayakovsky, and Eisenstein. She introduced me to their work and the work of other artists of the revolutionary period, who struggled to bring art and politics together. Learning about them gave me many ideas and encouraged me to continue their struggle in new ways.

Liz was central to the informal alliance within AIM that worked to keep art on the agenda along with politics and economics. She instigated and helped to set up local meetings and regional conferences on art and politics and solicited articles on the arts for AIM publications. For me personally, she arranged performances, came to previews, gave feedback, and urged me to write on dance and politics, which I did for the *AIM Newsletter* and its successor, *Modern Times.* Those publications were created to offer an alternative to the views of the *New Haven Register.* When I made my satirical dance *Newspapers*, I had the *Register* in mind and used it as the prop for New Haven performances. In other towns, I used the major local newspaper. Here's how AIM members responded to the premiere:

"The message of that dance is newspapers are good for anything but reading."

"I saw myself in that dance. As part of my social work training, I had to live on the street. Newspapers became critical for my survival. I used them to pad my socks, gloves, hat, all my clothes to keep warm. I sat, slept, and even stood on them."

"In one way or another, all the sections contrast a newspaper's flimsiness with its power."

Dancing for Kindergarteners

Unlike most adults and students in high schools and colleges, who sat back in their chairs, retreated when I danced near them, and were self-conscious about physical reactions, kindergarteners leaned forward, giggled, reached out, squealed, and touched if they could. They always found a way to participate.

They supplied a complete sound score for *When the Landlord Left…* They discussed each character:

"So sad, so sad."

"Stop hurting the person."

"Eek!"

"Help!"

One performance of *Newspapers* for kindergarteners turned into a match: dancer and newspaper vs. sixty tiny adversaries. From the start, I had to use the newspaper to fend off the ring of warriors, who kept closing in to try and touch the papers or me.

"Litterbug," accused one of the children during the first section, and the rest picked up on the theme.

"Why are you throwing the papers around?"

"Bad litterbug."

"Lying down litterbug."

Several of the sections ended on the floor, and there was always a child or a small group of children right in the spot where the dancing ended, imitating the final position. I shooed the children back with the newspaper, but as soon as I stopped attacking and started dancing, the aggressors moved in, encroaching more and more on the space.

Figure 05. Newspapers for a Greek Drama class at Yale (1968). Photograph by Dave Dickson

Figure 06. Downtown for a Greek Drama class at Yale (1968). Photograph by Dave Dickson.

"Ballerina litterbug."

"Put the litterbug in jail," and the ring of taunters surged inward.

"Back up, back up," I commanded and swatted and batted and stabbed with the papers. "How can I dance? I have no room."

For the final section, "Despair," I was lying on my back, face and upper body covered with newspaper. I heard thudding, rubbing, and other noises coming closer, as I began to rip free of the paper. By the time my face emerged, the warriors were all around, densely packed, on their knees, leaning over, and looking down: first grinning, then giggling, then laughing—mouths open, teeth showing—sixty carnivorous little faces, pinning me to the floor.

1968 Downtown

In the same year as *Newspapers*, I composed *Downtown*, the story of what happens when a person goes shopping. There were episodes of carrying home a heavy shopping bag, fantasizing about each of the new possessions, reliving the shopping trip, trying on all the items only to discover the impossibility of moving with them on, and taking them off with great difficulty.

The first time I performed *Downtown*, it had a certain integrity. It was about forty minutes long, and a viewer teased about the timing: "It's like a movie by one of those directors, who wants the action to be as sparse and deliberate as real life and doesn't mind boring the audience."

The piece didn't feel quite right, but I decided not to make changes before performing it for an AIM audience at a general meeting on the arts. About a hundred and twenty people came to see *Downtown*, *Newspapers*, and *When the Landlord Left...*

Some parts of *Downtown* received an uproarious response, others no response. During the discussion period, a question revealed one of the weakest moments in the piece.

"Why does the person come back and pick up the clothes after shedding them and freeing the body?"

I could answer the question politically: most of us have not freed ourselves from the temptations of downtown—we keep buying things and becoming angry and stopping ourselves, and then we're tempted all over again. But in dance terms, there was no reason for the person to come back.

Other comments were:

"The piece has some brilliant moments, but it doesn't seem to hang together."

"It was too cruel, too hard to watch."

"It's more like a poem than your other pieces, a real step forward for you as a dancer."

"I won't be able to buy anything for months." I liked that comment.

When I went back to work on the dance—trying to keep the good parts and fix the weak ones and figure out what was so cruel—the whole thing fell apart. With a performance coming up, the subject of downtown seemed important enough to do the piece even in an unresolved, patched-up state. Spectators talked freely about *Newspapers*, the other dance on the program, but eliciting comments about *Downtown* was hard work. The issue of compulsive consumerism registered, but the episodes that showed how that plays out in our lives, especially the lives of women, weren't articulate enough to discuss.

Back to the studio for major revisions. Moments that relied on acting were changed to dance moments. The original intention was not to have a story line, but to compose the piece out of short sequences, generated by the objects: boots, belt, pearls, hat, bracelet, gloves, wallet, shopping bag. Somewhere in the process, a story line crept in. I realized I had to stop fighting that and consciously arrange the sequences to tell the story.

The next performance indicated some progress. It was a benefit for the alternate school, started by AIM. About one hundred twenty-five people came, including the children from the school, who began the program by reciting poems they had written, one of those hard acts to follow. *Downtown* still wasn't right. The new ending didn't work. I tried giving the shopping bag full of discarded items to someone in the audience, who was insulted.

"Why me?" No one understood the meaning intended, which was giving away unwanted things to a friend or charity.

One viewer commented, "The piece looks too spread out. Is it the long narrow room?" I said I suspected the problem lay in the placement of the objects in space, which wasn't set, and therefore, the dance pattern wasn't set spatially.

Another viewer said, "The piece is too long." I had cut it from forty minutes to twenty. Until all the ingredients of a dance are right, it seems too long.

A parent from the alternate school telephoned the next day. "The neighbors from my block were very excited about the dancing."

"Did they make any specific comments about *Downtown?*"

"I can't think of any," she said, which indicated to me that the ideas still didn't read.

Back to the studio with a new work list:

- set the spatial pattern;
- change the ending again—try stashing the objects behind a desk or curtain or door;
- eliminate the bracelet, which didn't alter the meaning, showing how superfluous the bracelet bit was;
- tighten up the first scene by taking out the extraneous walking around;
- rehearse the piece over and over again to sharpen the timing.

Greek Drama Class at Yale

A performance for a Greek drama class at Yale was difficult. It took place in a newly renovated classroom with dead-white walls, an obtrusive structure at one end, and dangling crepe paper streamers left from some social event. Harris was there to cheer me on, as was a photographer from the AIM Newsletter, whose photos later appeared in an article I wrote on dance and politics. During the sections of *Newspapers*, which usually produced laughter, this audience of about twenty-five students was silent. *Downtown* felt better than at previous tries, but it still wasn't right—particularly the ending. I performed well—limbs, torso, and head did what they were supposed to do, the long string of pearls didn't break, the hat stayed on and fell off at the right moments, and the boots went on without much difficulty. The reactions of the students—hostility, snickering, shrinking back during the sexual gestures—indicated the dance had an impact.

The graduate student, who invited me to perform for the class after seeing me dance at an AIM event, commented that the theatre in ancient Greece was like mine, an arena for talking about the concerns of the polity.

Another graduate student said: "I didn't realize you could make dances out of ordinary human gestures. Then Rembrandt came to mind, how his subjects changed from aristocrats of the court to people on the streets. In his late paintings, even holy figures are just people."

I responded to that observation by saying that in moving away from formal dance vocabularies toward heightened human gesture, I had been studying the work of Rembrandt for ideas and encouragement.

The professor, who taught the class, didn't say anything until Harris and I were leaving. "In my opinion, politics and dance don't mix well. Which came first for you?" he asked.

"Dance," I replied. He nodded and left the room.

Leftist Retreat in New Hampshire

After months of work, *Downtown* still wasn't completely resolved. The beginning and middle sections seemed to be set. My umpteenth try at an ending had more potential than the others, because the dance ideas were stronger. I had a chance to try it out at World Fellowship, a retreat for Left activists and their families in New Hampshire. In 1969, the Women's Liberation Movement was just forming, and I was invited to dance *Downtown* as a catalyst for discussion. Announcements of the upcoming performance took place at each meal, and the words 'women's liberation' always produced laughter, until one of the most respected guests, who was scheduled to join me for the discussion, pointed this out. "Why is there always laughter at the mention of women's liberation?

Women's issues aren't a joke. That response is disturbing and inappropriate." The laughter stopped, but the reasons for it became an important part of the intense discussion that followed the dance.

The day after the performance a mother and daughter sought me out. The eight-year old child handed me a drawing she had made in response to *Downtown*. It showed a shop window with boots, a hat, beads, belts, a pocketbook, and the word SALE. A woman with a big package was going out the door of the shop saying: "I hate what I bought."

As I write many years later, I realize we were just beginning to find the words for a critical look at the issues of body image, women as sexual objects, women as shoppers, the destructive gaze, the silence of women, our absence from history, the need to raise consciousness. All these issues were part of the dance *Downtown*, but it took a television performance in 1970 to bring them out. The TV director pointed out that twenty minutes of silence wasn't advisable for TV, that viewers would telephone, asking if there was something wrong with the sound transmission. He suggested creating a sound score or running an announcement at the bottom of the screen saying the dance was being broadcast in silence. I decided to put together a collage of music, advertisements, and commentary on consumerism. With the sound score, the dance finally arrived. It became a play for solo dancer.

The TV director also questioned the props. He thought the boots and hat and other items should be more exaggerated, more theatrical. I saw his point, but chose to stick with the realistic items. They had special meaning, because I had bought them and worn or used them very little, if at all. The director found effective ways of making the subtle props read by zooming in on them; by focusing alternately on dancer and prop, thereby creating a dialogue; and by superimposing images of dancer and prop.

About costume, the director said, "no black or white" and recommended blue. I had a robin's egg blue leotard and tights that showed off the pearls, belt, hat, and boots very well. For live performances, I wavered between leotard and tights, which immediately identified me as a modern dancer, and pedestrian clothes, which had enough stretch for dancing, but could also be worn on the street. For television, I decided to play on the dancer side of the borderline between art and reality. The body-revealing costume proved to be right for underlining the critical issue of body image and its relationship to what we buy, and I wore it for all the subsequent performances of *Downtown*.

Harris was at work when the taped program, featuring *Downtown*, was broadcast for the first time. I had what turned out to be an unnerving experience of watching with my parents. During the introductory interview, I talked about my mother's support of my dancing and my father's objection to it, his preference for me to be a lawyer. I hadn't imagined hearing those comments with my parents sitting next to me. I could see how upset my father was.

"You don't understand," he said, "you work so hard for so little. That's what bothers me about dancing." I knew there was more to his objection, such as opposition to the public display of a woman's body and the class prejudice that it's better to work with the mind than the body: a lawyer is respected, but not a dancer. While the tension lingered as the three of us watched, I had to ignore it and focus on trying to view the performance without my usual unproductive doubts and criticisms. Because I knew all the steps, I was doing each and every move with the image of the dancer on the screen.

Downtown on Television

To the music of the popular song, *Downtown*, scurry a zigzag path with a loaded shopping bag hung on one shoulder, as if returning from a shopping trip. Topple to the side, letting the bag slip down to the ground. Hoist it, walk, and topple to the other side. Repeat—ending with the bag on the ground, head buried in it.

As the music continues, pull the purchases out of the shopping bag and try them on one by one. Who's in control—Dancer or Item?

Boots—kick high, medium, low, as the feet wobble more and more, compelling a fall to the floor. Pull off the boots and stand up.

Hat—tip the head sideways, backward, forward, and down—hat weighing the body down, until it drops off.

Belt—whip it in all directions, grab it in front with both hands, and jerk it toward the waist. Stamp and jerk, stamp and jerk, contracting the torso, until impaled on the belt. Fling it down.

Wallet—open it—shake it. Nothing inside. Close it—put it on the ground.

Pearls on a long string—dangle them in front of the crotch. Bump them forward several times, pressing the breasts out from under the pearls. Bend forward, turn into a backbend, pearls dangling and strangling. Keep turning and lowering to the floor. Roll until free of the pearls.

Gloves—stand up and put on one of the white gloves. Applaud! Cheerlead! Punch like a boxer! Shake hands! Try to shake off the glove. Impossible. Pull it off finger by finger and throw it down.

The music ends. The contents of the shopping bag are lined up on the floor. Pick up the empty bag and walk slowly, clutching it with both hands, as if obeying some inner command to go shopping. The sound score changes to a distorted recitation of the song's words that brings out the irony.[13]

"When you're alone and life is making you lonely, you can always go... DOWNTOWN!" *Strut slowly, swinging the shopping bag back and forth.* "When you have worries, all the noise and the hurry seems to help, I know, DOWNTOWN." *Change direction and strut with higher steps.* "Just listen to the music of the traffic in the city"—*strut, swinging the bag in figure eights.* "Linger on the sidewalk where the neon signs are pretty"—*strut and swing faster.* "How can you LOSE?" *Turn, plop the bag on top of the head, and thrust a hip out. Holding bag on head, scrape and slither forward.*

"The lights are much brighter there"—*sink into the hips.* "You can forget all your troubles, forget all your cares"—*undulate the body.* "So go, DOWN kick TOWN"—*kick—the voice on the tape rises.* "Things will be great"—*swagger along*—"when you're DOWN" *kick* "TOWN" *kick*. "You'll find a place, for sure"—*swagger harder. The voice rises to a shriek.* "DOWN" *kick* "TOWN" *kick*, "everything's waiting for you!" *Voice and movement stop.*

In silence, race around the displayed objects, elbowing invisible pushy shoppers left and right, as if reliving the experience in the store. The sound score resumes with ads designed to seduce the shopper.

Quick light voice: "Young looks on the move! You know, the kind of uncluttered little somethings you crave by the closet-full..." *Circle the boots on the run.*

Serious tone: "Get rid of ugly midriff bulge and protruding stomach. Trim inches off your waist instantly without diet or exercise. Talk body language with a collection of body belts." *Approach the belt with slow dragging steps, pick it up, and put it in the shopping bag.*

Alluring voice: "Not pale, simpering, or modest... they are wildly, madly, wonderfully baroque... weird, undersea shapes of indescribable beauty..." *Walk past the pearls, shifting the weight from hip to hip.*

Didactic voice: "Attention senior citizens. Every Tuesday, we feature special rates for senior citizens. Take advantage of this opportunity to save while you buy." *Scuff slowly to the gloves—yes—into the shopping bag.*

Enthusiastic tone: "Fur finds... We have fun furs, formal furs, furry boots. The looks you thought you would never find ... all here in our fur boutique—on fire!" *Circle the boots on the run—hold one up against the leg—yes—into the shopping bag.*

Slow delivery: "You just put it on and go—and what is more, it acts more like hair than real hair." *Take dragging steps to the hat—pick it up, put it on—no—put it back down.*

Alluring voice: "Otherworldly, imaginative, with shimmer and lustre extraordinaire... Wear them unconventionally, avant garde, and enjoy their savage beauty." *Hips shifting, walk past the pearls—still no.*

With punch in the voice: "Rich, riveting, unforgettable... the century's most splendid... glorious... inimitable... a mastermind behind it... If you are going to have only one indulgence, make it this one." *Slink backwards past the pearls, dash toward them, back away, dash toward, away, toward—yes—put the pearls in the bag.*

Sympathetic voice: "Imagine, even if your hair is dry and broken, beauty can be yours at last. All because of a radically new solution. Drop in and you may discover a whole new beautiful you." *Take dragging steps to the hat—lift it slowly—yes—into the bag.*

Crisp tone: "Be the best-dressed in town. Be the superstar at the party. Be one of their dreams. Be in style. Be a fashion plate. Clothes! Make! The person!" *Hips shifting, walk to the wallet, pause and look—no.*

Keep walking to the back of the space, steps becoming slower, heavier, and lower. "You are what you have and what others think of you; and what they think of you depends on what you have."[14] *Sit down on the floor.* "Buy yourself a self, piece by piece, installment by installment." *Dump the contents out of the shopping bag.* "What you have, you have. What you have, you are." *Put everything on as quickly as possible and assume one model's pose after another, as the commentary continues.*

"Mirror, mirror on the wall, who is the fairest of them all?" *Swivel around on the floor and stop, knees to one side.*

"O city of the thousand mirrors, the thousand magic mirrors with a woman in front of each one!" *Hug the knees, and move the head left and right to show off the hat.*

"None is fairer than you if you buy me, take me, wear me." *Swivel again and extend one leg to show off a boot.*

"Buy me for I do not cost much. I am cheap. I am a gift." *Rise to the knees, hook the thumbs under the belt, and lean back.*

"Do you recognize me?" *Sit, knees to one side, taking hold of the long string of pearls, and extend the arm to show them off.* "I am a commodity." *Clutch the pearls and extend the other arm to show them off again.*

"I am your own self whom you have been looking for, your dream, your coat, your shoe." *Rise to the knees and wave one hand to show off the glove. Turn the waving hand into a pointing hand and reach for the wallet.*

"Buy me the shadow of beauty, and you shall be the fairest of them all." *Crawl toward the wallet slowly and awkwardly, boots, hat, belt, pearls, and gloves acting as hindrances. Arrive at the wallet and pause.*

"The fundamental wrongness is that we are supposed to believe we can satisfy our real needs by buying things and by buying things only." *Use the arms to move the legs into a standing position and hoist the body into a crouch over the wallet. Grasp it with both hands, lift it, and put it down several times before letting it drop.*

"And, of course, it doesn't work—which is precisely the point. Unsatisfied, we buy more and more." *Rise to upright, take off the gloves, drop them, and wiggle the freed fingers. Using the hands, drag one leg forward, then the other.*

"Always a little hungry, always seeing fulfillment just a little out of reach." *Take off the hat, let it fall, and shake the unencumbered head. Take hold of the legs, and drag them forward.*

"Not that people shouldn't enjoy something new..." *Remove the pearls, let them fall, stretch the neck and circle the head. Raise the arms and undulate the upper body.*

"Not that we should give everything up and turn ascetic..." *Unfasten the belt, put it down, and undulate from the hips up through the fingertips. Twist at the waist, open the arms wide, and lower them.*

"But we just have to break the compulsiveness of buying." *Remove one boot and make a high circle of the leg from back to front. Remove the other boot and circle that leg.*

"Freed of encumberments, DANCE!" *Lunge, undulate, twist, circle the legs—stepping faster and faster—as the sound score switches to a countdown*: "ten, nine, eight, seven, six, five, four, three, two, one." *End at the wall.*

After the initial excitement of liberation from the purchases, the voice on the sound score asks: "WHO" (turn the head sharply away from the wall) "AM" (contract the torso) "I" (cross one foot over the other and reach an arm out)? "WHO" (look back toward the wall) "AM" (contract the torso) "I" (uncross the feet, step outward, and slap the thigh)? The sequence repeats, as the accent shifts from "WHO" to "AM" to "I."

The voice lowers to a whisper. "Who am I?" *Spiral down into a small knot on the floor.* "Who am I?" *Reach out toward each object that has been shed and pull into a knot.* "Who am I?" *Out and in.* "Who am I?" *Out and in.* "Who am I?" *End the struggle in a pose of maximum tension: body balanced on one side, back arched, head up, one hand grasping both feet.* "Who am I?" *Release and extend the body to full length.* "Who am I?" *Roll to the edge of the performing space.* The drone ends.

Ascend from prone to knees to standing, body bent over. Straighten up: ankles, knees, hips, waist, ribs, shoulders, neck, head. Walk slowly toward the front of the space, faster toward the back, faster still toward the front. Accelerate to a run around the space and out.

At the end of the broadcast, my father smiled and nodded and patted me on the back. He eventually accepted my dancing, saying: "If you're doing what you love, that's what's important." My mother commented that I spoke and danced well, and she thought people would find the program very interesting. A few days later I received the following letter from a viewer:

"Did making the dance *Downtown* cure you of compulsive buying—that old devil that haunts and saps the energy? It's distracting—an illusory cure for isolation and unhappiness. It's socially acceptable (everybody does it, therefore I feel like everybody when I do it—not like a stranger). It's thrilling like a vice: you can never get enough of it and you can never win. Because the goal is a fantasy that reality can never satisfy: the perfect outfit. It doesn't exist. We can't buy it if we shop from today until doomsday. Perfection is death. To think in terms of a perfect outfit is to think in terms of being an object, a fantastic dead thing that does not, cannot participate in life—imperfect, unpredictable life."

Dance and Politics

Backing up to the summer of 1968, my choreography of the moment had produced an environmental duet for dancer and architect, a mobile theater anti-war collage for nine activists, and three solos on social issues. In my journal, I made many attempts to put my ideas about dance and politics together and finally came up with something I could share at an AIM General Meeting on the Arts. After performing *When the Landlord Left…*, *Newspapers*, and *Downtown*, I gave the following talk, which was broadcast subsequently on a counter-culture radio station:

Dance Against Comfort

> Every thirty years or so, lots of new people like me get involved in dance—call us dancers against comfort or dancers to whom the art of dance becomes relevant—because it insists on a connection to the thoughts and activities of those who are working to change what they find unacceptable in society. Ideas generate movements, movements generate ideas: we dancers against comfort work back and forth. We break the pattern of dancers turning in on themselves, creating escapist fantasies, and playing movement games for a limited and special audience. Dance emerges from its cocoon and challenges new groups of people to rethink their notions about the gestures in which we move through life.
>
> Recently I was warming up outdoors. A group of political activists were on their way to a meeting. They glanced in my direction. Quickly I walked the perimeter of a space and began to dance—indicating the sky, earth, myself, them. One responded with a shake of the head, another sped past me, a third kicked a leg and waved.

At mealtime, I was in a dining hall. There were lots of people eating, reading newspapers, talking, making plans. Quickly I found an open space and began to dance—marching, hiding, saluting, stabbing with a newspaper. The diners looked back and forth between their newspapers and me.

At night I danced again. In a building threatened with demolition, a group had gathered. Quickly I cleared a space among them and began to dance—walking, looking at my hands, tap dancing, running, slashing, gesticulating. The group told stories and danced, but couldn't stop the demolition.

We dancers against comfort turn a field, a dining hall, a large room into a theater for dance. We claim the space by giving significance to the placement of movements. We build a narrative by dancing close to the audience or far away, on the perimeter or in the center; by gesturing in one spot or traveling from spot to spot; by moving in spokes or zigzags or in a circle. Everyday gestures take on as much importance as formal dance movements. An everyday object, such as a newspaper, becomes a starting point for a piece. Spectators are puzzled, provoked, unnerved, astonished, expectant, upon seeing an ordinary person dancing in their midst. They can hear the breathing, grunts, sighs, and see the effort. The dancer is set apart from them only by the work that goes into making and performing a dance.

Of course, we dancers against comfort have a hard time surviving. We disappear, and a period of polished but dead art ensues. The few of us, chosen and transformed into commodities by the entertainment industry, find ourselves cut off from the point of view of social injustice, escalating the technique (higher, faster, more violent), complicating the form (more elaborate productions), and playing to audiences that want to sit in the dark and be entertained. A chasm develops between performers and spectators. The door to the street closes. Dance becomes an end in itself. It loses its vital connection with the oppressed. The oppressed lose a voice, and the polity loses its conscience.

For the rest of us that the entertainment industry ignores, it's not at all easy to find audiences; to earn enough money for keeping a soloist, let alone a group, alive; to overcome doubt and go on dancing and believing.

A conversation with a childhood friend focused my thinking about the difference between performance as a commodity—approved, packaged, and sealed—and performance as a questioning of the status quo and a search for alternatives. After several years of auditioning for theater companies in the United States, my friend, frustrated but not yet cynical, auditioned and was accepted by a company in Israel. Within two years she had learned the language, performed major parts in two plays and a film, and made several advertisements for television. As she put it: "I had everything I always wanted—a lot of work, good parts, people were beginning to recognize me on the street. But one day after a shooting session for an ad, I sat down and asked myself what it all meant. What was I doing with my life? I felt so empty."

Since becoming a dancer against comfort or a dancer for 'Justice, fugitive from the camp of the conquerors,' I don't feel empty after a performance, because it's an exchange with people about issues that affect our lives. When I suggested that my disgruntled-now-idle friend come to an art and politics meeting, her response was a suspicious look. I understood. Subjects, such as urban renewal, compulsive buying, and haves versus have-nots, seem very far from the growth of a dancer, until a time of upheaval when Justice whispers: It's the willingness to challenge and experiment that keeps dancers and dance alive. Those who do not question and defy for fear of losing their comfort and security sink into parasitism. Once dancers confront, analyze, refuse to be channeled, recognize protest as a fundamental human cry, they dance for the oppressed, who are struggling—for they, too, are oppressed but struggling.

Whenever the clown baffles the officer,
whenever the joker makes the judge look silly,
whenever the fool defeats the machine—
comes a new sense of joy and freedom.

Chapter Two: Growing

1969 Rehearsal Space

Finding a place to choreograph and rehearse with no money was a frustrating task. I moved four times in less than three years and worked in temporary spaces, usually religious institutions, between the more permanent ones. The arts center auditorium where I began was lost to urban renewal. Loud thumps and crashes interrupted a rehearsal one morning. I rushed up the stairs to the sanctuary and found a wrecking crew dismantling the building without even checking to see if anyone was in it. I rushed downstairs and telephoned Harris, who was still working for the redevelopment agency. A debate had been raging about whether or not to save the old religious structure as part of a new arts complex for the city. As far as Harris and I knew, a final decision hadn't been made, and a small but influential group of planners and politicians favored rehabilitating the building to tearing it down. A car arrived with redevelopment officials, and the wreckers stopped, but I realized it was time to look for a new space.

The head of a large suburban synagogue agreed to let me rehearse on weekdays in whichever multi-purpose room wasn't being mopped and polished for a function. I often crossed paths with Morgan, the janitor. He didn't say much, but whenever he stopped to watch me dance, it was a sign that I was on to something interesting. One morning, he pushed aside his cleaning equipment, left for a while, and came back pushing a dolly, loaded with a set of well-used drums. He set them up, sat down, and started drumming. After a few seconds, I couldn't stand still. I slid my feet, circled my knees, swiveled my hips, thrust my ribs this way and that, rotated my shoulders—brought in lindy and charleston steps and any other steps I could think of. We jammed until the tune ran out.

"I didn't think you could dance like that," said Morgan.

"I didn't know you could play like that," I countered. From that session, I learned that he had played with professional jazz groups after serving in World War II. I invited him to come to a performance I was giving at the synagogue. I saw him peeking in from a doorway about halfway through, but when I looked again, he was gone.

One day the cantor asked if I would like to dance to medieval Jewish music. Although I had studied historic dance forms, it didn't dawn on me to draw on them. I looked closely at the sanctuary, moved through it again and again, looked and moved, moved and looked, searching for movements in response to the place and politics of the moment. I made a hodgepodge of notes in my journal.

Before the Law

Processional—confrontation with authority on its terms—acts of individual conscience—attempt to escape

What can a person dance in a sanctuary?

Comment on fact that dancing in a sanctuary, no matter how hard one tries, no matter what one does, the dancing is in a sanctuary. Once the decision to stand before the Law has been made, one's acts are immediately limited...

Part One—addressed to the altar
Part Two—the building: respond to aisles, steps/levels, walls, railings, carpet
Part Three—in amongst the congregation

Confront the Law in various ways:
Picket—gesticulate—reason—argue—bow—flagellate

From far away—from close up—from front, side, and back—from below—from above

violent—sweet—open—secret—frantic—indifferent—afraid—determined—hostile and defiant—obsequious—pleading

Obedience vs. rebellion
inside or outside an institution
accept, question, protest, reject, change the Law
imprisonment vs. freedom

How could dance tackle so many words? Somehow, out of the bits and pieces, I came up with a scenario for a group happening, long since misplaced or lost. The cantor, after a conference with the rabbi, rejected the proposal as unsuitable for the congregation and out of keeping with a religious event. I was told a dancer should stick to aesthetics and stay away from politics, a comment I often heard. My relations with everyone remained cordial, but I had had enough of the characterless rooms with their polished vinyl-on-concrete floors, which were taking a toll on my legs. I left the suburbs for the parish house of the First Methodist Church, an historic church on the New Haven Green. The large upper-story meeting room with a wooden floor and lots of windows looking out on the bustle of the city was a welcome change.

Teaching

When the money from jobs I held before returning to dance ran low, I agreed to take over the teaching positions of an acquaintance, who was traveling for six months. Harris was dubious. He thought the jobs would drain energy from my goal of being a choreographer and performer. More vulnerable to social pressures, both real and imagined, than he was, what ran through my mind was something like this:

An acquaintance has asked me to teach. I'm flattered and can't say no.

There are more opportunities to teach than to perform.

Teaching pays a little, performing almost nothing.

For someone who isn't famous, 'I teach dance' seems to be a more understandable and acceptable answer to the question 'What do you do?' than 'I choreograph and perform.'

Occasionally, I recognized the social channeling, and it made me angry. Why are so few dancers able to dance? As one friend put it: "You can't expect to be paid for doing what you love to do."

The fact that the teaching jobs required a lot of energy and gave nothing back became clear after the first classes. I did a great deal of preparation, constantly fell short of mythical expectations, fulfilled my obligations, and attached a big label to the telephone: TEACH ONLY AS ADJUNCT TO PERFORMING.

Jack Quinn: From Principal Dancer to Night Custodian

One of my temporary jobs was teaching dance exercise at an exclusive social club in downtown New Haven. The students were women, who found tennis, riding, and sailing insufficient exercise for their aging bodies. I had to enter by the employees' entrance, and one morning as I was coming in, Jack Quinn, the ballet teacher who had inspired my lasting love of dance, was going out. We hadn't seen each other since the last classes I took in 1957 before leaving for college. He was wearing the same coat he wore when I was a pupil.

"Mr. Quinn!" I exclaimed, addressing him as I always did. A startled look, and then he responded, "Baby!" He called me that from the first classes, when I was the smallest and youngest pupil at the more advanced level and wore shorts with suspenders and tops with puffed sleeves. They were costumes my mother had made for my dance recitals, when I was studying with retired vaudeville performers. I didn't discover tights and close-fitting tops until a dancer, who had studied in New York, came to take classes and became a model, not just for practice clothes, but also for many aspects of ballet technique.

Standing in the hallway, Mr. Quinn and I talked until I had to go and teach. He was employed as a night custodian, following a serious operation for cancer. He no longer had a studio in New Haven, but still taught one class a week in Waterbury. He wanted to know what I was doing, and I told him about Harris and the dances I was making.

"I use ballet sequences I learned from you. I've changed them, but you would recognize them." He gave me his address, so I could invite him to a performance.

When I entered the classroom, the women were waiting. I asked them if they knew anything about Jack Quinn, the club's night custodian.

"No," they said, and barely listened when I told them about his earlier life as a principal dancer with the Metropolitan Opera Ballet, where he had worked with two of the greatest choreographers of all time, Michel Fokine and George Balanchine. I asked if any of them remembered the Southbury Playhouse.

"Vaguely," said one person.

"Mr. Quinn owned it when it was a successful summer theater that did a ten-week season and hosted performances by dancers from the Ballets Russes." No reaction to anything I said. "He was also the best ballet teacher in the region. He kindled my passion for dance." I shook my head at the indifference of the club women, taught the class, and left, still thinking about the chance meeting with Mr. Quinn, which set off so many remembrances.

The walk to my rehearsal space in the church parish house took me past the platform on the New Haven Green, where a dance performance occasionally took place. The outdoor platform at Southbury Playhouse came into my mind. The summer I worked as a stagehand, I improvised dances on that platform before the Saturday shows, accompanied by a local accordionist. Aware of my limitations, I wanted Mr. Quinn to choreograph pieces for me, but he didn't have time. He trusted my youth and passion and the kindliness of the audience. Part of my job as a stagehand was searching for costumes in an attic storage room. One day I opened a trunk and found fragile old tutus, including one with the name 'Toumanova' on it. I was about to try it on when someone came looking for me. That's when I learned about the visits of the Ballets Russes dancers.

Bouts of heavy drinking led to Mr. Quinn's losing the Playhouse and cutting his full schedule of ballet classes to just a few classes a week. When I became a pupil, the alcoholism seemed under control, but a reputation for unreliability lingered. Without the advertising campaigns, promises of fame and fortune, and lavish recitals of other local dancing teachers, only two or four or six students at most appeared for a lesson with Mr. Quinn.

Walking to my downtown rehearsal space in a strong wind reminded me of a lesson on a day when it was not just windy, but snowing so hard the buses had stopped running. I couldn't bear to miss ballet class, even if I had to walk. My mother came with me as she often did, probably fearing I would dance myself into a snowdrift without her. Up the three flights of stairs to the studio with its splintery wooden floor and watering can for sprinkling to prevent slipping, just like the watering can in the painting of a ballet class by Degas that hung on one wall. Thank goodness the door to the studio was open. Suddenly the lights went out. Mr. Quinn found a few candles and set them on the floor along the wall that didn't have barres or mirrors.

Someone stumbled up the stairs; a pupil who came to every lesson, but never seemed to improve. Exasperation drove her name out of Mr. Quinn's head. "What's-your-name, *plié, plié* ... right foot front, right foot," placing the feet in the correct position ... "now the arms, arms, remember your arms ... You, hiding in the back, What's-your-name, why did you stop? How can you learn if you keep stopping?" In the flickering candlelight, even What's-your-name looked a little better. Mr. Quinn taught a complete class:

Barre —

Adagio — "The sweeping walk in a circle ending in pirouette is too light. Lean into it. Do it as if you have a heavy cape on your shoulders, sweeping out behind you. You have to know how to walk. That's the measure of a dancer."

Petit allegro — small quick springing steps, always my favorite.

Grand allegro — The challenge was to do the leaping combination at full speed and extension without blowing out or knocking down a candle.

Sauté turns, repeating *renversés, fouettés.*

Révérence.

No remaining after *révérence* to practice difficult steps. Mr. Quinn picked up a candle and accompanied What's-your-name, my mother, and me down the stairs. Glowing from the class by candlelight, I danced home through the snow with my mother following and laughing at my antics.

As my walk from the social club was ending, I realized my downtown rehearsal space was across the Green, but on the same street as Mr. Quinn's former studio and the Shubert Theatre, where the Ballets Russes de Monte Carlo and Ballet Theatre used to appear once a year. My mother was always the first in line to buy two tickets in the first row of the second balcony, the best of the cheap seats. Those performances meant not just the opportunity to see the classical repertory and professional dancers, but also to hear Mr. Quinn's reflections on a favorite ballet. I remember him finding the ensemble as important as the soloists; pointing out a dancer, who knew how to place the hands, turn the head, just stand; admiring virtuosity in the line as much as the height of an extension; exclaiming about a perfect phrase: a run along the diagonal ending in arabesque!

The unexpected encounter with Mr. Quinn resulted in the following scenario:

Performer/Teacher/Night Custodian

Part one: *Mazurka*
As many lights as possible, the whole room lit;
the audience seated on either side to create a corridor-like space;
Dancer in the middle does big energetic movements, flamboyant and abstract—leaps, jumps, turns—covering lots of space.

Part two: *Étude*
Only the corridor-like space between the divided-audience lit;
Dancer as teacher demonstrates movements taken from the dancing in part one—with talking: "head a little higher ... hold a moment after the *grand jeté* ... travel more on the *assemblé* ... the turns, keep the shoulders down ..."

Part three: *Nocturne*
Dancer as custodian carries a flashlight;
limited playing area determined by the beam from the flashlight;
sequence of everyday gestures and ballet steps pedestrianized, moving back and forth along the corridor-like space, interrupted by pauses;
words periodically: "third floor ... okay ... basement ... okay ... is anybody there?"

The scenario never developed beyond the written version, but I kept brooding on how to portray the skid from performer to menial worker, if employed at all—the skid of Quinn the ballet dancer, Morgan the jazz musician, and JoJo the clown—a trajectory all too common in a society that has little use for young performers, let alone old ones in poor health. Ideas, such as pedestrianizing ballet steps, contracting space, decreasing speed, lowering the elevation of movements, and using words, rumbled around in my mind.

Remembering Mr. Quinn's advice to practice balancing on one leg while waiting for the bus, I experimented with ballet steps at the bus stop as well as in the upper-story meeting room, and they became the vocabulary for the dance *Growing*. The urban rehearsal space was turning out to have almost as many interruptions as the bus stop. When I arrived one day, the floor was covered with splinters from railroad ties, lying helter-skelter in the middle of the room. I went to the office to complain. The minister, who was sitting behind a heavy antique desk, explained that a theater group used the space a few evenings a week.

"I apologize for not telling them to clean up. Where are the brooms and dustpans? They're around here somewhere." The telephone rang. "Ask my secretary."

The secretary directed me to a broom closet. By lugging and sweeping, I worked off some of the anger and frustration of not having a reliable practice situation. The minister appeared just as I was finishing and sat down on the only upholstered chair in the room.

"Tell me about what you're working on."

"I've been rethinking ballet steps and how they're put together."

"'Think before you leap'—are you acting on that old proverb?"

"I'm asking what's the beginning, middle, and end of a leap. Can the parts be separated and rearranged and new elements inserted?"

"Will a leap be recognizable after you take it apart?" asked the minister.

"Maybe not—and therefore full of new possibilities. Would you like to see what I've done with an exercise for the arms?"

"A private performance? Please ..."

Port de bras

I stepped forward and thrust one arm down, simultaneously exhaling with audible breath sound and bending the knees. Made three circles of the arm growing higher and bigger, each beginning with a thrust, body curving with the motions. Pivoted half way around, and thrust the other arm toward the floor, lifted it to the side and overhead and dropped it down across the face.

Twisted and reached both arms to one side. Pivoted a quarter turn from feet apart, one forward and one back, to feet apart in the same plane, and lifted the arms high with the head following. Hold!

Kept the arms reaching while the body bent forward in six clocklike
ticks
un-
til
hands
touched
floor.

Heaved the body and arms back to high. Opened the arms out to the sides and bounced them down and back up to high, the legs echoing by bending and straightening. Pivoted from legs apart in the same plane to one forward and one back and lowered the hands by crossing and re-crossing them with rhythmic slaps:

slap
slap slap
slap slap slap
slap.

With curves and counter-curves, pivots and clocklike ticks, the sequence built to a repeat of the rhythmic slaps, ending with a slap of the hands on the thighs.

I walked toward where the minister was sitting to explain. "I explored several ballet ingredients: circling the arms—*port de bras*; bending the knees—*plié*; and a pivot between legs apart, forward and back, and legs in the same plane—between fourth and second positions."

The minister used the armrests to straighten up in the upholstered chair. "I guess what strikes me about ballet dancers is how upright they are."

"There are bends, tilts, twists, reaches in ballet, but they are hidden or minimized. I expose and exaggerate them."

"Your breathing out loud caught my attention. Was that intentional?"

"Another example of exposing the hidden."

"The breathing and slapping became a kind of music. What about making music in the feet?"

"You're ahead of me. In the next sequence, the sound comes from the feet. It begins so slowly that the folk rhythm is almost obliterated."

Pas de Cheval and Passepieds

With the feet together and the knees bending and straightening, I lifted the right leg slowly to the front, brought it down on the heel, and scraped the foot back in like the pawing of a horse (*pas de cheval*). Repeated the slow pawing with the left and right legs.

Then lifted the left leg slowly and heavily to the back, came down on the toes, pivoted half way round to the left, and thumped the left heel forward.

The pawing sequence continued, and as the tempo increased, the deep bends and rises turned into springs and the pas de cheval became lighter quicker passing steps or *passepieds*, which revealed the folk dance: spring **heel**—spring **heel**—spring **heel toes heel**.

The minister sat back in the armchair. "I think of ballet dancers floating, their toes barely touching the floor. Your moves look different."

"Ballet originally took steps from folk dance and lightened them."

"Are you reversing the process—giving the steps back to the earth?"

"I go from a heavy to a light version of the steps, and I could go the other way."

"Do ballerinas ever bang their heels and toes the way you did?"

"In modern ballets, the point shoe is occasionally used like a weapon to stab the floor and jab the air, but classical ballet separates the light from the heavy, the airy from the earthy, the high from the low."

The minister picked up the thread: "The ballerina from the chorus, the aristocrats from the peasants: am I getting at the class politics of ballet?"

"Yes, there's hierarchy everywhere in ballet: stories, characters, even movements. By contrast, modern dance has made everyone a soloist and widened the range of topics and movements."

"Democratizing dance, I like that," said the minister. "But if you turn ballet upside down and inside out, will it survive?"

"That's the only way to keep it alive."

"Is it possible to watch ballet in terms of social class as well as beautiful dancing?"

"The experience has more significance."

"Another aspect of rethinking ballet?"

"Yes, rather than denying its characteristics."

The minister prolonged the discussion. "Let's go back to what you just danced for me. Your arm movements had one kind of line and rhythm, and your leg movements another. Without music, how do you blend the different ingredients together?"

"*Growing* is the title and also the organizing concept of the dance. The movements are arranged to grow in speed and space. I begin in one spot and move in larger and larger circles, alternating between sections of modernized ballet movements and sections of ordinary walking."

"A verse/refrain structure like many of the hymns. Would you be able to dance *Growing* in the sanctuary?"

"If I can adapt the spatial pattern."

After we discussed the best times for rehearsing in the sanctuary, the minister headed back to the office, and I began working on the phrase that followed the *port de bras* and *pas de cheval* sequences. My rethinking of ballet continued as an inner monologue:

Plié, bend

Relevé, rise on the toes

Developpé, extend one leg by bending and straightening it

Tombé, lunge

Cambré, circle the upper body

Reach

All motions done in ballet, all motions done in everyday life: the challenge was to make them dance on the borderline between the school form and the vernacular form. What developed was a breathing, twisting, sensual sequence that talked about the dancer's body in relation to turning inward vs. reaching outward.

Feet together, start the hands at the crotch and mark an invisible line up the center of the torso and face and into the air, as the knees bend and the body descends to deep *plié*. No staying there. On the breath, reverse and ascend with gentle twists, the arms opening out to the sides and lowering.

Rise to the toes (*relevé*), arms moving out to the sides again and up until the hands touch overhead—a narrow elongated position difficult to maintain. On the breath, lower the heels with a gentle twisting motion of the body, the hands pressing down the face and torso and ending at one thigh.

Extend a leg (*developpé*) with the hands moving down the thigh, knee, and calf to the ankle and then back up the leg, as it bends, extends, and lowers to the front (*tombé*).

Keep the hands progressing up the body, until it arches backward, and the arms reach up and out—a gesture of suspension and tension. Release the pose by circling the upper body and the arms (*cambré*), leading into a lunge and a reach to the audience.

Turning inward vs. reaching outward

My exploration of turning inward vs. reaching outward, a fundamental paradigm of modern dance, began during a period of deep personal crisis, when Bessie Schönberg, my composition teacher at Sarah Lawrence, assigned a "generosity" study. I agonized in the dance studio, in the library, on pathways between classes, at meals, and in bed. One morning, I went to the studio and stayed all day, trying this movement and that one, watching other people at work on their studies, anguishing alone and anguishing with others. I couldn't come up with a single true gesture, nothing, blank. Everyone left. It was nearly midnight and I was down on the floor on my knees, crumpled over in total misery. I lifted my head and body enough to reach both hands forward, palms up—lifted a little higher, lunged forward, and extended the reach—a gesture of "generosity," and I knew it! Tears of release ... From that gesture, it was possible to build a study, which led to many other studies. Bessie's gift as a teacher was coming up with an assignment that went to the heart of a personal struggle and turned it into a creative struggle with profound implications for going on in dance and in life.

For the dance *Growing*, the individual movements lay on a continuum from inward-turning to outward-reaching, while the whole scenario was about moving outward. At a high school performance, a student asked why the movements grew larger rather than smaller. When questioned, he defined growing as increasing concentration. Based on his comment, I tried reversing the sections, running them from grand allegro to adagio, from big circles to one spot. Impossible. The dance material insisted on growing outward. Maybe a future dance could employ the opposite scenario of narrowing and slowing down, like the scenario written for the portrait of my ballet teacher, Mr. Quinn.

Because gestures of reaching out were more difficult for me, I considered them more important than inward-turning ones, until some years later when a teacher in Italy confronted me. I was leading a workshop in her studio in Siena, carrying on about how wonderful it was to work in a circle, to look across at each other, to join hands and dance together, when the teacher suddenly stopped translating, switched to English, and spoke vehemently: "Don't say that to them. Reaching out is the only gesture they know—family and community. They never leave this town. In order to grow and change, they have to turn inward and find their own individuality."

In AIM, the issue of the group vs. the individual sometimes turned into politics vs. art. Discovering the power of group political action was so meaningful to me that at first I ignored accusations of selfishness and individual chauvinism, characteristics linked especially to art. No one actually said, "Give up dancing and hawk leaflets," but the pressure was there. Harris and I defended the necessity of art at meetings, and others voiced concern about the group's inability to respond to the needs of individuals. I took charge of the New People's Program, because so many of the newcomers to AIM, when asked, said what they most wanted to do was paint or write or dance or play an instrument. It was clear that building individual strength was as important as building group solidarity. In both dance and political terms, no part of the continuum from inward-turning to outward-reaching gestures can be neglected.

Renversés

I continued the run-through of *Growing* with turning *renversés*, oriented to the four diagonals. *Renversé* is a particularly interesting step because of the complex action of the torso from leaning forward to rising to arching back to tilting side, as the leg circles from front to side to back (*rond de jambe*), echoed and accented by a circle of the same arm as leg. I did three *renversés* with quarter turns, two with half turns, one with a three-quarter turn, and the last with a full turn. The first one was lumbering, the body hovering over the foot as it dragged along the floor. With each succeeding turn, the leg was higher off the floor, and the body leaned, rose, arched, and tilted more rapidly.

Turns in my dances are always unusual—broken, slow, isolated, alternating (first one way, then the other)—often with elaborate build-ups. Multiple or repeating revolutions are impossible because of motion sickness. On some days, even one turn can cause dizziness and nausea. Spinning blurs details of the revolving body; it is motion as an end in itself that matters. A dancer with motion sickness works at the opposite end of the spectrum, using turns to emphasize change of direction and reveal the body as a multi-faceted entity.

A walking refrain, oriented to the floor, followed the *renversés*. I was tracing a small circle of slow forward steps, looking at the floor, feeling it under my feet, bending down and running a hand along the surface, when the door to the meeting room opened and a tall young man in raggedy clothes stumbled in, ran, and crashed against a wall—crumpled to the floor, scrambled up, stumbled and ran to the opposite wall. Another crash and fall and stumbling run and another, but this time the intruder reached a back exit, and I heard uneven steps and thuds going down the stairs.

Exit Coffeehouse and Exit Players

After my fright subsided, I followed and ended up in the basement of the church, where there was a coffeehouse called The Exit, a hangout for the young and rebellious. Much to the congregation's chagrin, on evenings when it wasn't raining or snowing, the wide outdoor steps leading to the doors of the sanctuary were crowded with singing, guitar-playing, shouting, screaming, hugging, staggering, nodding, and sleeping people.

"They have to have some place to go," the minister was saying to a wraithlike person with prominent cheekbones and long straggly hair, dressed in a fringed vest, leggings, and moccasins. On a sofa against the wall, a person who looked like the one that zigzagged through the upstairs meeting room was stretched out. "Enough of the board and congregation are still on my side, but who knows for how long."

The minister turned to me and seeing my face, apologized for the frightening interruption. "Let me introduce the program-director of The Exit. I have to leave, but you two should have a lot to say to each other. In addition to scheduling activities and handling emergencies, he leads the Exit Players—acts, directs, and even writes his own plays.

Exit-director and I shook hands. "Tell me about the Exit Players."

"A new group—just people, not actors. We work together two nights a week in the meeting room." Exit-director spoke in a quiet voice with little inflection. "Sorry about the railroad ties."

"Even without the railroad ties, that floor is so splintery I have to rehearse in sneakers all the time, and sequences along the floor are impossible."

"What kind of dancing do you do?"

"Sometimes I call it political dance." I gave a brief description of *When the Landlord Left...*, *Newspapers,* and *Downtown.*

"Issue-oriented pieces—I've written a few of those myself."

"Do you direct the plays of other writers?"

"Yes. The minimalist playwrights like Beckett—they capture basic ideas with a minimum of words."

"Do you dance?"

"Not a step. The Exit Players stand, walk, sit."

"I use everyday gestures in my dances, but the core vocabulary for my newest piece, *Growing,* comes from ballet."

"Why ballet, the most aristocratic dance form?"

"We have to claim ballet for our own purposes. Not too long ago, I met my old ballet teacher—once a principal dancer, now a night custodian—hardly an aristocratic pattern. The steps I learned as a young dancer started coming back, steps that are hundreds of years old. Why turn our backs on all that history?"

"Too constricting. And not relevant."

"Not so constricting and irrelevant if one picks and chooses the moves and explores them from a contemporary point of view."

"What do you mean?"

"Watch someone on the street, trying to jump over a puddle. A spring off one foot and a landing on two feet, one at a time—a street *pas de chat,* step of a cat."

"But a cat springs with its whole body."

"In our time, all kinds of torso and arm gestures can be done with ballet leg gestures."

"Don't ballet dancers usually turn their feet out?"

"Turning the feet in is a way of pedestrianizing a ballet step. Let me show you a fragment from *Growing.*"

Pas de Chat

Leaning forward, hands clasped behind the back, I stepped forward and thumped a heel—stepped and thumped with the other foot—then
pas de chat, slap the thighs
pas de chat, clap forward
pas de chat, slap the thighs
and a half-turn jump to bring the feet together and the hands behind the back for a repeat backwards.

Exit-director clasped his hands behind his back and turned his feet out and in. "Finding the familiar in a ballet step."

"Yes, giving it the weight of an everyday gesture." I stood in a turned-out position.

"On the other hand, formalizing a pedestrian move like a walking step." He lifted his leg before stepping forward.

"Or a slap." I slapped my thighs, and he imitated.

"It seems to me composers used to turn street cries into sonata themes. Now we turn sonata themes into street cries."

"The same in dance. I like to work back and forth between the theater and the street."

"In my plays, people speak and move the way they do every day. No one has any dance training. You clearly know modern as well as ballet."

"I explore both. After the street *pas de chat*, I use a swing from modern dance to lead into a ballet step. I'll show you."

Swing into Petits Pas Courus en Tournant

I swung the body and arms from side to deep down to side, each swing culminating in a half-turn of tapping steps on the toes (*petits pas courus en tournant*) to change from facing inside the circle to outside to inside to outside. My hands dropped down and reached progressively higher on each swing and turn, until they arced overhead with the final and only complete turn.

I came to where Exit-director was standing.

"A large buildup for a small turn broken into many parts," he observed. "It looked difficult to do those moves going sideways."

"I wanted to bring out the effort and the change of orientation from inside to outside the circle."

"I thought of a worker twisting this way and that, bending and lifting, until the task was done."

"Interesting. I want to do more with work gestures."

Shuffling footsteps and giggles interrupted our exchange. The religious institution's kindergarten class had come to visit. Exit-director looked over at the sleeper on the sofa, who had not budged, then led the children to the other end of the cavernous space and turned on more lights. I offered to dance part of *Growing* for them.

"I know how to dance," a child lifted both arms and turned on her toes.

"Me, too." Another child spun around.

"Me, too ..."

"Me, too ..."

The teacher helped me seat the children on the floor in a large circle. "This dance is called *Growing*, because my movements and circles of the space keep growing larger. There's no music, but listen for all the different sounds the body makes. After I dance, it will be your turn to dance."

Battements Développés

Begin circling the space with low kicks, legs bent to straight (battements développés)—side, side, front—a half turn and a kick to the back—like three 'hellos' and a 'how-do-you-do.'

Keep circling with higher kicks, hands at the waist and elbows out. The children alternately leaned forward and backed away.

Hands clasped behind the neck, repeat the kicks, still higher, and on the half-turn, thrust the arms down with a loud exhale to intensify the backward leg strike. The children edged back.

End the kicks with one to the front as high as possible, arms and hands flung high overhead, and a grand battement back on the exhale, body leaning forward, arms sweeping back like wings.

To complete the orbit, change dynamics with steps backward, drawing the other foot in by contracting the torso. Repeat the backward steps, the rhythm accenting the inwardness of the moves: step D R A W — step DRAW step — DRAW step DRAW — sustained turn on the toes (soutenu en tournant).

End the turn with the torso in deep contraction, hands crossed at the crotch, and head down. The children were silent.

Balancé, Arabesque, Soutenu en Tournant

Start making a bigger circle with slow waltz steps (balancés)—an arm reaching high on the forward steps and low on the backward turning ones.

"How old are you now?" a child asked.

"Not very old," I answered, while continuing the lyrical phrase: s*tep forward and lift the other leg backward into arabesque, one arm reaching forward, the other back, a powerful reaching out gesture from the ballet vocabulary.*

Step another arabesque with the leg higher.

"Are you grown up yet?" a second child picked up on the question-and-answer game.

"Not yet."

Return to the sustained turn on the toes (soutenu) to resolve the phrase on an inward-turning note.

"When will you be grown up?" a third child added to the sound score.

"Not for a while."

Launch into faster waltz steps that covered more space, followed by three arabesques. Again a soutenu turned the action inward momentarily.

To complete the larger circle, waltz (balancés) backwards, swaying from side to side, ending with a reaching arabesque and a turn with crossed arms moving up the body to overhead and opening out to the sides. The children wiggled and squirmed forward and stretched out their hands to try and touch me, as I waltzed by them.

Chassé, Reach, Pas de Bourrée, Pirouette

For the next still larger circling of the space, the tempo picked up and the movements lightened. *Gallop forward (chassé), lunge and open one arm in a big torso-motivated reach to the children.*

"How old do you think I am?" I asked, *repeating the chassé and reaching to the other side* against a roar of number calling.

"Fifteen" ... "Sixteen" ... "Seventeen" ... "My cousin is twenty."

Travel sideways with a crossing step front, open step side, crossing step back (grapevine in folk dance, pas de bourrée in ballet), body twisting, arms wrapping around the waist, ending with a spin (pirouette).

"Are you twenty-two?" ... "Twenty-five?" ... "Thirty?" The children couldn't imagine anyone older than thirty.

Repeat the gallops and reaches, grapevine steps and spins, finishing with a heroic pose—legs in a forward lunge, head lifted up and back, and arms extended like wings.

"Let me stop there." The children clapped, and I walked around clapping and getting them on their feet to go through the fundamental gestures of *Growing*.

"Reach up to the **sky**..." I spoke and demonstrated.

"Bend down and touch the **ground** ...

"Turn around, hugging your**self** ...
"Reach out and join hands with your **neighbors** ...
"**Circle** the space by walking eight steps ...
"Again—**sky** ... **ground** ... **self** ... **neighbors** ... **circle** ..."

We varied the pattern by moving into the center of the space and reaching up, backing out and touching the floor, turning on axis in different ways, joining hands and circling with skips and slides. "Give yourselves a round of applause." We all applauded and then the teacher and children left, clapping and jumping, skipping and waving.

I waltzed to the small desk where Exit-director was sitting and drawing on a sketch pad. "Dance in silence for kindergarten kids," he said and looked up at me.

"I'm still responding to ballets I saw as a child."

He continued to draw. "You don't compromise."

"I compromised today."

"Explain." Exit-director alternately looked up and drew.

"I once tried to do all of *Growing* for second graders. Some watched with great intensity, but I worried about the others and lost confidence in the dance and myself. Since then, I've performed only a fragment for children."

Exit-director switched to another pen. "Today there was talking."

"I encouraged it. Another compromise, though it may be the key to performing the whole dance for a young audience."

"Talking throughout might bury the dance." He put down the pen and sat back.

I looked at the sketch he had made of me. The gesture was accurate and full of life. "You draw as well as act, direct, write, and do programming for The Exit."

"I work part-time as a graphic artist."

"Would you make a poster for me?"

A nod, yes. "When can I see all of *Growing*—without children and talking."

"A few friends are coming to a rehearsal in the upstairs meeting room where I rehearse, and the minister has asked me to perform at a service."

"How can you dance circles in the sanctuary?"

"I think I can adapt the expanding pattern for the main aisle and cross aisle in front of the altar."

"Circles in a t-shaped space? Let me know the date of the sanctuary performance."

Exit-director went over to the sleeper on the sofa, and I walked slowly up the back stairs to the workspace. No more interruptions that day, but I kept listening for unfamiliar sounds in the stair halls and rearranged the furniture so that intruders would be noticeable immediately.

Rehearsing for an Unusual Retired Dancer

Liz Henderson brought a retired professional dancer, who had performed in China and the Soviet Union, to see *Downtown* and *Growing* in the upstairs meeting room. Under five feet tall and slight, costumed in a straw hat, embroidered blouse, wrap-around skirt, and sandals, she entered and floated around the space before being introduced to Harris and me. After a brief exchange, she circled the room again before deciding on a seat for the showing. I performed both dances, trying not to worry about the presence and approval of Unusual-Dancer.

At the conclusion, Liz immediately voiced a criticism: "One section of *Growing*—not the last one, but the one before that—was so fast, it was just a blur." She was referring to the *petit allegro* section that had been giving me a lot of trouble. I had to circle four times in widening orbits with small fast motions that reached up, down, in, and out, and traveled backward and sideways as often as forward.

"I danced the section too fast, an ongoing problem for me."

"There was sensuality in some of the movements. You could bring that out," said Liz.

"Good suggestion, I'll do that."

Unusual-Dancer entered the discussion. "You obviously think of dancing for the ear as well as the eye. Why not make the different sounds more emphatic?"

"Another good suggestion. Thank you."

"You're following in the footsteps of other political artists by making a collage or montage of dance materials," mused Unusual-Dancer.

She stood up and walked toward the windows before saying more: "I liked the alternation between dancing and walking sections. You ran both in counter-clockwise circles. In some mythologies, a counter-clockwise circle symbolizes death." (Whether or not other audience members would be aware of this symbolism, the comment made me re-consider the directions of the orbits. After experimenting, I decided it was best to keep them all going the same way, each one contributing a little more to *Growing*.)

The windows were open, but the room was warm. Unusual-Dancer took off her hat and used it as a fan. "When I began to dance, I did pieces like yours—pieces about everyday life in China. I still might be dancing today if I had continued, but I was sidetracked by a Soviet choreographer I admired. Major theaters, large audiences—when the company collapsed, I couldn't return to experimental dance."

"Do you remember your early dances?" I asked.

"Yes. I've taught them to dancers here and there, now and again."

"Would you teach one to me?"

"No. You're too good a dancer. You're making your own dances, and you should continue."

Unusual-Dancer turned away from me and then turned back. "I have another suggestion for *Growing*. In the walking circles, you touch the floor, walls, objects in the room, and yourself. Why not touch the people in the audience as well."

I realized immediately that would add emphasis to the dimension of reaching out. "I've been successful with audience participation in one of my dances and wanted to do more."

"Audience participation ..." Unusual-Dancer put on her hat, adjusted her skirt, and floated to the door. "Experiments are for the young. Now I prefer traditional dance with music on the stage of a theater."

After Liz and Retired-dancer left, I went back to the *petit allegro* section and danced parts of it for Harris, slowing down the movements and bringing out the sensual qualities and sounds.

Step on to the toes (piqué), the other foot slithering up the ankle, one hand moving up the abdomen, and step down—
Step up again, the free foot slithering up to the calf, the hand continuing to move invitingly up the torso, and step down—
Third step up, the free foot slithering up to the knee, the hand rising along the neck and cheek, and step down to set off tapping steps on the toes in a half circle, the hand lowering into a pushing away motion toward Harris—
He laughed.

I tried another fragment. *From a lunge, inhale and lift the front foot to the knee, hands rising up the center of the body; exhale and drop the foot behind (passé), followed by a big breathy circle of the torso and arms—side, back, side, forward—ending with a slap of the hands on the floor.*
"That breathes," said Harris.

I moved on to another fragment. *Step and rock forward, one arm sweeping out to the side and across in a big embrace, and then undulate the torso to propel swooshing steps backward, the other arm moving up the body and face and reaching backward to extend the arch of the body toward Harris—*
"Like a maenad," he said.

I tried a springing fragment. *Step hop (sauté), leg back in arabesque, hands slapping the thighs—repeat, changing legs—run forward, opening the arms wide—and jump to turn half way around, snapping the arms across the middle. Repeat the playful sequence backward, leg rising forward on the step hops ...*
"Looks like fun," said Harris.

The last orbit of the *petit allegro* section was an accelerating tattoo of traveling steps sideways with the feet crossed, the front foot stamping and the back foot tapping—
stamp tap, stamp tap, stamp tap ...
punctuated by a spring like a cat (*pas de chat*) at nine o'clock, six o'clock, three o'clock, and home, the hands reaching out on the stamp taps and moving down the sides of the body on the pas de chat, all the way to the floor on the last landing.
Harris walked toward me with a big smile. "Better," we both agreed.

1969 Growing in the Church Sanctuary

Exit-director came to see *Growing* in the sanctuary of the First Methodist Church, a performance that almost didn't happen. I sent a brief description of the dance and a resume to the minister, who responded by saying that the Worship Committee wanted a meeting with me for further explanation. I wrote him back saying that I would appreciate his handling negotiations with the Worship Committee, that I was eager to dance, but if there was too much opposition, we could call off the performance.

A few days later, the minister greeted me on the way to rehearsal with a victory sign. "About three-quarters of the way through the service, the organist is going to play a religious dance tune, which will be your cue to enter. Maybe you could begin with a few introductory words—something like that description of *Growing* you wrote for the Committee."

I forgot how many verses the organist was supposed to play and entered too soon, making it necessary to stand in front of the congregation, trying to look interested in the music and move minimally to the rhythm, while feeling very exposed in a white leotard and black tights. Worst of all, the sanctuary was unheated, and my bare feet grew colder and colder. The walk to the pulpit to speak and the walk to take up the opening position were painful. My circulation improved once the dance started, and I turned my full attention to making articulate gestures that didn't look truncated within the restricted spacing.

The slower and more deliberate sections of dancing and walking fanned out quite easily from the intersection of the main and cross aisles in front of the altar. Because the sanctuary was resonant and the worshippers silent, even the sounds of quieter movements were audible. The reaches up and out were particularly meaningful in the vast, high-ceilinged space lit by stained glass windows, while the earthy, sensual, and personal gestures were more difficult to communicate. I used more and more of the t-shaped aisle space. By the *grand allegro* section, the slides, circles of the legs, hops, jumps, and leaps grew too big. The dance could no longer be contained in the sanctuary. I left by the main aisle, reached out and shook hands with those who reached back, opened the doors and went out to the steps that faced the streets, buildings, and central Green of the city.

Exit-director and I had made plans to meet outdoors on the steps after the service.

"The aisles were a challenge, but you used them well," he said.

We stood and looked out at the Green.

"Do you know the elevated platform out there?" he asked.

"The one that's used for arts festivals?"

"Yes. Could you dance on it?"

"What kind of shape is it in?"

"The boards are warped. No two come together."

"I've had nightmares about dancing on that kind of stage."

"It's a clear space. You could dance in circles."

"The *grand allegro* section of *Growing* might work better than it did in the sanctuary."

"I'm looking for someone to perform on Saturday night at this year's festival. The usual groups with the city and university stamp of approval aren't participating. They say that since the inner-city riots, their people don't come to the Green."

"Sounds like our kind of situation."

"I've lined up painters, sculptors, and photographers for the tent exhibits. The best rock groups that play the Exit will perform—and the Exit Players."

"What about a rock group for Saturday night?"

"They have paying gigs."

"A solo dancer in silence?"

"Do you always perform in silence?"

"Actually not. I've danced *Newspapers* to eighteenth century music. *Downtown* has a taped collage of pop music and words, and I've been thinking about a jazz piece for *Growing*. Then only *When the Landlord Left…* would be in silence."

"Maybe we could use microphones to amplify the sounds you make."

"Will there be a good sound system?"

"The city has agreed to provide lights and sound. Come the night before and check them out. The platform is always there for rehearsing."

"You've laid down the gauntlet for me." I bowed.

Exit-director bowed in return. "Oh, I almost forgot. One of the Exit Players is getting married and wants someone to do a wedding dance—for a fee. I recommended you."

Growing as a Wedding Dance

Exit-player telephoned that night. "We're creating our own ceremony, and in a book on old customs, we read about wedding dances. Both of us come from religions that frown on dancing, but stop short of total prohibition."

"Do you want the dance as part of the ceremony or the reception?" I asked.

"The end of the ceremony. Our argument is that we're honoring tradition and keeping it alive by challenging it."

"Where will the wedding take place?"

"At the ocean front in a big old frame hotel that looks like an overgrown cottage—white clapboards, black shutters, an attic storey—"

"All in need of repair—I know the place. Folk singers used to have hootenannies there." I talked about *Growing* as a possible wedding dance and set a date for Exit-player to see a rehearsal in the upstairs meeting room.

She was tall and broad and walked across the room with long strides to greet me. I was warmed up and ready to go and suggested we talk after the dancing. She sat down on one of the chairs. I walked to the starting point, took a few breaths, and performed the circles growing larger, often making contact with her through looks, reaches with the legs and arms, and during the walking refrains.

I had been working and reworking the *grand allegro* section, trying to dance the big fast movements as talking gestures rather than technical feats. When do we do *grand allegro* in everyday life? We gallop forward and open our arms to greet someone (*chassé* with open arms); circle a leg over an obstacle (*grand rond de jambe*); run and jump for joy (*pas couru, assemblé*); skip and kick, leap and slide with excitement (*ballonné, pas de basque*); waltz forward, backward, and around in ecstasy (*grands balancés*). For the last and most exuberant moves (*fouettés en l'air, sautés, grands jetés*), a folk tune came into my mind:

"Whoever treasures freedom"—*slide and turn in the air, legs flying*
"Like the swallow"—*skip fast, skip high, skip higher*
"Has learned to fly"—*run and leap, run and leap*

The flying arms and legs came to an abrupt stop at the starting spot. I took a breath, turned, walked the final orbit—*touching the floor, walls, myself, the Exit-player*—and walked toward an exit door. "That's the end."

Exit-player applauded and approached me. "Would it be possible for the wedding couple to join you at the end of *Growing*?"

"Of course!" I reached out a hand, Exit-player took it, and we started to walk in a circle. "A dancer suggested that I touch people. You've pushed the notion one step further."

"Joining you seems the obvious conclusion to what's come before."

"Sometimes it takes an outside eye to see the obvious. The ending of *Growing* has been anti-climactic, but I haven't known how to fix it."

As we continued walking, Exit-player said, "I wanted to study ballet. My family opposed the idea for religious reasons, and I was always too tall and too wide. Your gestures are looser, freer."

We arrived at the chairs and sat down. "At one performance of *Growing*, a modern dancer in the audience said there was too much ballet, and a ballet dancer countered that there was no ballet at all."

"I saw ballet movements, but they were changed, because you truly dance in the round."

"I like to handle gestures from the multi-point perspective of the dancer instead of the one-point perspective of the best box in the theater."

"Off the stage, we see backs and sides of steps as well as fronts." Exit-player paused and then went on: "Without music, the steps are less flowing, more uneven. A person my size can identify with that."

"There was a ballet master in the eighteenth century, who urged dancers to go out on the street and observe how people moved. That idea seems to reappear when dance goes through a period of change."

"Like now."

"Yes, a time to rethink what's meaningful."

"Just what we're trying to do with the wedding ceremony. *Growing* will be the perfect ending." Exit-player and I stood and headed for the door. "I'll call you with directions for reaching the hotel, and we can try to figure out a rehearsal schedule. I hope the room will be large enough."

Exit-player's fears proved to be justified. With all the wedding guests seated on the perimeter, the space was small, and I had to be careful not to trip over feet or fall into someone's lap, but the concept of growing came across—and with new meaning because of the group ending. For the first time, it was clear that a person can grow just so much without the participation of others.

After performing the final circles of dancing and walking, I arrived at the wedding couple and extended both hands. "Will you join me?" The advance planning ended with the three of us taking hands and walking together, but whether inspired by their reading about wedding dances or by the spirit of the occasion, the couple started inviting the wedding guests to join in, including the anti-dance relatives. No one could resist the invitation, and the three of us led the whole assembly in a serpentine march through the space. "Form an arch," I coached the couple, and I led the line of guests under the arch and out to form one big circle with the newlyweds in the center.

Dancer-in-Residence

A wedding guest who worked for the Connecticut Arts Commission approached me during the reception. "The state is starting an artists-in-education program. Would you be interested in doing a two-week residency in a suburban high school?"

"If I can give a preliminary performance for the students and let them decide if they want to work with me."

"The principal and teachers will probably go along with that. This is a pilot program to bring the experience of practicing artists into the schools."

"Good, because I would like to work with the students as if they were members of my dance group."

At North Haven High School, when the only space available for the preliminary performance turned out to be an auditorium with a stage too small for seating the audience in-the-round, a daunting challenge arose: I had to perform my dances on the stage for the first time. Would they read with the dancer separated from the audience? How could I pull off the participatory ending of *Growing*?

About two hundred and fifty students made their way into the six-hundred-seat auditorium and sat scattered in clusters and rows. With the stage and house equally lit, I started clapping and soon everyone was clapping. Aware that dancing was more likely to hold the students' attention than talking, I had prepared a brief announcement about the program and my upcoming residency and had just begun to speak when loud laughing and whistling erupted from the back row. I stopped in mid-sentence, left the stage, and marched up the aisle to confront the troublemakers. "Either behave or leave," I said. They were stunned into silence by the presence right next to them of a determined performer, weight planted on both feet, hands on hips. "If you leave, you'll miss the best dance performance of your lives." I did an about face and returned to the stage. A door opened and closed, and the back row had fewer people when I resumed speaking.

There was no sound in the auditorium through the rest of the introductory remarks and the beginning of the first dance *Newspapers*. Finally someone found the courage to giggle when I hid behind a paper—then more giggles when a folded paper became a fan—and when I invited a member of the audience to come up on stage and hold a paper as a flag, give-and-take between performer and audience was established. There was sighing when I lay down on a paper and rolled up in it, silence to catch soft shoe and breath rhythms, murmuring and chuckling that seemed to alternate with the crackling, rippling, and crunching of the newspaper. "Despair" elicited the most demonstrative reaction with its variations on murder, suicide, and burial. I ripped free of the papers and announced, "That's the end." The students applauded, and I nodded, bowed, and clapped acknowledgment.

"The next dance is called *Growing*. A person can grow just so much alone—without reaching out to others. At the end of this dance, I'll ask you to join me. Your participation is voluntary."

Walk to the back of the stage and begin with circles of the arms, then moves of the legs, the whole body, and the body turning.
Walk the first orbit—small and oriented to the floor.

Move out into the stage space with circles of street pas de chat, low swings into high tapping half-turns, broken kicks, a waltzing phrase, and slides and reaches concluding with pirouettes.

Walk the second orbit—larger and oriented up and out.

Cover more of the stage space with growing circles of high steps and low steps; rocks forward and sweeps backward; springs in arabesque, slides, and jumps; running steps forward and turns on axis; accelerating stamp-taps, alternating with high-springing pas de chat. It was much more difficult to reach out to spectators from the proscenium. With the lights on, I picked out rows and clusters of students and directed gestures to them, but was unsure what was communicating. Stop worrying and do the dance as choreographed, an inner voice prompted.

Walk the third orbit—larger still, running the hands up the front of the body, up the face, over the head, and down the back. The obvious reference to self preceded direct contact with the audience. I went down the steps and walked along the first row of seats, touching seats, jackets, and books before touching knees, hands, shoulders, and heads of students.

I returned to the stage for the final orbits of dance: *slides, big circles of the legs—arms opening and reaching out—running steps, jumps; bounding ballonnées and pas de basque; waltz steps that swept high and low; a climactic phrase of hops, slides, turns in the air, runs, and leaps that passed dangerously close to the edge of the stage; and finally, repeats of run run skip, run run leap!*

Pause ...

The students were very quiet as I walked forward, descended once again to where they were, and reached out a hand: "Will you join me?" The student took the offered hand, a second joined, and a third. Suddenly there was lots of buzzing and movement. "Shall we?" ... "Are you going to?" ... "Yes?" ... "No?" ... I went up the aisle, looking at each face, reaching and asking: "Will you join us?" Some students hesitated, some left, some scattered to the far walls, but at least half joined the group and linked hands. There was no cross aisle at the back of the auditorium. I had no choice but to open the door and go out into the corridor.

This was a dance performance, not a political demonstration, but the energy generated was formidable. The principal and other staff members had come out of their offices and stood in frozen positions, unsure how to react. I opened another door to the auditorium and led the students back in, down another aisle and up on to the stage, where everyone started to jump, clap, shimmy and shake, laugh, shout, spin, kick, and slide. Everyone danced and danced until the bell rang, announcing the end of the period.

By my standards, the pay was quite good for the two-week residency, but with four classes a day, one and a half to two hours each, it was impossible to do anything but prepare, teach, eat, and sleep. As I expected, the two classes of students, who had chosen to work with me on the stage, went much better than the music and drama classes that had been assigned and met in large classrooms. The volunteers learned parts of *Growing* and *When the Landlord Left...*, to which they added ideas from their own experience and ethnic backgrounds that gave me new material to think about. At the final showing, the arts commission representative was impressed enough to ask: "Would you be willing to do more residencies?"

"Yes, I said, but only two classes a day—and not for the next few months. I have performances scheduled and want to work on some new choreography."

"An elementary school principal in Groton is looking for an 'experimental dancer.' It's a bit of a commute—about forty minutes."

"An 'experimental dancer'—how can I say no?"

"The principal will call, and you can negotiate the terms."

I was glad to return to dancing after the teaching stint, though the upper-story meeting room had a new problem. A neighborhood marching band now used it for pre- and post-parade activities and always left a mess. Each time after cleaning up, I groaned and moaned—if only I had my own space.

For all the ballet steps in *Growing*, I hadn't been doing a ballet warm-up. Grueling *ronds de jambe en l'air* and grands battements had seemed unwarranted for works that had as many pedestrian as formal dance movements. I had been experimenting with freer ways of warming up—walking, running, swinging the arms, circling the head, collapsing, rising. During the two weeks of teaching at the high school, the less technical warm-up worked well with the untrained students, but returning to the studio to rehearse and choreograph, I noticed a loss of control, tightness in the legs, weakness in the back. Running warms the body, but doesn't prepare it for the kind of strength, precision, balance, stretch, and changes of weight that dance requires. I went back to the disciplined, formal ballet barre, and within a few days, felt stretched and controlled enough to move out into the space and try ballet combinations that remained in my muscle memory. *Barre, adagio, petit allegro, grand allegro*—I realized how much *Growing* grew like a ballet class: from the basic, deliberate positions and steps in one spot—to the first moving out into space, building on the basics with simple combinations of steps—to more demanding balances, rhythms, and coordination of body parts—to full-out locomotion through space, pausing at will. Rehearsing the dance in the studio could feel like a remembrance of a class with Mr. Quinn.

Although *Growing* had been working well in silence, I felt that for performances on television and the downtown Green, the dance needed music. Not having a sound system in my rehearsal studio, I improvised to recordings at home in our third floor apartment—stumbling over furniture, tripping on the rug in the living room, sliding on the vinyl in the kitchen, stubbing my toes on the uneven wood floor in the bedroom, and ricocheting off the walls of the narrow corridor that linked the spaces. (Fortunately, the tenants on the second floor had jobs that kept them away all day.) Classical, jazz, rock, folk, electronic, environmental sound—no one piece seemed suitable for the whole dance, nor could I find four short pieces, one for each section of the dance.

A favorite jazz cut by the great saxophonist John Coltrane was the right length, but the divisions by instrument (clarinet, piano, bass, and percussion, in addition to saxophone) synchronized oddly with the verse/refrain, dancing/walking structure of *Growing*. I had been listening and improvising to the piece all through the composition of the dance, letting its rhythms affect the phrasing and its sounds bring out the emotional and sensual sides of the movements. When I danced *Growing* in silence, that jazz cut ran through my mind. I showed parts of the piece with music to Harris in our small living room. He made a few suggestions, and with doubts, I decided that for my performances on television and the Green, I would dance to Coltrane.

1970 WNHC Television, New Haven

The making of the television program was so rushed, there was no possibility of confronting the challenges of filming dance. Unlike my first television appearance, which had commercial sponsors, this was a weekly, fifteen-minute free spot that the channel gave to the council of religious groups in the city. The pre-broadcast taping took place at night, either the last job or overtime for the director and camera person, who were harried and impatient. They had three different groups and lots of announcements to cram into the time slot. I had no choice but to do the axial opening section of *Growing*, given the four-minute time limit and closet-sized performing space. (Rehearsing in the third floor apartment turned out to be good preparation.) No run-throughs—no previews—stand there—wait for the signal—go tape—go dance and music—do it—get it over with—next group. The one good thing about the appearance was the chance to tell people to come out and see the whole dance at the arts festival on the Green the following weekend.

Summerfest '70, New Haven Green

Since the founding of New Haven in 1638, the Green has been the heart of the city. Used as a communal pasture by the original settlers, over the years it became the scene of town meetings, plots and trials, parades and festivals, and in the 1960s and 70s, civil rights and anti-war demonstrations. Privately owned by descendants of the original settlers, groups that want to stage an event must get permission from the owners, who tend to be open-minded and usually grant it. As I rehearsed for my performance on the outdoor platform, sometimes I was facing Yale University buildings, which occupied about half the Green frontage, and sometimes civic buildings—city hall, courthouse, post office, library—or downtown businesses, which occupied the other half.

A strong part of urban renewal rhetoric had been the commitment to making the Green and adjacent business district—the historic center of the city—competitive with suburban shopping centers. What fighting migration to the suburbs had meant, in fact, was removal of low-income housing, shops, and people from inner-city neighborhoods to make way for highways, corporate headquarters, Yale buildings, and other projects that served the interests of the rich. The commission, which investigated the cause of the terrible summer riots of 1967, concluded that so many housing units had been destroyed that people, who had neither the money nor status to relocate out of the inner city, had no place to go. Since the riots, tension between the advocates and victims of urban renewal had remained at a high level. I had been invited to perform at the summer arts festival, because the usual organizers from Yale and the city had turned it over to the counter-culture, and the usual groups weren't participating. They thought the Green was too dangerous since the riots, and there would be no audience or the wrong audience.

On the day of the outdoor performance, the weather was threatening. Would it rain? Would the wind make it impossible to perform *Newspapers*? I was troubled about the proscenium situation—performer in light, audience in darkness. The elevated platform was hazardous; the boards were so warped and separated that the ground was visible in some spots. About two hundred chairs had been lined up auditorium style with a gap large enough for a full symphony orchestra between the chairs and the platform. The sound and light technician had a full-time job and no time for a rehearsal with microphones, tape deck, speakers, and lights, which were mounted on tall stanchions on either side of the platform. Harris agreed to sit at the control table and give cues. My greatest doubts and fears, however, centered on whether a solo dancer could have an exchange with a volatile urban audience downtown on a Saturday night.

When I stepped to the microphone, about a hundred people had gathered—political people, alternate life-style people, street people from different neighborhoods, all kinds of people except those, who normally attended the arts festivals on the Green from the arts and crafts clubs, suburbs, and Yale.

Newspapers was a warm-up for the audience and me, and for the technician, who turned both microphones on for the introductory statement and forgot to turn them off. The sounds were amplified as I walked forward scattering pages of newspaper; backed up hiding behind a page; folded a page into a thin strip, lifted it like a weight, and let it open into a fan; crept across the papers on hands and knees and rolled up in one like a homeless person. I heard Harris's voice from the control table: "Leave the microphones on. They're picking up the sounds of the dance, which is great." And they stayed on for the rest of the program.

The witty eighteenth century music allowed me to add mannered looks at the floor before leaping or stamping to insure that my feet landed on the boards of the platform rather than between them. The audience participation moment of having a spectator hold the newspaper as a flag was successful, as usual, and another spectator became a performer by picking up a paper that flew off the stage and bringing it to me on cue for the section of racing to collect all the papers and pile them into a stack. There was an audible response to the alternation of goose-steps with paper held high and scraping steps with paper on the bent back—and to the scrunching of a page into a ball, hugging it, and spiraling to the ground. The mock murder, suicide, burial, and final ripping free of the newspapers brought laughter and applause.

After taking off the shirt and pants worn for *Newspapers*, leaving only a robin's egg blue leotard and tights and red sneakers as costume for *Downtown*, I felt naked. Each movement sequence—in relation to boots, hat, belt, pearls—exposed another part of the body. What setting could be better than downtown for a dance with images of the fantasies and frustrations of shopping? A person starts out with a shopping bag full of dreams, but finds that

the boots, which are supposed to make the feet fly, pinch;
the hat for height and style is heavy and clumsy;
the belt, bought to streamline the torso, stabs and constricts;
the pearls for elegance and allure strangle;
the wallet is empty; and
when the whole outfit is on, the body can move only in fixed poses or not at all.

While the lights of the stores that faced the Green beckoned to the audience (*You can always go downtown ... Everything's waiting for you*), the script, which I wrote and recorded as the sound score, argued with buying as a solution to all problems. I ended the dance by acting out the struggle to free the body from commodities, which inhibit and prevent us from moving freely.

After *Downtown,* I had to take a pause to breathe and change costume. I wondered if the audience would leave. Quite the opposite. More people seemed to be coming. Most of the chairs were occupied, and there were people sitting on blankets in the orchestra pit and to either side of the chairs. I reappeared in baggy black leggings, orange long-sleeved leotard, and black knitted vest (with the red sneakers still on, of course) and announced: *When the landlord left, I did the only thing a poor soul can do, I walked around the room and scratched my head*—that's the title of the next dance.

Laughter came from near and far.

"Tell it like it is," said a spectator.

I told the background story of an inner-city tenant, who was forced to move five times by urban renewal.

"You got it," said a voice close-by.

"Sounds like my story," said a voice from farther away.

In listing the groups working to change the city's priorities, I left one name out. An audience member ran up to the edge of the stage and shouted the name of the omitted group. I apologized for the omission, and the audience member acknowledged it with a nod.

Sighs, grunts, groans, guffaws, and comments greeted the various characters in the dance and their dealings with the chair:

Inner-city Tenant
Landlord
Police Officer
Social Worker
Housing Inspector
Student
Concerned Citizen
Bulldozer

As I ended with a reprise of **Inner-city Tenant**, who picked up the chair dropped by **Bulldozer**, and carried it out into the audience, a co-worker from AIM whispered, "I don't know how you're doing this performance."

"Neither do I," I whispered back.

"You look so confident."

"I've been terrified."

"The audience is with you," said the co-worker.

I returned to the platform for *Growing*, the last and hardest challenge of the program. Coltrane turned out to be an irresistible ally. There was an influx of new people, leaning on the stage, perching on the light stanchions, and reclining, sitting, or standing on the grass all the way out to the sidewalk. Even the wind seemed to acknowledge the rhythms of the music and the dance. Not intrusive for the first three pieces, it came up and built to great gusts that whipped the muslin backdrop up and around and back and forth during the climactic orbits of waltzing, turning in the air, running, skipping, leaping, and reaching.

The arts critic for the *New Haven Register*, who was in the audience, wrote:

One cannot compete with Coltrane. Though, towards the end of a piece that had me listening more than watching, Stone seemed to acknowledge the music's force and worked towards instead of against or with Coltrane. Her movements grew; she seemed to be 'growing' vinelike. We witnessed their romance. Indeed romance is the only way of being with Coltrane.

Maybe the whole audience had a romance with Coltrane and me by extension. As impossible as it seems, when I came down off the lit platform into the unlit audience and asked, "Will you join me?" many people did. A line formed that snaked through and around the chairs and then broke into clusters. Some people kept dancing, others came and talked to me or stood and talked among themselves, and the rest drifted off into the downtown streets.

Exchange with Balletomane

Not long after the festival on the Green, Harris and I went to see a visiting ballet company at the Shubert Theatre. In the lobby after the performance, I bumped into an acquaintance who was a ballet devotee and sometimes wrote dance reviews for small publications. I had read a few of his pieces and usually disagreed with his views. We hardly talked about the ballets we had just seen. Rather, our exchange turned into a surreal academic battle between conservative and innovative forces in dance. Harris couldn't believe it went on for as long as it did.

"What are you doing at a ballet performance?" Balletomane asked.

"Ballet was the starting point for my new dance *Growing*," I replied.

"The one you did on the Green? I didn't see any ballet in that piece."

"Maybe you were sitting too far away."

"Don't be rude." People were scurrying past us on their way out of the theatre. We dodged them and went on arguing.

"Early in the dance there was a *renversé*, a big sweep of the leg from front to back." I demonstrated with an arm.

"No need for a definition or demonstration. One step in isolation."

"Actually I did several *renversés*, but only the last one was complete."

"Awkward. If you break a ballet step apart, it's no longer a ballet step."

"Or it becomes a new kind of ballet step." Harris was standing by us, looking uncomfortable, but not speaking.

"Your torso moves are twisted, bent, totally unballetic."

"Do you expect dancers in our time to stay vertical?"

"A patronizing question. Of course not, as long as the wider use of the torso doesn't destroy the ballet line." A cluster of people walking and talking separated to keep from bumping into us.

"I broke the *renversé* apart to make the lines of the legs, torso, and arms more visible."

"Then legs, torso, and arms become separate entities."

"Free to form new steps."

"*Voila!* The ballet line disappears—in fact, the whole step disappears, so why insist on calling what you do ballet?"

"To maintain the link to dance history." I bowed.

"A strange thing for an experimental dancer to say."

Harris had sat down on a bench near the exit, and we walked towards him. "You do a lot of walking in your dance," said Balletomane.

"Yes, I alternate circles of dance moves with circles of walking steps."

"Obviously not ballet."

"There's walking in ballet."

"Not in sneakers, clothes for the street not the stage, and to music for listening not dancing."

"What about jazz ballets?"

"The classicism has to be even stronger. A random juxtaposition of steps won't do."

"Such as rise, kick, lunge, circle the body, reach, which looks random, but isn't." I turned and reached to Harris, and he nodded.

"Nonsense as a ballet sentence."

"I could name the steps in French."

"It would still be nonsense. You're one of those conceptual choreographers, who write ballet steps."

"The early dancing masters wrote steps," I said. We sat down on the bench next to Harris, who was reading his program.

"They wrote long, unreadable treatises."

"I find the Renaissance and Baroque forms fascinating to study and do."

"The dances were dull."

"Galliards and gigues are quite lively and challenging to do."

"No comparison to the bravura technique today. Ballet has come a long way since then."

"I agree that ballet has changed and keeps changing. You want to stop it at a particular moment."

"You want to be historical and free of history at the same time," countered Balletomane.

There were only a few people left in the lobby, and the ushers were cleaning up.

"Isn't the present part of history? Can't past forms be updated?"

"For ballet to be ballet requires staying within certain parameters. Conceptual choreographers quickly stray outside of them."

"Like taking apart *renversés* and giving connecting steps as much importance as climactic ones."

"Yes, ideas that disrupt rhythm and nullify phrasing."

"Or change the sense of time for dancers and spectators." The ushers were locking the doors. Harris stood and walked to the exit, and we distractedly followed him.

"Speaking of time, your moves are more disconnected than flowing."

"Flow is an illusion in dance. I like to reveal the unevenness."

"Disrupted flow is for dolls and puppets, for grotesque and old characters," pronounced Balletomane.

"That kind of thinking limits ballet to technique and romance."

"A model of civilized behavior that goes with a particular state of mind."

We left the theatre by the only open door and turned to face each other. "Can the vocabulary be claimed free of that state of mind?"

"It ceases to be ballet."

"If that state of mind is no longer relevant, dance has to change to fit a new state of mind."

"With movement material other than ballet steps."

"As you said, once the steps are broken apart, they no longer look like ballet. They can serve new purposes."

"I go to dance concerts for enjoyment, not for mental acrobatics." Balletomane hurried away, as the lights of the marquee went off.

I took a deep breath and turned to Harris, who was looking across the street at what was once the College movie theatre. "Isn't that the building where Jack Quinn had his studio?" he asked.

"Yes," I said, "on the third floor—up a dingy dark staircase to ballet class, music, and dreams!"

We walked slowly toward the Green and the oldest buildings on the Yale campus. "You know how much I still love ballet ... the influence of Mr. Quinn ... respect for the development of western dance for centuries. But I'm choreographing now. I have to record our struggles."

"I have the same dilemma with past and present in architecture."

We stood at the corner of College and Chapel Streets, looking toward the concrete shopping mall that had been constructed in place of three old department stores, so well built they were hard for the bulldozers to knock down. "That Front Block is so ugly," I said.

"Urban renewal," Harris shook his head as we started for our car, "too much destruction of history."

1972 Anti-War Teach-in

Growing had a long life on potpourri programs and as an essential part of my portrait of the Socialist revolutionary, Rosa Luxemburg. In 1972, I gave a particularly memorable performance of the dance at an anti-war teach-in at Southern Connecticut State College. As the event was finding its stride, I whispered to Harris that I was going to do a warm-up at the back of the room. Using a piano for support, I did a ballet barre in a corner of the large multi-purpose room. When the organizers of the event invited me to perform, they expressed concern about the hard slippery floor, concrete covered with vinyl. I felt out the floor during the exercises and hoped that my red sneakers would provide enough cushion and traction.

The audience of about 150 people was seated in rows of chairs classroom style. All the speakers were well-informed and deeply committed to what they were saying, but their talks were long. By the end of the third talk, a pair of folk singers, who had been humming and strumming guitars near the door, moved into the hallway, and other students followed. A fourth speaker, a fifth—even people I recognized from other protest activities, who remained drawn-in by the cogent arguments in support of our cause, were beginning to sag in their seats. It was time for political action in a medium other than words. It was time for dancing.

When my turn came, I started shouting and clapping: "Help me clear this space. Move the chairs to the edge—way out—against the wall. I'm going to dance in the middle." Harris stood up immediately to help. Other people struggled to their feet, stretched, and moved into action, pushing and carrying and dragging chairs. Those, who must have been hanging around in the hallway, were attracted by the activity and noise, and the audience, which had begun to shrink, started to grow again.

Even before everyone had settled down, I walked into the center of the space: "There have been powerful words, but enough words for now. I'm going to dance. The title of this piece is *Growing*, and that's what it's about—that's what this teach-in is about—growing and changing. I start in one spot and move in larger and larger circles of dancing and walking until I can't go any further without asking you to join me. You've cleared this space. After I dance, it will be your turn to use it."

A migraine had been threatening, and with the first moves (*arm circles, followed by folk dance steps*), I knew it was going to get worse. An inner pep talk began, as I executed the steps: Forget your head (*extend a leg, lunge, circle the body*). Think about those, who are dying in the war (*seven broken turns with ever-higher leg circles*).

First orbit of walking.

Inner pep talk continued: Dance can get to people (*small leaps, runs, and jump*s) in a way that speeches cannot (*deep swings*). You are not just performing against the war (*big kicks*), but for the art of dance (*waltz, waltz, arabesque, turn*). Inner voice kept pushing: Look at the audience (*gallop, reach*). They are coming to life (*grapevine, spin, reach*).

Second orbit of walking.

Inner voice cajoled: Each movement is one more accomplished (*high steps, low steps, turns on the toes: tap-tap-tap, tap-tap-tap*) and one less to do (*big circle of the arms and body, slap the floor; rock forward, run backward*). The pounding in my head grew worse (*hop in arabesque, glide, glide, brush jump*), as the movements grew faster (*runs forward, turns on axis*) and more pounding (*stamp taps that accelerated around the space*).

The third orbit of walking was a respite—I ran my hands up my body and held them at my pulsing temples—before reaching out and touching the audience. I went to Harris and two political co-workers first and touched their knees and hands. The audience quickly picked up the idea, and as I went around, reaching and touching, they reached and touched in return.

Finally came the fastest section of the dance (*slides, big circles of the legs, runs, jumps*). The throbbing in my head was so fierce (*hops, kicks, slides, and leaps*), I was sure it must be visible (*sweeping waltz moves—high, low, sideways, turning*). Oh no! I had noticed bits of trash on the slick floor and saw the cigarette butt (*gallop, three skips turning*) a split-second before sliding on it and taking a dive. The migraine climaxed. I was up and moving so swiftly (*run run leap, run run leap*), the audience probably thought the fall was part of the dance (*hop, slide, turn in the air; leap, slide, turn in the air*). The migraine began to release, as I launched into the last circles (*run run run skip and run run skip*) with joyous, rhythmic words running in my head—comes a new sense of joy and freedom!

It was easy to get these spectators to participate. They were on their feet and ready to move when I walked the last orbit, pausing long enough to extend a hand and ask: "Will you join me?" Soon some of them echoed my question: "Will you join us?" The group formed a big circle, and I coached, "Into the center"—people instinctively raised their arms—"and out." The arms lowered. "Again: into the center and out," I directed. "Now circle around: three steps forward and two back."

"That's life," said one of the participants, and everyone laughed. A particularly enthusiastic person decided to break the circle and lead a string of followers in a weaving pattern. Other quintets and quartets broke off and started weaving. Pretty soon, the group was hopelessly tangled up, limbs twisted and bodies crushed against each other. Someone started clapping. Somehow limbs untwisted and bodies freed themselves, and suddenly everyone was clapping, jumping up and down, and shouting "Out! Now!"—followed by laughing, dancing, and embracing one another.

As Harris and I left, the pair of folk singers who had re-entered for the performance moved into the center of the space. Their strumming turned into music, and their humming into strong singing. Two other guitarists and a recorder player were taking their instruments out of the cases. A percussionist was pulling drums into the room. People were either singing along or rocking and swaying or just sitting and listening, and in a corner, a faction was talking and arguing politics. The audience had taken over the leadership.

I've moved ahead of my story. Back to the struggles of 1969 to find a rehearsal studio, search for new choreographic ideas, and go on confronting political issues of the moment through dance.

Chapter Three: If You Don't Jump In...

Search for a New Studio

One day I went to the upper-story meeting room to begin work on a new piece, opened the door, and saw folding tables and cardboard boxes blocking the space. The floor and furniture were strewn with the remains of a parade and party, no doubt left by the newest users, a neighborhood marching band. I returned to the hallway, sat down on a step, wrote the minister a cordial note of 'thanks and farewell,' delivered the note to the office, and went out in search of another studio. No more religious institutions. The performances and teaching were beginning to pay enough to consider a cheap rental. I read and responded to newspaper ads, asked friends for suggestions, even visited two real estate agents. All the cheap rentals were too small.

A trip to a downtown store for fabric to make tights solved the problem. I was a well-known customer, since I sewed everything from costumes to coats to bedspreads. Furthermore, my father had worked in the store for a short time after closing his own fabric business. The friendliest of the store owners came to one of my performances, and the two of us often chatted about dance and fabrics and everyday things.

"You look upset," he said.

"I left my old rehearsal studio and can't find another."

"We have an empty space in the warehouse. Let me show it to you." Friendly Owner led me to an adjoining building, and we took the freight elevator to the third floor. "The heaters are shut off above the first floor. The space might be cold in the winter." When the elevator stopped, he pulled out a pocket flashlight to find the string that turned on a lonely light bulb. It was too dark to see much.

"Why are the windows covered with cardboard?" I asked.

"The pigeons came in through the broken panes. We can get someone to replace them."

I slid a foot forward and around a few times and tried some jumps. "A wooden floor, thank goodness. It seems splintery, but strong and springy."

"It took a lot of punishment, when the building was a paint factory." Friendly Owner ran a finger down the wall and scuffed a foot. "Many layers of dust and dirt ..."

"But lots of space and privacy," I observed, my eyes having adjusted to the dim light. "How much will it cost to rent the space?"

"Nothing. It's been empty for years. Use it!" Friendly Owner looked toward the boarded up windows on what was once the front façade. "In years to come, we can put a plaque on this building, saying: STONE DANCED HERE!"

1969 Making a Studio in a Warehouse

Saturday morning

The Saturday after Friendly Owner offered the warehouse space for rehearsing, Harris came with me to help make the new studio usable. We removed the cardboard and found that only a few of the window panes were broken.

"You can cover the broken panes with clear plastic," said Friendly Owner, who had appeared to check on our progress. "There's some in the store that I can give you."

I had been moving around the space. "Definitely not enough light from the windows for rehearsing, and we want to begin working with video."

Friendly Owner pointed to outlets on the ceiling for lights.

"We can buy floodlights," said Harris. "How much power is available?" Friendly Owner and Harris checked the fuse box and figured out it had sufficient capacity.

I tried a dance sequence. "We need to buy new flooring."

"That will be an improvement," said Friendly Owner. "Will it be okay to glue the flooring down?"

"Sure. You need a stable surface to make masterpieces, so we can put a plaque on this building."

Harris and I left with Friendly Owner to learn how the elevator works, get the plastic for the windows, and borrow an industrial vacuum cleaner.

Saturday afternoon

We went in search of lights and flooring. We found floodlights at a lighting store in a suburban shopping center and vinyl on sale in a downtown store, which was willing to deliver the rolls the following week to the first floor of the warehouse.

Sunday

Friendly Owner gave us a key so we could enter the warehouse with the store closed. Vacuuming, sweeping, and mopping the space and washing the windows were exhausting tasks, made especially difficult by the lack of water on the third floor. Down and up, down and up by stairs and elevator to fetch water. Then up and down, up and down a ladder to clean the windows and cover the broken panes.

The following Saturday

The first job was lugging the heavy rolls of vinyl and containers of adhesive to the third floor. Then down and up, down and up for tools and water. We argued over each stage of laying the vinyl: it keeps curling ... well, straighten it ... I can't ... do it this way ... no, that way ... you're not holding it down firmly enough ... I can't help it ... stop pulling so hard ... it's crooked ... then fix it ... I'm trying ...

Sunday

We dragged the heavy ladder from one end of the space to the other and climbed up and down, up and down, putting in new double sockets and twelve pairs of floodlights. All the tasks had dirtied the new vinyl, so we had to wash it—down for water and back up, down and up, down and up. When we finished, we were so tired all we could do was sit and stare at the clean rectangle.

Monday morning

I came up the stairs and stood at the edge of the new vinyl, then sat, then stood, then sat. Having a space used by no one else ... what a luxury ... new opportunities ... new responsibilities ... I thought of the legendary modern dancers in their studios, discovering the central springs of movement: the solar plexus, wave motion, breathing, contraction and release, fall and recovery, the arc between two deaths ... Cold weather and no heat forced an end to my reverie. It was freeze, leave, or dance. I plunged into a banal new study, named almost immediately If you don't jump in, you won't be able to swim.

Point one arm forward in a more and more commanding way. Answer with a growing number of procrastination gestures that stay in one spot—lunge, lean sideways, cover the face, cross the arms, jump to face away. By the sixth and most vehement arm command, answered by five stuck-in-one-spot gestures, the impetus finally came to rev up the legs and use the arms to push off into a backward skim on the toes across the space to the opposite edge of the vinyl.

Harris laughed when he saw the study, knowing I was playing on a personal foible, indicated by the title. When we went to the beach, he would dive in immediately, even when the water was cold, while I would procrastinate and go in slowly, slowly, stand and wet my arms, stand and wet my face, stand some more, and then I would suddenly turn around and plunge in backwards. I tried to develop the material into more of a dance, but it worked best as a fragment. The other fragments, sketches, and studies I turned out during the first months in the warehouse were also more valuable as raw material for future development than as finished dances. Harris called the process 'mining.'

1969 SAVE-THE-NEIGHBORHOOD/ANTI-ROUTE 34 EXTENSION RALLY

The windows of my new studio looked out on State Street, a street of small businesses scheduled for demolition to build a six-lane by-pass or highway connector. At a public hearing, when AIM members, including Harris, protested against putting a six-lane highway in that location, urban renewal officials said, in all seriousness, that there was nothing to worry about, it was just two three-lane roads. While that project was still a ways off, the city was concentrating on the Route 34 Extension, which would cut a wide swath through some of the better parts of the neighborhood where I grew up, an area of modest, but mostly well-kept, two- and three-family homes. Some of them had gardens in the backyard for growing flowers and vegetables. One family raised rabbits, which the whole neighborhood liked to visit at Easter time. Another family flooded the backyard in the winter for ice-skating.

Like all the other urban renewal projects, the Route 34 Extension was planned by government and university personnel to benefit the corporate and institutional interests they served, with little consideration for the people whose homes and small businesses they were tearing down. When the AIM Urban Renewal Committee decided to stage a rally in opposition to the Route 34 Extension, I put together a mobile theater event with Harris's help.

The rally took place at Troup Junior High School, where I was a student from 1951 to 1954 and staged my first ballets: *Peter and the Wolf*, based on choreography by my ballet teacher, Jack Quinn, and *Coppélia*, which I choreographed myself. For the Anti-Route 34 Extension Rally, I wrote and directed something very different from those ballets: a protest skit called HIGHWAY ROBBERY. In keeping with "clear a space and I'll dance," the AIM cast of fourteen performed not on the stage of the auditorium where I once performed, but in the three-quarter round in the cafeteria. About two hundred neighborhood people and a handful of city legislators turned out for the event.

As the Narrator, I stepped forward and began:
SPECTATORS, FOR YOUR PLEASURE AND ENLIGHTENMENT, MOBILE THEATER PRESENTS—HIGHWAY ROBBERY.

INTRODUCING OUR CAST OF CHARACTERS—FIRST AND FOREMOST, THE HEROES OF THIS STORY: THE PEOPLE OF THE CITY! *Each of the eleven cast members playing the People thrust a fist in the air and held up a poster, on which Harris had drawn colorful elevations of homes and businesses in the city.*

NEXT, THE VILLAINS OF THIS STORY: THE AUTOMOBILE, OIL, AND CONSTRUCTION CORPORATIONS. *The Corporations character was holding a poster, looking at it closely, and flashing it every so often so that others caught a glimpse. On it were the highways planned by the corporations and city officials as secretly as possible.*

The Narrator said in a loud whisper:
LET'S SEE WHAT CORPORATIONS IS HOLDING. IT SAYS:
MASTERPLAN
MAJOR INTERCHANGE X
DOWNTOWN CONNECTOR _
INTERSTATE 91 _
ROUTE 34 EXTENSION _
SIX-LANE BY-PASS _
INNER RING ROAD _
EAST CONNECTOR _
OUTER RING ROAD _
THERE'S AN X NEXT TO MAJOR INTERCHANGE. THE OTHER SEVEN HIGHWAYS HAVE A BLANK, WAITING FOR THE **X** OF COMPLETION.

The Narrator returned to the introduction of the characters:
LAST, THE FLUNKY IN THIS STORY: THE HIGHWAY AND URBAN RENEWAL PROGRAMS. *Harris, as the Flunky, swept his arms and body into a deep bow. In one hand he had a stick, to which a ball and string had been attached, labeled WRECKING BALL. In the other hand, he had a roll of gray cloth, labeled HIGHWAYS.*

SPECTATORS, YOU ALSO HAVE A PART TO PLAY. YOU CAN MAKE YOUR VOICES HEARD BY APPLAUDING THE HEROES OF THIS STORY—THE PEOPLE OF THE CITY! *The Spectators applauded, conducted by the Narrator.* AND BY BOOING THE VILLAINS OF THIS STORY—THE CORPORATIONS AND THEIR FLUNKIES! *The Spectators booed, conducted by the Narrator.*

PLACES PLEASE! *The eleven people formed two lines, representing two sides of a Street. They held the posters of homes and businesses so the audience could see them. Corporations and Flunky stood apart from the People. Flunky brought a chair for Corporations to stand on.*

THIS IS STREET FIFTEEN YEARS AGO. STREET IS VERY LIVELY, RENOWNED THROUGHOUT THE REGION FOR ITS BAKERIES, BUTCHER SHOPS, AND DELICATESSENS. *Chatter and gesticulation from the Street.* IT HAS ITS PROBLEMS, TO BE SURE. SOME OF THE BUILDINGS LOOK SHABBY AND NEGLECTED—A LITTLE SHABBINESS AND NEGLECT, PLEASE ... *Six of the eleven posters trembled.* BUT FOR LOTS OF PEOPLE AND SMALL BUSINESSES, THIS IS A THRIVING STREET. *Loud chatter and energetic gesticulation from the Street.*

ENTER, THE VILLAIN—THE AUTOMOBILE, OIL, AND CONSTRUCTION CORPORATIONS, FOLLOWED BY THEIR FLUNKY—THE HIGHWAY AND URBAN RENEWAL PROGRAMS. *Flunky helped Corporations down from the chair, and the two started toward the Street.*

THE CORPORATIONS ARE LOOKING FOR BUSINESS AND PROFITS. *Corporations looked up, down, left, and right repeatedly, hands either clasped in prayer or raised in innocence.*

WITH FLUNKY'S HELP, THEY GAVE STREET THE BUSINESS *pause for irony to sink in,* BUT CERTAINLY NOT THE PROFITS. LET'S SEE WHAT HAPPENED ... *Flunky set the chair down somewhat removed from the Street. Corporations got up on it with the MASTERPLAN poster, pointed to DOWNTOWN CONNECTOR and then to the Street. Flunky went down the Street with the WRECKING BALL, knocking down the posters of homes and businesses one by one. When all the posters were down, he went back to Corporations and picked up the roll of HIGHWAYS cloth. As Flunky rolled out the cloth, the People picked up their posters, moved to another part of the performing space, and formed a Square. When the first length of cloth had been laid down and all the People had moved, Flunky went back to Corporations and MASTERPLAN, took a black X out of his pocket, and pinned it next to DOWNTOWN CONNECTOR. Tableau.*

The Narrator resumed. SO MUCH FOR STREET ... WHERE DID ALL THOSE PEOPLE AND SMALL BUSINESSES GO? SOME OF THEM MOVED TO SQUARE.

The scenario repeated for SQUARE with a few changes. SQUARE was renowned for its religious festivals as well as its fruit, vegetable, and fish markets and family restaurants. It had fewer problems than Street—only three of the posters trembled—and when Flunky came with the WRECKING BALL to knock it down, two of the Square People resisted, before all eleven moved with their posters to a third location and formed a cluster, representing a NEIGHBORHOOD. Flunky laid down a second length of HIGHWAYS cloth, and put an X next to INTERSTATE 91. Tableau.

The scenario repeated for NEIGHBORHOOD, which audience members immediately recognized as the neighborhood where they lived. They moved to the edge of their seats, as the Narrator summarized the action so far.

THIS CITY SEEMS TO BE A HIGHWAY TO A POT OF GOLD FOR THE CORPORATIONS! WILL THEY, WITH FLUNKY'S HELP, ROB AND DESTROY NEIGHBORHOOD FOR THE ROUTE 34 EXTENSION, AS THEY ROBBED AND DESTROYED STREET FOR DOWNTOWN CONNECTOR AND SQUARE FOR INTERSTATE 91? WILL OTHER STREETS, SQUARES, AND NEIGHBORHOODS BE ROBBED AND DESTROYED TO BUILD SIX-LANE BY-PASS, INNER RING ROAD, EAST CONNECTOR, AND OUTER RING ROAD? THE CORPORATIONS AND THEIR FLUNKIES SAY 'YES.' BUT MORE IMPORTANT, WHAT DO THE PEOPLE OF THE CITY SAY? LET'S SEE.

The action began as before. The Neighborhood posters with their homes and businesses were knocked down, but there was more resistance than at Square, and when Flunky tried to lay down a third length of Highway cloth, the cluster of eleven People turned into a fighting unit and drove the character from the room. Meanwhile Corporations took the MASTERPLAN and tried to sneak away.

The Narrator concluded. THE MORAL OF THIS STORY IS THAT WHEN WE, THE PEOPLE, COME TOGETHER, WE CAN CERTAINLY STOP A HIGHWAY. WE COULD EVEN STOP THE CORPORATIONS. IT'S UP TO US!

As the Narrator was speaking the final words, the people in the audience stood up and moved into action. They were furious with Corporations, who was trying to sneak out with the MASTERPLAN, and rewrote the ending of the scenario on the spot. They cornered Corporations and took away the MASTERPLAN to wild cheering and clapping and singing— "We shall overcome ..."

Among the rebelling audience members were two of my Troup Junior High School classmates, who were activists in the inner-city civil rights group, the Hill Parents Association. We stayed on after the performance to talk about politics and dance. They teased me about the change from classical ballets on the stage to a protest rally in the basement cafeteria. One of them had been a hunter in *Peter and the Wolf* and said he could still do the moves. The other one reminisced about how I made ballet dancers out of athletes and anyone willing to rock-and-roll at lunchtime in the gymnasium.

Mobile Theater performed *HIGHWAY ROBBERY* only once, after which AIM turned to other tactics of protest: neighborhood meetings, letters to city officials, press releases to the local newspaper, and articles in the *AIM Newsletter*. But our efforts to save the neighborhood were futile. The wrecking ball leveled all the buildings with frightening speed. At first, protest activities continued in the form of sporadic attempts to reclaim the land. Some protesters declared themselves squatters and pitched tents. Others turned over the earth with thoughts of farming it, often finding plants from the old gardens still growing amidst the rubble. Anyone who was caught was arrested and fined for "trespassing." After awhile, the Route 34 Extension disappeared from the city's building plans. The leveled neighborhood remained a wasteland, waiting for the city to seek developers to rebuild what was so wantonly torn down.

Mining for New Ideas

In my warehouse studio, as part of the mining process, I explored how to portray bodies under stress:

- a person up against the wall, moving in sustained or broken gestures—leaning, tilting, turning, falling and rising—with some part of the body in constant contact with the wall;

- a person whose bulk inhibits movement—how to turn my thin body into a fat one, the torso a fleshy blob, from which head, hands, and feet protrude and execute slow pressing and wringing motions;

- a person on the run—a game of tag that turns into running and running to keep warm or escape.

I brought a history of art books to the studio. Thinking of sculpted, painted, or photographed gestures as frozen moments stimulated my imagination: what came before and after? How could I move into and out of the gestures? What were the possible rhythms?

I imitated gestures of Michelangelo that spiraled and twisted into uncomfortable balances and falls.

Inspired by William Blake's illustrations of poems, I treated the torso as an axis that could tilt this way and that, while the arms and legs extended into space.

Henry Moore's gestures of miners set off motions of crawling and shaping the torso and extremities to fit into tight spaces.

Imitating figures by Alberto Giacometti and the Etruscans before him, I elongated the body as if it were on a high pedestal, squeezed the legs together, and pressed the arms close to the torso.

My body was forced into unfamiliar territory, as I turned a fixed gesture from the history of art into a moving gesture and wove seemingly incongruent gestures into sequences.

Another part of the mining process involved experiments with speaking while moving. I gave the dominant role to the gestures, having them precede the words and allowing the gestural rhythms to distort the verbal phrasing. Being neither a trained actor nor singer and wanting the words to be understood, I spoke in an everyday voice. However, I also tried out ideas from books by Antonin Artaud and Jerzy Grotowski for letting involuntary or repressed sounds like breathing come out and be heard, making words resonate from different parts of the body, and bouncing the voice off the walls, floor, and ceiling. One of the most complete studies from this period of experimentation was set off by a poem from a book on the Chinese revolution.[1]

Rich Man Poor Man

I spoke and *moved* simultaneously:

A man is rich—*stride directly to a chair at one end of the space*

Ever fatter, ever whiter—*sit down on it like royalty*

Goes to borrow fifty pieces—*make imperious gestures, extending a fist to one side and then the other*

Has hundreds pressed upon him—*stand up with fists raised in triumph and sit back down, hands on well-fed abdomen*

Turns to go—*look at an imaginary watch*

Is urged to stay and drink—*sit back, look around, and acknowledge a circle of admirers with nods and smiles—widen the look around, no longer smiling—widen the look farther, growing more tense and fearful— finally look around sharply, body pinned to the chair, and fall to the floor.*

Figure 07. Climactic Poor Man gesture (1970). Photograph by Virginia Blaisdell.

Upon rising, I became the poor person, running from side to side in front of the chair:
A man is poor—*run forward*
Ever thinner—*run backward*
Ever blacker—*run sideways*
Goes to borrow fifty coins—*approach the chair as if it were a throne, kneel, and clap fifty times*

Is asked hundreds in return—*roll into a climactic twisted agonizing gesture, back pinned to the floor, pelvis thrust to the ceiling, palms begging for mercy*

Turns to go—*roll to kneeling*

Knows he's taken for a thief—*rise slowly and walk backward with open hands—knot the hands into fists, and then cross them in a 'fuck you' gesture.*

The swearing gesture never felt quite right, but I couldn't find another, until I realized all I needed to do was raise my fists—an ambiguous gesture, signaling anger, power, threat, or possible rebellion.

A critic at a coffeehouse performance of *Rich Man Poor Man* wrote:

"A piece of about five minutes. Pin-pointy: wealth, reversal, ungrounded power, unabashed reality, internal power struggle. Stone was inviting ... seemed too strong for someone so sleek ... worked directly at us ... The piece was clean, sharp ...

For the young people's branch of AIM, I performed *Rich Man Poor Man* in our office—
Striding down the middle of the space as the **Rich Man** between the line-ups of discarded and donated furniture—
Sitting down on the best of the mongrel chairs—
Gesturing with hands and body, the chair creaking—
Falling to the floor, hoping for no splinters—

Standing slowly as the **Poor Man**—

Running back and forth from the sofa with exposed springs to the lopsided stool to the bench that kept collapsing to the folding chair that no longer folded—

Kneeling, clapping, and rolling into the agonized pose, aware of the unmopped floor—

Rising from bent over to upright, while walking backward to the window end of the office.

Two of the young people immediately began a dialogue:

"Only the rich guy sits in the chair after marching to it. The chair represents a possession."

"And it represents comfort. Everyone wants comfort and possessions."

"Not everyone."

"Who wants to be poor?"

"The poor guy has the whole space to move in. The rich guy's path is more limited."

"But the poor guy runs back and forth, begs before the chair, and then backs up. So the chair still wins."

A new voice: "Is anyone free?"

Another voice: "I've thought the things in that dance, but I could never say them out loud."

More Experiments

On a cold windy day, as I entered the fabric store on the way to rehearsal, Friendly Owner's partner, who was in charge of property maintenance, was on his way out. I stopped him and asked about heat for the studio.

"It will cost fifty dollars to fix the circulator," he said. "I don't want to spend the money."

"What if I pay for it?"

"Well, our fuel bills are enormous, and I don't want to heat that building. Why not get some infra-red bulbs and an electric heater?"

"I borrowed a little heater, but it blew the fuses and didn't heat the space."

"Well, try the bulbs. I don't want to get involved with heating that building."

"What if only the one heater where I dance were turned on. The rest could be left off."

"You wouldn't be able to be there when that heater was on. It would blow you out of the room. You would have to turn it on, wait, and then turn the thermostat off." He backed away from me, saying: "Some heat comes up from the first floor." Going out the door, he added: "I don't think it will be cold this winter."

I went up to the studio. It was cold! Harris suggested putting the heater in the bathroom on the second floor. I did that and was delighted when it worked without blowing the fuses and took the chill off the little room in no time. Now there was a spot to go if and when the studio became too cold. I changed into a sweat suit, heavy socks, and jazz shoes, ran up the stairs, and went through a fast-paced warm-up. Then on to exploring a striking sequence of gestures from a painting by the Spanish artist Juan Genovés.2 The painting was composed like a photographic contact sheet, showing a person on the run—

caught in a spotlight, arms raised in fear
running away from us, towards us, sideways
lunging, twisting, bending over as if shot
stopped with arms and legs open wide and palms forward pleading
falling—hands up in innocence
falling—hands gripping the face
The last frame was just the light from the spotlight.

I tried a gesture—it took a while to translate it into dance. Tried another and another, treating each gesture rigorously as if it were a step from a formal dance vocabulary. One gesture lent itself to variation: small, large, fast, slow, in the air, on the floor. It led into an old study—dead end, the idea petered out. I experimented with maintaining the same gesture while jumping, galloping, and running. I tried all the gestures in sequence, forgot a shape and had to check the painting—forgot the order—started and stopped, started and stopped. Enough. It was time for lunch.

On my way to the restaurant, I walked past a line-up at the unemployment office. There was a person standing with shoulders hunched, head down, arms hanging, not on the run, but looking just as trapped as the figure in the Genovés painting. How were the other people standing? I walked past, assuming different postures. At lunch, I thought of a Van Gogh painting of prisoners in the yard—torsos slumping, shoulders sagging, hands groping, heads tilted, faces staring into nowhere.

I headed back to the studio, mimicking people scurrying against the wind, hands in pockets, bodies forward, heads down. No sun. It was as cold in the studio as it was outside! I ran, skipped, galloped, hopped, jumped, inserting gestures from the Genovés painting. Occasionally a gesture came to life, took on an unusual rhythm, and led to other moves. By late in the day, I knew the gestures well enough to run them in sequence percussively: *Freeze! Freeze! Freeze!* Holding each gesture for one count, then five counts, then ten. I also tried the sequence in slow motion, which shifted the emphasis from the poses to the transitions between them. The slower I danced, the more gestures resulted.

Harris's maxim, which helped him to write four books, was: "Always finish with an opening for the next day." I tore a piece of paper into eight pieces, wrote a gesture on seven of the pieces and left one blank, shook the pieces in a bag, drew them out one at a time, and wrote down the random order. Then I shook, drew out, and wrote twice more. The plan for the next day was to dance the three lists and see if one order was more meaningful than another, if any interesting phrases emerged, and what happened to the movements with different words or tunes running in my head.

I rode the bus home. The driver stopped for a rider using a cane: one foot up, the other foot to the same step, stop—one foot, other foot, stop—one foot, other foot, stop. The driver waited. The money was in a change purse buried deep in a pocket. The rider balanced on the cane, dropped the coins in the box one by one, and put the purse away. There was a seat in front, but he looked to the back and started going there: step, drag the other foot, wait—step, drag, wait ... The driver watched in the rear view mirror and finally took off. The unsteady rider almost fell, used the cane and a seat handle to regain balance, and took out a handkerchief to blow his nose. The driver stopped for another customer. The still unseated rider lurched and then continued stepping and dragging until he arrived at a seat at the very back. He balanced on the cane, gripped a pole with the other hand, shuffled his feet into position, hesitated, and finally sat down. Everyone on the bus sighed with relief.

After dinner I lined up chairs in the living room and demonstrated the bus rider episode for Harris, who laughed in recognition: "empty seat in front ... gimpy leg ... determined to sit in back."

I put the chairs back and sat down on the sofa. "I worked on the Genovés gestures today."

"Do you want to show me?" Harris asked.

"No, it's too soon. The gestures are strong, but I don't know what order to put them in, the rhythms aren't right, and I need an idea to hold everything together."

"You're putting the movements out on the floor. You always say you can't tell anything until you've done that."

"The best dancing of the day was done by the unemployed and the bus rider."

"Sounds like new studies to me."

"Maybe."

While I was mining for new dance ideas, AIM was going through a period of growth, experimentation, and fragmentation. It was necessary to form a New People's Group to orient the influx of newcomers about the who, what, when, where, why, and how of the organization. Everyone still pulled together to protest war and urban renewal and to fight for alternative electoral politics, but the issues of equal rights had begun to divide the group by race, gender, and age. There were enough people from different neighborhoods of the city with particular problems to form neighborhood groups. The organization had started a small newspaper, a press, a children's school, and a coffeehouse. Those interested in art and politics worked together on projects to keep the arts on the AIM agenda. Gone were the long difficult meetings ending in consensus. The meetings were still long and difficult, but were likely to end in grumbling and dissatisfaction. Some group or individual's interests were being mishandled, slighted, or ignored.

Study: On the Wall

My endeavors with the Genovés gestures finally resulted in a study, structured by a Bertolt Brecht poem.[3] I made On the Wall as a requiem for the Kent State students, who were shot and killed at an anti-Vietnam War demonstration.[2]

The first part of the poem was spoken (*on the wall*) while walking an increasing number of steps (*in chalk*) along one side of the space, voice rising (*is written*). The sound and action intensified with a run (*THEY*) that spiraled into the center (*WANT*), ending with a high-pitched shout on the word (*WAR!*)

The second part of the poem was a descent in movement and voice, each word and gesture punched out like a gunshot, until the sustained collapse:

SHE—*stretch the body and arms up as if nailed to a wall*
WHO—*contract the torso and cover the head with the arms*
WROTE—*double the body over, arms clutching the middle*
IT—*lift the body and open the legs and arms wide, hands up*
HAS—*lunge and reach both arms forward*
ALREAD—*kneel down on one knee with fist raised*
FALLEN—*collapse—fold the body over the knees and lower the fist*

Study: I Want the Pen

A line from a poem by Vladimir Mayakovsky became the basis of *I Want the Pen*, another anti-war study.[4]

I want the pen
to be on a par
with the bayonet.[3]

Although Mayakovsky wrote the line in three phrases, I worked with it in two—a four- and an eight-beat phrase—with accents on the fourth and eighth beat:

I want the pen
to be on a par with the bayonet.

Moving around the space, sometimes saying the words while dancing and sometimes just dancing, I ascended from a crawl to low lunges to walking to marching to triplets (down up up) to runs—with the words **pen** and **bayonet** marked by pauses, hand thrusts, kicks, hops, and finally leaps. The ending was never resolved—no leaping off into the wings when performing in the round. I tried reversing from runs to crawling—slowing down—traveling backward, sideways, curling into the center. Nothing worked. Definitely a fragment for future development.

Performance of New Studies

For a political group in the region that met at a small private college, I performed the three new studies—*If You Don't Jump In*, *Rich Man Poor Man*, and *I Want the Pen...*—along with *Newspapers* and *Growing*. The audience and I began in one lounge, had to move to another after *Rich Man Poor Man* because of a conflicting event, had to move again after *Newspaper*s to make way for the president's punch-and-cookie party, and ended up in a basement space with a large stone pillar in the middle and wet, sticky stuff on the floor. (Clearly the political group had no power with the scheduling of rooms in the college.) A few spectators found paper toweling and helped me clean up the floor, so the program could resume.

Most of the audience members weren't phased by the disruptions and having to sit on the floor for *Growing*, but a person I recognized from a couple of modern dance workshops became more and more agitated with each move and exploded during the discussion period.

"Theaters were invented so a person could sit in a seat and watch the stage. This was a hassle and an anti-performance—no music or lighting or even a proper costume."

"I've been searching for an aesthetic including costume that says I'm a person like any of you, but also a dancer." I pulled up my homemade gray slacks, pulled down my orange and yellow patterned jersey, and looked at my red sneakers.

"What about leotard and tights?" asked the workshop dancer.

"I sometimes perform in leotard and tights, but they call too much attention to the body as a technical entity. They emphasize the dancer more than the person."

"Some modern dancers have come up with neutral costumes."

"The neutral costume isn't really the answer. I dance about different subjects, and costume should somehow reflect that."

"You didn't change tonight," the workshop dancer pointed out.

"Dancing the way I do often makes it difficult to change costume." I looked around and asked if someone else had a question or comment.

A person in jeans spoke up: "I think you want the ideas for your dances to come through the choreography."

"Yes, even costume can be evoked through gesture." I demonstrated by running my hands up one leg as if pulling up a stocking, by circling a wrist to indicate ruffles, cupping my breasts like the braid on a Renaissance gown, by putting my hands to one shoulder and tilting my head as if wearing a rose.

"Why wear anything at all?" The workshop dancer's question provoked responses from several audience members:

"I saw a performance, in which all the dancers undressed. Once their clothes were off, the dancing was an anti-climax."

"The audience came for the striptease, not for the dancing."

"In our society a naked body is anything but neutral. So nakedness becomes another kind of costume, the most provocative or numbing of all."

"This evening, we had to move twice. A naked dancer requires a more controlled setting, unless she wants to be arrested."

The spectator in jeans brought up another issue: "Your outfit could be worn on the street as well as on the stage."

"That's my intention, though occasionally it turns into a problem. I once arrived at a performance and realized I'd forgotten my dance pants. It was winter, and I had to perform in what I was wearing—heavy corduroy slacks with lining. The room was hot, and my body became sweaty. The lining stuck, and the slacks wrapped around my legs like chains. Interestingly enough, a member of the audience found it especially meaningful that I danced in the outfit I was wearing when I arrived."

As I looked around the audience, a number of people seemed to be surveying what they and their neighbors were wearing. "I worry the most about costuming when I'm full of doubts about my dancing and dances. I forget the hours and months of work on the ideas—who cares about those? I fall into a preoccupation with what our society tells me I can manipulate: my appearance."

"A dancer has to think about appearance." The workshop dancer was exasperated. "What you have on isn't a costume. That offends me."

"Did the everyday outfit keep you from seeing the dance?" asked the person in jeans.

"The whole pedestrian aesthetic puts me off," concluded the workshop dancer.

"It draws me in," countered the person in jeans.

One audience member wrote me a note:

> Art gains a lot for me when I'm compelled to remember that it's the work of people and not some super-package all by itself ...
>
> The humor in the *Newspaper* piece was a relief after the polemical tone of *Some Rich Some Poor*, and the emotional intensity of *Growing* was a surprise again ... I must admit that I respond in a very verbal and theoretical rather than physical way, but I think what you're doing is expressive in both ways and reflects all the thought and work you've put into it.

1969 PEOPLE VERSUS WAR-BOSS

In response to a meeting with members of AIM and representatives of area colleges, who wanted a theatrical event as part of the ongoing anti-war offensive, I ventured into mobile theater again in collaboration with Liz Henderson. Our idea was to make a "living cartoon" that could be put together and performed anywhere—indoors or outdoors—with a pick-up cast and very little rehearsing. No words, the meaning revealed through action and props. "Clear a space and we'll dance." An audience would assemble, get a vivid message in a few minutes, and the "living cartoon" would move on to a new place, new performers, new audience.

We came up with *PEOPLE VERSUS WAR-BOSS*, which required a cast of seven: **War-Boss**, two **Peasants**, and four **Soldiers**.

War-Boss had the most elaborate props: a whistle, a sash worn diagonally that said WAR-BOSS on the front and MILITARY-INDUSTRIAL-COMPLEX on the back, and a giant circular portfolio made of two poster boards covered with a map of the world, sewed together at the bottom and sides with long handles on the top. The person who played **War-Boss** had to wear a business suit, shirt, and tie.

For each **Peasant**, there was a wide belt that wrapped around the waist, a cloth cap, and a flag with the word PEASANT in appliquéd letters. One set of belt-cap-flag was green, the other purple.

For the **Soldiers**, there were official army jackets and hats, contributed by veterans, who were members of AIM.

The scenario went as follows:

War-Boss is playing with the world-portfolio—opening and closing, bouncing and swinging it.

Peasant-In-Green enters and circles at a distance, writing the name of a country in the air with the flag.

War-Boss pivots, beckons to **Peasant** to no avail, points a warning finger, and begins to tremble, pulls a whistle out of a pocket and blows.

Four Soldiers march out of the audience and surround the **Peasant**, who has been walking short rows as far from **War-Boss** as possible, using the flag as an agricultural tool.

The **Soldiers** spin the **Peasant** around and take away the belt; grab the cap and turn the **Peasant** upside down; drop the **Peasant** on the ground and take away the flag.

Not sure of their next moves, the **Soldiers** push, shove, change places, and toss the belt, cap, and flag around.

Meanwhile the stripped **Peasant** crawls away.

The confusion subsides, and the **Soldiers** manage to form a line-up so they can pass the stripped **Peasant's** items to **War-Boss**, who stuffs them into the portfolio.

As the **Soldiers** march out and disperse, **Peasant-In-Purple** enters.

Repeat of the gestural standoff between **Peasant** and **War-Boss**, but when **War-Boss** blows the whistle, only **Three Soldiers** come out of the audience.

The **Fourth Soldier**—military jacket and hat on the ground—is standing near the playing area next to the stripped **Peasant**.

The **Three Soldiers** take away **Peasant-In-Purple's** cap and belt and pass them to **War-Boss**, but when they try to take the flag, the **Ex-Soldier** and stripped **Peasant** run to the victim's aid.

Three against three!

Form two opposing lines for a contra dance:

into the center, bow, back out;

into the center, do-si-do, back out;

into the center, circle, link arms, and form one line of **Resisters** facing **War-Boss**, who has been frantically beckoning and blowing the whistle, pivoting, and pointing.

A tug-of-war for the world-portfolio ensues.

The **Soldiers** and **Peasants** wrest the world-portfolio from **War-Boss/Military-Industrial-Complex** and carry it triumphantly through the audience.

War-Boss flees.

Liz and I wanted to stop the scenario at the face-off between **War-Boss** and the others, but the first cast that performed the piece insisted on the decisive ending—as far as they were concerned, there was no alternative: "the world belongs to the people"—and each performing group after that concurred.

The first performance of *PEOPLE VERSUS WAR-BOSS* took place outdoors at a suburban community college, where a moratorium-on-war rally was scheduled for noon. At eleven, some of the performers still had not arrived. Somehow within the next hour, Liz and I led a political discussion and a rehearsal.

One of the cast was a Vietnam veteran, who spoke up immediately after hearing the scenario: "Don't make me play a soldier. I want to play a peasant."

The performers came up with additional staging ideas and the decisive ending, and by noon, they were making their way toward the crowd, discussing the 'skit' and coaching and cueing each other. At first, they wanted to be on the platform with the other speakers, but Liz convinced them to perform in amongst the audience. Along with the props, I had brought a tambourine for sound accompaniment, which allowed me to direct and prompt a bit while the action was going on. The students were so enthusiastic about the results that they agreed to do another performance at the Bread and Roses Coffeehouse, founded by AIM, to rally people for a national anti-war march.

Unlike the casual community college cast, the students from a small women's college in New Haven wanted to rehearse *PEOPLE VERSUS WAR-BOSS* the night before their performance. Liz and I waited about an hour and a half while the organizers collected the participants and found someone to let us into the locked auditorium. The students were very apologetic about the delay. They got into their parts hesitantly—were apprehensive about playing roles so distant from their daily lives—handled the props with care and even folded and packed them up at the end of the rehearsal—wanted to do everything perfectly—kept looking to us for approval—we kept throwing the responsibility back on them.

The college auditorium was long and narrow with a small stage at one end, but fortunately there was a platform that ran from the middle of the stage out into the audience. It was just wide enough to perform on, so the 'living cartoon' could be enacted primarily on this platform and in amongst the audience. The students found wonderful costumes for themselves and gave a strong performance for all their hesitation and apprehension at the rehearsal. Liz and I were thrilled when they took the lead in answering questions from their classmates about the theater piece and the anti-war movement during the follow-up discussion.

Of all the casts, the one from our political group was the most harried. We rehearsed at one end of the office just before the meeting at which we performed. The phone didn't stop ringing—mimeographing, mailings, and meetings were going on at the other end of the space. At one point I looked down at the tambourine and noticed it was splattered with blood—I was trying so hard to drown out the din, I kept gashing my fingers on the cymbals. The distractions of the rehearsal showed in the performance—people dropped props and costumes fell off—but there was a lot of laughter, our co-workers had a chance to see the scenario that was being performed in their name, the idea of a "living cartoon" came across clearly, and we had a good discussion afterwards about the feasibility of developing the idea into a "living newspaper."

A labor organizer from the 1930s, who sometimes came to AIM meetings, spoke up: "Living cartoon—living newspaper—wonderful ideas—I thought they all died out. At the People's Center, we had speakers and put on plays. We could attract large audiences by word-of-mouth, leafleting, and driving through the streets with a megaphone and signs, if someone had a car. We didn't perform outdoors, and there were fewer colleges—only for the rich. You're using the old ideas in a new way. Bravo!"

About two hundred and fifty people turned out for a Stop-the-War Rally on the central green of a small town north of New Haven. One of the performers from the first cast invited Liz and me to stage *PEOPLE VERSUS WAR-BOSS* and recruited public and private high school students to perform the parts. The rehearsal was nerve-wracking. We had about twenty minutes to work in the small, obstacle-filled living room of a house that fronted the green. But the show went on with very few mistakes—the cast even adlibbed battle cries and exchanges with the audience, which was a very responsive one. People watched intently—waited for things to develop—laughed and frowned at the right moments—and finally clapped and cheered. Afterwards many came up to us and told us how much they enjoyed the skit—they liked the fact that there were no words—they were glad the people won for a change. A faculty member was amazed and delighted to see some very shy students performing in public.

I think the success of the event was due to the enthusiasm of the cast members, who had been on a national march the day before.

"We couldn't believe our eyes," said one student, "so many people against the war."

Another reported they had seen some guerrilla theatre. A third exclaimed proudly: "Yesterday we were spectators, but today we're performers!"

Stuck in the Warehouse Elevator

The warehouse had its difficulties other than being too cold in the winter and too hot in the summer. Friendly Owner warned about the agéd freight elevator. "Be sure to close both doors, the one to the floor and the one to the elevator."

For all my carefulness, other people used the building, and on the way to rehearsal one afternoon, the elevator stopped between the second and third floors. I looked for an emergency signal, but there was none. I shouted and shouted—could see the door to the third floor but couldn't climb out of the cage—rattled the cage—shouted and stamped—tried the start lever again and again, the elevator wouldn't budge—shouted and rattled and stamped—no response, no one was around.

An inner voice said: Eventually someone will come into the warehouse for something, but when? Will I have to spend the night here? Better not dwell on that possibility.

There was a light in the elevator. I pulled out a book, sat down in a corner, and tried to read. Stood up periodically to shout and jump. Thirty minutes ... Did whatever other moves were possible in the cage to keep from freezing. Forty minutes ... Tried to rehearse a sequence about being trapped. An hour ...

Finally the glorious sound of footsteps on the second floor.

"Hello! Hello! Can you hear me? Help!"

The footsteps stopped.

"Hello! Help! The elevator is stuck!"

The footsteps came to the elevator door. "Joan?" Friendly Owner's voice.

"Yes. How do I get this thing going?"

"The door here is ajar. Someone must have forgotten to close it." As soon as he closed the door, I was able to start the elevator and arrived at the studio, just as my rescuer was coming up the stairs.

"My punishment for being lazy and not walking up the way you did."

"You need your energy for dancing. Everyone gets stuck in that elevator. Good thing I needed some fabric." Friendly Owner walked toward the bolts of material stored next to the dancing space. I followed.

"Maybe the muse of dance trapped me in there for a reason. I'm working on two studies about being bound or free. They're going badly, and I'm supposed to perform them soon. One is called *How a Calf Can Become a Swallow*."

Friendly Owner searched through the tall rolls of cloth.

"Maybe you know the folk song I recited while dancing. Joan Baez recorded a version of it."[5]

On the wagon lies a calf,
It's lying there bound with a rope.
High up in the sky flies a swallow,
Joyfully darting back and forth.

"Do you recognize it?"

"No." Friendly Owner pulled out a bolt of fabric and stood it on end. "Go on ..."

"Here's the refrain:

The wind is laughing in the cornfield,
Laughing, laughing, laughing,

Laughing loud the whole day long
And half the night.

"The second part of the refrain is just one word, Dona, repeated to a tune that sounds like a bird in flight. I sing that part."

Friendly Owner rocked the bolt of material back and forth. "How many other verses are there?"

"Two."

The calf is screaming. The farmer shouts in reply:
'Who told you to be a calf?
You could have been a bird,
You could have been a swallow!'

"I dance the refrain and then comes the last verse:

Poor wretched calves get bound with ropes,
They get transported, they get slaughtered,
But whoever has wings, flies up higher,
And is not a slave to anyone!

"Strong message," said Friendly Owner. "What kind of movements?"

"The study starts on the floor, progresses to the knees, to standing, to moving through space. During the Dona refrains, the arms gesture like wings."

I demonstrated: "First clipped and broken, hands clasped behind the neck and only the elbows flapping. Then the hands move to the shoulders, widening the span, and the elbows flap and circle. Finally the arms open out to their full width, the closest we can get to wings for flying."

"A struggle for liberation. Did you practice it in the elevator?"

"No. I tried to work on the gestures for the other study: *Mouse, Cat, Swan, Chick, Bitch or Human Being.*"

"Women's liberation. I thought you'd be involved in that."

"There's lots of precedent in dance for using animal imagery. While playing Peter in a production of *Peter and the Wolf,* I learned all the animal parts and can still do them. But I'm trying to find new moves for the women's issue."

Friendly Owner rocked the bolt of fabric again. "Start with the old moves. You have to start somewhere."

I lifted one arm like a wing. "With a gesture ..."

"One gesture and then another ... Keep working." Friendly Owner hoisted the heavy roll to one shoulder and trundled off.

Women's Group Meetings

The conversation helped me make peace with the elevator incident. Instead of leaving in a state of agitation, I stayed to work on the troublesome studies. *Mouse, Cat, Swan, Chick, Bitch or Human Being* was the least resolved—a reflection of the women's group meetings I had been attending? Personal confessions in tears, whispers, shouts—no to channeling, no to obligations, no to traditional interpersonal relationships—yes to collective living, promiscuity, any wild alternative to the status quo. At the first meeting, I said nothing. The leaders set up a private session and demanded an explanation of my silence.

"What excited me about our political activities was the opportunity to understand myself better by discovering the world outside myself. I'm interested in gender as one of several political issues," I said.

Leaders: "You were impatient with personal confessions."

"Yes. I work out personal issues alone and with Harris."

Leaders: "Maybe that's unhealthy."

"I also try to objectify personal issues by dancing and writing about them."

Leaders: "Maybe that's why art is unhealthy."

"There was pressure at the meeting to throw all our values out the window. Turning our backs on existing relationships is easier than struggling to maintain them in more positive ways or searching long and hard for alternatives. My priorities are Harris and dance."

Leaders: "In that order?"

"Harris would have me put dance first. In any case, politics comes third, and I have limited time for it."

Leaders: "You would rather put your time in political projects other than gender?"

"Vis-à-vis the larger organization, gender groups are particularly divisive."

Leaders: "Mixed-gender groups are repressive. Only by meeting separately can we women discover our strengths. Look at the leadership of AIM. You're the only woman with a say in major decisions."

"Thanks to a gender-conscious lawyer, in legalizing our entity, she said: 'You can hold any office except secretary. Why not be the treasurer and control the money.'"

Leaders: "And you think there's no need for gender politics?"

Even for a choreographer, who was not upset and confused, the gender issue would have been too complex to handle in a study, but I felt compelled to try and speak. Where to turn for a vocabulary? During the personal confessions at the women's meetings, there were gestures in words and motions that could be interpreted as

crouching, unable to stand—
pouncing and clawing in all directions—
flying high—
hiding the body, flaunting the body—
stomping, wringing, slashing—
running away from this, backing away from that—
turning away, reversing, sweeping aside, starting anew.

Small Cities Organizers Conference

Why is it so difficult to translate raw gestural observations directly into dance? Instead I dredged up animal movements and phrases from ballets performed in childhood and from modern dances attempted in college. The muddled *Mouse, Cat ...* fragment was brief, and I danced it only once for the audience at a Small City Organizers Conference, where the AIM cast performed *PEOPLE VERSUS WAR-BOSS*, and I performed my experimental short pieces in the following order:

If You Don't Jump in You Won't Be Able to Swim
How a Calf Can Become a Swallow
Mouse, Cat, Swan, Chick, Bitch or Human Being
Rich Man Poor Man
On the Wall ...
I Want the Pen ...

The response to the collage was surprisingly positive. Probably because all the seams and flaws were showing, the pieces were encouraging to those struggling to stand on their own feet as artists in a way that more finished works would not have been. A student organizer, who had been majoring in literature, realized it might be possible to switch to his real love, dance, without losing literature. Several of the activists remarked that the words made the dance more understandable. A dancer among the spectators found the words distracting, but said she disliked dance in silence even more. I was distressed. Why can so few people read dance in and of itself?

An actor-organizer, whose acting class at the university had been struggling to move while speaking, requested an encore of the gesture/word descent in *On the Wall.* I demonstrated and then invited the people, who had gathered, to try and do the gestures—first percussively and then in slow motion—first without the words and then with them. The actor-organizer asked if I would perform and lead a workshop for his acting class.

As the event was about to break up, a few people from AIM and other organizations, and the 1930s organizer gathered around a table and sat down for more discussion.

"*Mouse, Cat, Chick,* etc.—banal imagery for a serious issue," said one person.

"Sometimes the banal and abstract play intriguingly off each other," countered another person.

"In this case," I said, "the movement material was too weak."

"I was dubious about the combination of words and dance, but you pulled it off," commented a third person.

"What about the singing in *Calf to Swallow*? I was very dubious about that."

"I didn't expect to like the singing, but I did, especially the way the changing motions distorted the Donna refrain."

Harry Henderson entered the discussion. "*Calf to Swallow* goes from down to partially up to standing to moving. That occurs in several of your dances."

"And the reverse: from up to down, standing to prone—a basic formal device for a choreographer," I said, "and a composer—like going up and down the scale in music."

"Up to down, down to up—do you know the concept of the fortunate fall?" Harry's comment stayed with me and became very important for a future dance about standing Eve on her feet, which was titled *Eve and the Serpent.*

The 1930s organizer, who had come to a performance of *PEOPLE VERSUS WAR-BOSS*, held back to let others speak before claiming attention. "*If You Don't Jump In* and *Rich Man Poor Man* made me think of the stories of Jimmy Higgins in the old IWW (Industrial Workers of the World) newspaper. He was the person, who fought hard for truth and justice, for a better life for workers—did all the menial tasks and got none of the glory. Using those wonderful labor songs, you should do a dance about Jimmy Higgins:

organizing marches and cultural events—

1930s organizer raised a fist

collecting signatures on petitions—

mimed writing a list of names on the table

folding, stuffing, sealing, stamping, and sending out a mailing to raise money to send out another mailing to raise money to send out ...

used his hands to indicate the tasks

wearing out shoes on a picket line—

stamped with his feet

writing and printing flyers all night—

wiped sweat from his forehead

then standing and talking on street corners all day to distribute them—

indicated words rolling out of his mouth

sitting at meeting after meeting, thinking maybe this will be the one out of twenty that accomplishes something—

lifted a hand and rested his cheek on it

negotiating and winning—

put a hand forward and did a handshake

negotiating and losing—

fist up and thumb down

knocking on doors and recruiting—

knocked several times in the air

one—

knock

by—

knock

one—

knock

hounded by investigators—

looked over one shoulder

running from the police—

looked over the other shoulder

enduring brutality—

lifted his chin

fighting misunderstanding—

put hands on thighs and leaned forward

getting through it all by laughing, talking, marching, singing, suffering, and celebrating with other like-minded souls"—

stood up, walked around the chair, and sat down with a laugh.

We all applauded. "Thank you for the performance." I stood up and bowed, and 1930s organizer nodded in response.

"What about the descendants of Jimmy Higgins?" I asked, "is there new dance material?"

Nineteen thirtees organizer leaned forward: "The young seem to care more about the 'millions' and the 'diamond rings' than about the 'right to live' and a 'union job.' They don't have the joy of joining together to put on a play or hear a speaker say 'every day is one day closer to socialism.'" He paused before going on. "Jobs and workplaces have changed, but in the system, workers are still workers. There are periods when corporate power manages to keep them fooled and repressed. Some become bitter and angry. But Jimmy Higgins lies buried in every worker's soul and will come to life again when the conditions are right." He looked around the table and then at me. "So make a new dance about workers."

Figure 08. Gesture from Passion in newspaper article about portrait of Rosa (1971).
Photograph by Virginia Blaisdell.

Chapter Four: Passion

I feel the need to say something great, but how, what, where?" I copied the quote of the socialist revolutionary, Rosa Luxemburg (1871-1918), on a three-by-five card, taped it to the wall of my warehouse studio above the sound system, and looked at it often during the months it took to choreograph *Passion*.[1] I was reading Rosa's writings and biographies of her, in which the word 'passion' often appeared to describe her zeal as a person, activist, and writer. But I was unaware at the time that this new dance would become part of a full-evening portrait of her.

Along with others in AIM, I saw the late 1960s and early '70s as a period of revolutionary change and was trying to figure out how to play a role as a dancer. I was drawn to Rosa, not because of any references to dance in her writings (though she was passionate about walking), but because she was a woman revolutionary and a Jew, who came from Poland, where my father grew up. When I asked him if he knew anything about her, he said no, but revealed that as a teenager, he had walked ten miles to hear Leon Trotsky on the Red Train. His hope was that Trotsky would come to power and make life better for everyone, especially the Jews. No doubt these ideas were in my mind while I was choreographing *Passion*, but my immediate concern was a formal struggle with dance.

After making many studies and short dances, I wanted to compose a longer work and turned to Beethoven's *Appassionata*, an acknowledged masterpiece in sonata form for solo piano. Never having undertaken such a complex argument in dance, but familiar with music visualization as a choreographic device and with sonatas as a piano student, I set out to learn about the form, Beethoven, and the chosen piece by reading music history texts and studying the score. To come up with a movement vocabulary appropriate for the music, I searched through art history books, and in Kenneth Clark's *The Nude*, found poses from sculpture and painting that resonated with passion when brought to life in the dancing body.

Having purchased a tape deck for my studio, I went there day after day, listened to the music, followed the score, listened and improvised gestural sequences—went home and listened to the recording, experimented with dance material in the apartment's constricted spaces, played parts of the piece that were difficult to analyze on the piano.

The whole sonata is in duple meter (two beats or a multiple of two beats per measure), which Beethoven unbalances and distorts for expressive purposes. Just looking at the score gives an indication of the urgent, driving, frenetic quality of the music with its occasional halt to breathe or pick up the pieces. Section One is in twelve/eight time—twelve eighth notes (often in four sets of three), twenty-four sixteenth notes (often four sets of six)—sometimes just six half notes—twelve invites the play of two against three. A lot of notes—easier to translate into footsteps than movements for the torso.

Sections Two and Three are in two/four time, which indicates "keep moving," but they are very different in the way they propel the body forward. Section Two is the calm that follows one frenzy and precedes another. It begins with a theme in quarter-note chords, moves on to a variation in syncopated eighth notes, then a variation in sixteenth notes, played very smoothly. For the third variation, thirty-second notes rock and run over the keyboard, while eighth notes spring and tap above and below them. And then a return to the quarter-note chords, embellished by singing passages of sixteenth notes.

The ending of Section Two becomes the beginning of Section Three: two rippled chords, the first questioning, the second dissonant and terrible. The frenzy returns, all the more intense after the brief respite.

The great turn-of-the-century writer and music historian Romain Rolland described Section Three as "a fury that rarely ceases," and "a tumult of voices" (which I translated as a tumult of gestures), "combining, clashing, heightening, rekindling lines and rhythms."[2] The galloping two/four meter is relentless. Exhilaration is the command. No time for exhaustion.

While I was choreographing *Passion*, Harris was commuting to an architectural job in Westport, Connecticut, to keep us going financially. In his spare time, he was working on the text and drawings for his first book, *Workbook of an Unsuccessful Architect.* With *Passion* and *Workbook*, each of us was setting off in a new direction.

When Harris drove away in the morning, I took the bus to my downtown studio. After a warm up and two or three hours of choreographing and rehearsing, I would take a lunch break, and then return to the studio for more hours of struggle, sometimes breaking the routine for a visit to a library or a shopping trip. I continued to perform, teach, and participate in AIM, but tried to wrest as much time as possible for composing *Passion.*

At any one session, I worked alternately on the three sections of the dance. Doubt, frustration, despair—not a single moment of the piece came easily. The general argument of Section One was the hardest to build. It took an incredible amount of effort, sweating, and swearing to block out two contrasting themes: one based on knotting and twisting, the other on releasing and breathing—tension and release—a contrast basic to life and dance. Now many years later, I see that the first section was the most difficult to compose, because it was the most personal. My journal writings at the time say: inward-turning, the burden of self, reaching up out anywhere for help, back and forth in the same rut, stamps of angry resistance or acceptance, a few moments of release and hope. To paraphrase the poet Pablo Neruda's lighter way of putting it: I opened up and closeted myself with my own most treacherous enemy, Joan Stone.

For the knotting and twisting theme, I rose from doubled over to stretched up high, arms crossing in front and behind as if lacing a bundle with rope from ankles to knees to buttocks to crotch to waist to chest to neck to hands tied above the head, legs squeezed together, feet crossed—the final excruciating pose. For the breathing theme, I faced forward and made visible and audible breaths by expanding the torso on the inhale and contracting it on the exhale. The breathing also set off accelerating patterns of stepping and stamping, based on the rhythms of Beethoven, including the well-known—ta ta ta TUM, stamp stamp stamp STAMP—which occurs in the *Appassionata*, as well as the *Fifth Symphony.*

Once I had the knotting and breathing themes, the problem was how to develop them in relation to the spatial concept of advancing and retreating along the spine of the space. Moving forward and back along a pathway is a well-known structural device in choreography. In my dance, it enabled me to embody how I heard the music and saw my work in dance and politics. I came up with multiple ways of advancing by moving sideways and along the floor as well as forward, only to have the advances, which grew longer and more complicated, turn into relatively quick and direct retreats. I progressed and regressed again and again, until at last I had overcome enough difficulties and built enough momentum to break out of the channel and sweep around with the simplest knotting and unknotting step in dance: the grapevine, in which the feet cross and open while moving sideways, and the body and arms twist and untwist in harmony with the feet. At the very end, just walking steps forward (breathing in the feet) brought me to the starting point for Section Two.

If we think of mind in every cell of the body and the body in every pulse of the mind, a dance becomes a complex philosophical argument, which brings me to something the philosopher Ludwig Wittgenstein once observed: philosophy (dance) unties knots in our thinking, hence its result must be simple, but philosophizing (making the dance) has to be as complicated as the knots it unties.

From the start, Section Two in the simpler form of a theme and variations was somewhat easier to choreograph than Section One. What emerged was an evocation of the simmering, sensual, amorous side of passion. I built a theme on a walking base that called attention to different parts of the body. The sensuality was evident from the first strokes of the feet along the floor. A casual walk turned into circles of the knees that reverberated through the torso. More walking steps led to a bend from the waist, followed by a thrust of the pelvis forward to rise, and a half turn to change direction. Then came the upper body. I walked with shoulders rotating seductively forward and backward and shimmying down and up. Circles of the rib cage came next, and finally a nonchalant walk, culminating in a circle of the head to change direction.

With much exertion and moments of inspiration, the variations evolved: JAZZ, SLOW MOTION, FOLK, and COURTLY. What held the change of styles together was the erotic undertone, even in the courtly variation, and the spatial pattern of snaking back and forth invitingly over the whole dancing ground. In my mind, I was always going toward Harris, seeing him at the end of each row of movement.

Section Three posed yet other compositional challenges. When I told Harris about the five motifs—DESPAIR, TALK, STRIVE, PLAY, FLY—he said it sounded like AIM with more time spent despairing, talking, and striving than playing or flying. (The dance reflected that imbalance in its time structure with longer more frequent sections of struggle than play.) By 1970 when I was working on Passion, we knew that the revolutionary changes we were hoping for weren't going to happen soon. Bob Cook had run for Congress in 1966 and '68, but didn't plan to run again. The organization had split into small groups by neighborhood and interest. It still had a strong local presence through its newspaper, *Modern Times*, its coffeehouse, small press, and children's school. It also remained central to the ongoing protests against the Vietnam War and urban renewal and to the support of equal rights issues. Harris and I went to meetings of the central organization, the art and politics group, the urban renewal group, and he often participated in neighborhood projects as an advocate architect. We all despaired, talked, strove, and occasionally played and flew to keep the organization going and thriving.

As in Sections One and Two, the spatial configuration was critical to the meaning of Section Three. DESPAIR and FLY, at opposite ends of the emotional spectrum, were done on axis in the center. To dance DESPAIR, I came up with a balance on one leg, one hand covering an eye, interspersed with contractions, reaches, swings, and arcs. FLY was realized through undulations and vibrations in the torso that raised the arms like wings.

TALK, STRIVE, and PLAY moved out to the corners and edges and back to the center. To TALK, I came up with deep squat jumps, interwoven with raps, taps, and slaps in the feet. The squat jumps were so deep and the footwork so fast that in racing from center to corner and back, I often stumbled—passion veering out of control. For STRIVE, I traced the pathways out and in with long strides, arms reaching forward and back, which narrowed to small jumps, arms pulling in—and the reverse: from jumps to strides. PLAY was fun to do with its prances, lifting the knees high, and step taps sideways with the feet crossed, traveling in a big loop out to the edge, around a corner, and back to the center.

Not unhappy on days when *Passion* seemed to be progressing, miserable on days when nothing seemed to go right, I painstakingly assembled all the bits and pieces into sections and the three sections into a whole, and then switched from the tasks of composition to those of performance: run-throughs of the individual sections, run-throughs of the whole, rehearsals of bits and pieces that needed attention; run-throughs and rehearsals, rehearsals and run-throughs; sections, the whole, bits and pieces, sections, the whole ...

At the end of the first performance for Harris, I cried.

"Why are you crying?" he asked, as he approached with arms open wide for a hug.

"Fait accompli ... a release ... happiness ..."

For all the work and emotion of composing *Passion*, the dance was a failure—at least as performed on a gray, autumn afternoon in 1970 at my alma mater, Sarah Lawrence College. The audience was packed together in a little bank of seats at the dark end of the dance studio, and at the other end, under harsh white theatrical lights, I began with five studies in silence or with spoken words, danced *Passion* to Beethoven in the middle, and ended with *Growing* to Coltrane. Bessie left immediately after the performance—didn't stay to hear the student comments, which ranged from excitement about my belief in the dances and strength and endurance as a dancer to questioning the audience participation ending of *Growing*.

"It almost worked," said one dancer.

"It came closer than any other attempts I've seen," said another.

"Would it have worked better if we sat in-the-round on the cushions we sometimes use—and without the theatrical lights?" asked the head of Dance Group. The answer was definitely 'yes,' but it took the mistake, doing the wrong thing, for me to realize that.

Bessie had invited Harris and me to dinner and waited until after lots of vodka and wine, served with a sumptuous meal, to deliver a "brutally frank" critique.

"The piece of music for *Passion* is too big, too famous—it does not need you—it dominates the dance—you imitate it too closely. The dance is repetitious and redundant—the themes always run the same way: why not backward or interrupted?"

(I did run them backward and interrupted, but somehow that didn't read.)

"Find a new piece of music at the right scale for your work, preferably one written for the dance—take out the repeats—re-do the piece totally or drop it," she said.

"The structure of *Growing* is interesting, but the music is wrong. It is a lament, and your dance is the opposite, an affirmation. Do a new piece, a lament, to that music. For your dance, I am not sure. You have always been rhythmically strong. The wrong music hides your strength."

(I had danced the piece in silence before the performance on the Green. Return to silence?)

"You had everyone join at the end of *Growing*," she continued, "and then you did nothing with them. Could you circle, wind into the middle, a folk dance—something?"

(That happened spontaneously at other performances. I had to make it conscious.)

Bessie also criticized my opening remarks. "Why do you feel you have to speak before you dance? You underestimate the audience. Force them to work. Your words were misleading. You called yourself a political dancer. What you are doing is not agitprop, the only art that can be called political. Your dancing is social, humanist. Get rid of the word political—find a different way of describing your position.

"Why did you talk about the ballet in *Growing*? It is a modern piece, and you are a modern dancer. You have made yourself a strong performer. You should try out for a company in New York."

From Bessie, that was high praise.

Other issues she raised were also troubling. "A choreographer must have a vision—new ideas about theatre as well as movement and sound ... Group is more interesting to an audience than solo—the variety of faces and bodies ... Merry (Meredith Monk) and Cindy (Lucinda Childs), who were in the college with you, are pushing the frontiers of dance."

Bessie's critique gave Harris and me much to brood on during the trip home, which took longer than the usual hour and a half because of a driving rainstorm. At first we said nothing, each sinking into a private gloom, until on the verge of tears, I broke the silence: "Should I continue to dance at all?" We both agreed that I should, but not without deep consideration of Bessie's comments.

The rain beat down on the roof and windows of the car for quite a while, before I spoke again: "The attack calls into question future dances planned to the music of great composers. Should I drop those ideas?"

Harris answered with a question: "Can you drop the music and save the dance ideas?"

I paused to sniffle and blow my nose. "Maybe ... I think so." Were the sniffles due to tears, nerves and exhaustion, an allergy attack? Probably all of those things.

The car was old and had a poor heating and defrosting system. The windshield kept steaming up. I chided Harris about not keeping a rag in the car (though it was just as much my fault as his) and wiped ineffectually with tissues and his handkerchief. "Should I discard *Passion* and *Growing* and go back to more explicitly political dances, such as *Downtown?*"

"Is that possible?" asked Harris, knowing the answer.

"No. Agitprop is important, but I can't stay there." I blew my nose. "Do you agree that Bessie's definition of political art is too limited?"

"Yes. Your dances are political in the way that Brecht's poems are political. You have to find new words to explain what you're doing."

The windshield wipers were of little help in the downpour. Harris and I disliked using them, because they made a terrible noise, but there was no choice in this weather. The screech of the wipers added to our misery.

"Should I look more to the avant garde? With my motion sickness, I wouldn't be much good at climbing on walls or performing on rafts."

"Nudity isn't your thing," said Harris, "and you love dancing too much to do anti-dance."

"Bessie said my work is too real. I haven't learned the art of distortion. Even as a student I was drawn to the representational. The abstract only made sense to me as abstraction from reality."

"Too real"—Harris disagreed with Bessie's criticism—"the realness of the work is its strength."

Suddenly the rain came down so hard, it was impossible to see. "Pull over!" I shrieked. Harris tried to turn the wheel, but nothing happened. The car had hit a slick and was hydroplaning. I clutched the seat and strained forward, trying to see. Harris clutched the wheel. There was nothing to do but hang on and wait, hang on and wait, hang on and wait. The rain let up a bit and the tires made contact with the road again. No accident. Fate, if not the muse of dance, was with us that night. We stopped at the first roadside gas station to collect ourselves.

"How about a cup of coffee?" Harris suggested.

I searched in my pocketbook for change and a tissue for my nose. "If you call what comes out of that vending machine coffee. Even without sugar, it tastes like candy." Standing in the snack room of the station, which was deserted, we shared one cup, passing it back and forth, and resumed talking—not about the hydroplaning, which was over in a few seconds, but about Bessie's critique, which would have consequences for a long time to come.

Harris took a sip of coffee. "Should we take Bessie's criticisms to apply only to the most sophisticated New York audiences? When you performed Passion for our political friends, it was clear that most of them had never heard the music." He handed the cup to me.

"More of them knew the jazz piece I chose for *Growing*. One even commented that the music and dance had nothing to do with each other, but I ignored the comment."

"As you've said, a dancer never knows who's in the audience."

"I learned that from Bessie, and my performances have verified it. There's usually at least one sophisticated and knowledgeable viewer, and I have to dance for that viewer." From my pocketbook, I took out an anti-histamine for my running nose and asked for the last sips of coffee.

Harris handed over the cup and looked out the window. "We should drive home, while the rain is less blinding."

We got back to the car and on to the highway without incident. The rain was steady, but not frightening, and there was almost no traffic. We said little to each other, until we neared the exit ramp a few blocks from our apartment. "Can I, will I, be able to dance *Passion* and *Growing* in silence?"

"That's how you began and how you tend to work," said Harris.

"If I forget about music except as a composing tool and perform in silence, the stage is out. It can tolerate a short piece without sound, but not a long piece or a whole program. Silence will restrict me to performances on an intimate scale."

Harris asked, "How serious were you about becoming a proscenium performer, about enlarging the scale of your works by theatrical means?"

"I haven't thought much about that. I've been focusing on making myself a choreographer and performer."

As we pulled into the garage, words of the novelist Honoré de Balzac came into my mind: "art or success." Dance in silence and in small venues might be art, but it was unlikely to be a success.

Neither the tumultuous day nor the vodka and wine at dinner could bring on the weariness that leads to sleep. Harris couldn't help but be caught up in the crisis. We sat close to each other on the couch in the living room, drinking tea and alternately thinking our own thoughts and talking, thinking and talking, through the night.

A few days later, I wrote to Bessie:

> Your comments set me reeling. It will be a while before I regain my equilibrium, but you were right to be so brutally frank. As Antonin Artaud put it: "Cruelty is rigor." You should know that the students, who remained and talked with me, were also critical, though they couldn't articulate the problems as you did. I cannot say more at this point, except that I'm dancing Passion and Growing at a college and at an arts festival in the next month with the following changes from what you saw: no music and no theatrical lighting, and the audience will sit in the three-quarter round. I think both those dances are good, but it was impossible to see them because of the way I performed them. The head of Dance Group asked if I would return in the spring and dance for and with the students on the lawn. What a kind way of saying: get rid of the canned sound and get off the stage. I won't return until I've done lots more thinking and dancing.

I went back to the studio and tried *Passion* in silence. The music ran in my head, and I quickly realized that the rhythms and phrasing, in fact the whole time structure, was in my body. Without the recording, I could be a little looser with the timing, could make the involuntary sounds like breathing and gasping louder, and could bring out the rhythms by turning my body into a percussion instrument. In other words, I could let the dance take over.

When I showed it to Harris, he applauded, as he walked toward me. "The music was like scaffolding on a completed building. It was hiding the dance. Now the development of the ideas is clearer. The passion keeps growing."

"I needed the scaffolding to construct the dance."

"But now it can stand on its own. The music is in the dance."

"Do you remember there was a blind person at the premiere of *Growing*, when I was doing it in silence? She said she could imagine what I was doing from the different sounds she heard."

Harris nodded. "And the high school kids, who said they enjoyed the dance in silence—they could see it better."

"I remember one student saying music doesn't require dance, why should dance require music? And another wondered what a ballet would look like in silence."

Harris and I sat down on two of the chairs I set out for people who came to see a performance in the studio. "Working with music and then discarding it gives me a new compositional tool. I can use a score to guide the rhythms, phrasing, and duration—to construct my own time score."

"Gestures from art history"—Harris put a hand over one eye, imitating a distinctive gesture from Michelangelo in the last section of *Passion*, and we both laughed. To see what a movement looked like, I sometimes used him as a model.

"I learned to design my own spatial score from your chair arrangement for *When the Landlord Left...*"

"You're developing a method."

"Three scores—temporal, gestural, and spatial—time is the hardest element for me."

"You composed *The Landlord...*, *Downtown*, and *Growing* without music."

"Not really. The Bob Dylan song with the refrain, *It's a hard rain's a-gonna fall*, was in my head when I choreographed the central character in landlord. I sing it silently every time I perform to shape the moves. Other tunes shaped other characters. *Downtown* improved when I added the sound track of ads and political commentary and the song, *Downtown*. And you know I was always listening to Coltrane for rhythms and phrasing when I was working on *Growing*."

"You're building a vision," said Harris.

"I think that's what the dance *Passion* is all about: tapping the forces within and molding them to continue the struggle no matter what." I stood up and walked toward the sound system, where there was a bottle of water. Passion was a marathon that made me thirsty and sweaty even in the coldest weather. Harris followed.

"'The struggle goes on,'" he said, reciting a mantra of the '60s and '70s.

I took a sip of water and looked at the quote from Rosa taped to the wall. In her own passionate way, she had expressed that same thought many times.

A student organizer from Trinity College in Hartford, who saw me dance at a small city organizers conference, arranged a performance at his school. Acting on Bessie's advice to find new words, it was advertised as "dances of our time" instead of "political dance." I wondered if the substitute phrase was a factor in the composition of the audience, which was mostly dancers, not political people, according to the student organizer, who invited me. Harris set up chairs in the three-quarter round in the center of the huge ballroom. No stage, no special lighting, no music. I didn't speak except to announce the program, which began with *Five Sketches*, renamed to link them into a suite of basic human characteristics: **Procrastination** (*If You Don't Jump In*), **Frustration** (*How a Calf Can Become a Swallow*), **Anger** (*I Want the Pen to be on a Par With the Bayonet.*), **Protest** (*On the Wall*), and **Contradiction** (*Rich Man Poor Man*).

Next on the program was *Passion*, the first public performance of it without music. At the end of the relentless knotting, twisting, stamping, breathing, up and down, back and forth motions of the opening section, the audience applauded. Surprised and pleased, I looked at the spectators, as I grapevined and walked close to them. They were with me.

From the first gestures, the second section was lighter and more outward reaching. The passion was there, but indirect, smoldering. The THEME and variations advanced in a serpentine pattern without hurry. Going across the space and back brought me face to face with viewers at the end of each sequence.

I walked the THEME, feet slithering, knees circling, hips responding. As I bent over and came up with pelvis forward and body undulating, there was a person sitting directly ahead. After an exchange of looks, I turned to start walking back. The upper body took over—shoulders rotating, ribs thrusting and shifting, and at the end, a quick circle of the head. I directed it at two people, who were sitting a few paces away. One looked down, and the other smiled.

The JAZZ variation moved sideways with faster syncopated steps, drags, and shuffles. A side bend ended with a pop up recovery that made the audience laugh. Going back the other way, toe-heel steps and little jumps propelled the shoulder and rib action, and as I circled my head, I almost jumped on the feet of a spectator. He rapidly tucked them under his chair and grinned.

For the SLOW MOTION variation, I traveled backward, extending the legs slowly, circling the knees smoothly, bending over and rising with a sustained undulation of the whole body that produced an involuntary sigh. A viewer sighed with me. I changed direction and slithered across with leg extensions forward and side, interrupted by shoulder, rib, and head gestures. Slow motion magnified the sensuality. A viewer sitting on the floor stretched out sideways, as if the elongated motions were contagious.

Little springs with the toes tapping and heels rapping replaced the walking steps of the theme in the FOLK variation, and a cutting and whipping step became the folk version of knee circles. Why was the audience tittering? With all the fancy footwork, I didn't realize that a large brown dog had entered the ballroom, until it bounded into the center of the dancing space. Thinking that a member of the audience would solve the problem, I continued to brush and leap and whip my legs, while the friendly intruder alternately sprung and backed away in response. When no one came forward, I took hold of the dog by the collar, led it out an open door of the ballroom, closed the door, and returned to the center. The audience laughed and clapped, and I resumed the folk variation where I left off, with step taps forward and turning squat jumps. At the edge of the space, a spectator answered the saucy display by crossing one leg over the other and crossing her arms, making herself into a sitting folk dancer.

For the next lap of the FOLK variation, I step-tapped backward, hands at the waist, and then jumped with elbows and shoulders fanning in and out to turn myself around. Facing the viewer whose arms and legs were crossed, I echoed by springing and crossing my arms and legs while bending forward and rising. At the end of the line, my head said YES, feet tapping forward and back, and then NO, feet tapping from side to side. Another YES, and I turned and ran around the space, past the starting and ending points of all the previous sequences, barely missing the toes and knees of audience members. The run finished on the opposite side with an authoritative step and point forward.

Ballet steps, which originated in the courts of Europe, were the obvious choice for the last variation, COURTLY. I made my way across the space, walking slowly and deliberately with legs turned out and toes pointed. There was sensuality in the feet sliding up and down the legs and circling along the floor—and in the body rocking forward and back. Curved arms and gentle shifts of the head and shoulders that accompanied the body moves could be directed to members of the audience, some of whom responded with a nod. The final phrase consisted of a deep bow all the way to the floor, a push off to standing, a circle of the head while turning, and a final balance on the toes, full of anticipation.

There was no break between the second and third sections of *Passion*. I backed into the center of the space and plunged into the five motifs. Pitted against each other were DESPAIRING sequences, trapped in the center—TALKING gestures that slapped and tapped their way to the edge and back—heroic STRIVING gestures that struck out to the corners and retreated—a PRANCING and twining phrase that carved the space into quadrants—ecstatic movements in the center that embodied FLYING. In the coda, the motifs coalesced into a commanding sweep of the periphery with quick squat jumps, prances, and step taps, followed by flying gestures that lifted, dipped, and lifted in the center. The final move was a twist and a DETERMINED STRIDE FORWARD!

The program at Trinity ended with *Growing*. Although I originally performed the dance in silence, the new version was different. Working to music had changed the dynamics and integration of the fragments and made the piece more like speaking. Coltrane's music ran in my mind to shape the phrasing. With the audience sitting close and in-the-round, I reached out to nearly every spectator as the dance grew, and to the critical question after the final orbits of dancing and walking: "Will you join me/us?"—everyone said: "Yes."

I had designed a participatory ending to avoid a repeat of the fiasco at Sarah Lawrence. The audience formed a big circle, and I directed:

"Five steps into the center, raising the arms; five steps to back out, lowering the arms; five steps to turn in place, hands over your heart; five counts to join hands with the person on either side. Circling to the left: three steps forward and two back."

After several repeats of the sequence, I led the group in a coiling figure, called "escargot" or "the snail" in folk dance. The large circle became a line that coiled in on itself, coiled in and coiled in, until those in the center were in danger of being crushed.

"Reverse!" I shouted. "Reverse, reverse," echoed along the coil, and the uncoiling started with slow steps, but the momentum built rapidly to a run. The line started to whip, and people screamed and dropped hands and broke away to spin and jump. When the commotion subsided, they applauded.

Most of the audience stayed for the discussion. They made a small circle and settled down in a variety of postures on the floor. The one faculty member at the performance, who had left a modern dance company in New York, was the first to comment: "The dog walking right into the middle of the dance wasn't disruptive, because your dance isn't separated from life."

"People go to see dance to get away from life," mused a woman, who had spread a cape on the floor and was perched on it. "Escape is more enjoyable."

"I found Joan's dances very enjoyable. They made me want to explore my own ideas," said a tall gaunt dancer, who had been trying to do flying gestures, before sitting down with the others.

"I forgot about the lack of music after the first few minutes," commented a person, who was sitting with crossed legs, hands tapping his knees.

"Is there any advantage to discarding the music?" asked the cape woman.

"The dance is more visible," said the organizer, who invited me.

"People are used to having music with dance. Silence is challenging."

"Silence makes them watch the dance."

"Or it turns them off, and they leave," said the cape woman. Other people in the circle laughed or grunted or nodded.

The organizer took a slightly different tack. "I went to a lecture-demonstration where the choreographer showed the same dance to two different pieces of music. The movements fit the change so well that some people didn't realize they were seeing the same dance twice. I guess it was just a formal experiment, but I wanted something more."

"Good that it made you think," said the faculty member.

The tall dancer entered the discussion. "Merce Cunningham sees dance and music as independent entities. He says they're just sharing the same space at the same time."

"That's an important new idea about dealing with dance and music," said the faculty member. "Some choreography teachers encourage using the lesser works of great composers or the best work of lesser composers, music with more room for dance."

I raised another possibility. "I worked with a great piece of music and then discarded it."

"Isn't that cheating?" asked the cape woman. "Shouldn't you play the music?"

"Until recently, musicians and especially visual artists considered it essential to work from precedent, from models. Architects build scaffolding and then remove it. Van Gogh had a perspective device for putting things in the right places. I use a musical score the same way."

"Too many questions, too much discussion," said the cape woman, as she rose and put on her cape. "I want to stay with my vision of a dancer growing passionately." With one shoulder forward and the other back like a ballerina making an exit, she glided away from the gathering and out of the ballroom.

The organizer restarted the discussion. "There were lots of different dance genres in your pieces—modern, ballet, jazz."

"I also saw folk and tap," said the tall dancer.

"That was very clear in the middle section of *Passion*," said the faculty member.

"A theme and variations," I explained. "My movement theme calls attention to different parts of the body. I do it first like everyday gestures. And then come the variations."

The faculty member stood up and addressed the audience: "The pioneers of modern dance turned their backs on history in order to find new ways of moving. They invented personal vocabularies for their dances, which can be limiting. Joan and I are working with a wider vocabulary, drawing upon many genres old and new. That's the step our generation of choreographers is taking."

"That can be confusing," said a student, who hadn't spoken before, "too many choices."

"Good comment—something your generation will have to face," I said, and the faculty member agreed.

The student sitting with crossed legs spoke up again: "*Passion* was about tying ourselves in knots. Why do we do that again and again? Why are there so few moments of release?"

There was no verbal response, but audience members shifted their positions, as if thinking about knots in their own bodies. The student took another tack. "I read somewhere that passion brings disorder into society."

"Maybe because it can set off revolutionary acts," ventured the organizer.

The tall dancer folded his knees to his chest and wrapped his arms around them. "I could hardly breathe until the ending of *Passion*." He stood up. "One pose made me think of hanging on by a thread. How do you

Figure 09. "Clinging to oneself to keep from splintering." Passion, Section Three (1971).
Photograph by Virginia Blaisdell.

Figure 10. “Counter motions that seem to be tearing the body apart.” Passion, Section Three (1971). Photograph by Virginia Blaisdell.

do it?" He stretched and extended his torso and arms upward.

"You could have been a model for that gesture," I said and demonstrated. "It comes from an ancient Greek sculpture of Marsyas, who challenged Apollo to a musical contest, and lost. He was bound to a tree and flayed alive."

The tall dancer stamped: ta ta ta TUM.

I stamped in response.

Other dancers stood and stretched up as high as they could.

I stamped and lowered my arms, and the dancers answered. In call-and-response fashion, we arrived at standing with our arms down, and the faculty member claimed the floor for a final announcement: "As the students know, I'm moving to a farm at the end of the school year. I gave a performance something like this one in New York. The critics flayed me alive. Dance, dancer, audience—and to hell with the rest. Why is that such a challenge?"

1971 Metamorphosis I: Women's Arts Festival

I submitted an application, which was accepted, to perform *Dances Against Comfort* at Metamorphosis I, a Women's Arts Festival open to performing, visual, and literary artists, seeking a new consciousness of their power as women. The Festival was held from April 29 to May 2, 1971, with most of the events taking place in the Center Church Parish House about a block away from the Church's location on the New Haven Green. Participants came from New York and Philadelphia as well as many towns in Connecticut.

The evening I performed began with an original musical review. Seven singers, costumed in long pastel-colored gowns, a pianist at a grand piano, and a narrator all squeezed themselves on to a small raised platform with microphones and makeshift lighting at one end of the multi-purpose hall of the parish house. A lieder singer and accompanist in formal dress followed. The audience of about a hundred, mostly women, sat in darkness in rows of moveable chairs, facing the shallow lit area. Trying to keep warm at the back of the hall, I realized that hardly anyone could see because of the flat floor, yet modern and Haitian dancers had performed the night before, and a ballet was scheduled for the following night.

I was standing by the light switches when the lieder singer finished and switched on all the overhead lights. People blinked and gasped and looked around. "Let's move the chairs back against the walls," I announced. "I'm going to dance right up close to you."

There was some difficulty in rearranging the chairs because of the carpet, which was not firmly attached to the wood floor. An audience member tripped and quipped: "No wonder they're calling this event *Dance Against Comfort*."

Another woman, scuffing and bumping a chair, asked: "How can anyone dance on this?"

I had asked the same question during rehearsal and tried to have the carpet removed, but the floor underneath was worse. The answer, of course, was to make the difficulties of the carpet—shifts, resistance, muffled sound—part of the performance.

When the flurry of resettlement died down, I put the chair for *Rich Man Poor Man* in place and announced the dance as a prologue to a portrait of Rosa Luxemburg, on which I was working. After a brief summary of Rosa's life, I launched into the poem, speaking as I moved.

A man is rich—ever fatter, ever whiter (*marched down the center of the space and sat on the chair*). The carpet didn't hinder **Rich Man**, who spent most of the prologue sitting and speaking in a voice that boomed off the walls and ceiling. Goes to borrow fifty pieces (*extended the hands to the sides with palms up that turned into fists*). Has hundreds pressed upon him (*raised the arms, clasped the hands, and lowered them to rest on the belly*). Turns to go (*looked at an imaginary watch*). Is urged to stay and drink (*looked side, forward, side, and behind several times, facial expression changing from smiles to nods to frowns to fear*). Fell to the floor.

The reversal of fortune segued into **Poor Man**, who ran laps at racing-speed. A man is poor (*run forward*). Ever thinner (*run backward*). Ever blacker (*run sideways*). I almost tumbled on the runs because of the unstable carpet. Goes to borrow fifty coins (*knelt and begged with fifty claps, starting loud and slow and becoming softer, quicker, and more desperate, as the body slumped down*). Is asked hundreds in return (*rolled over, pinning the back to the floor, knees bent, pelvis and hands heaving upward*). Knows he's taken for a thief (*rolled to prone, pushed off on to the feet, and backed up with open hands, clenching into fists and rising into a threat*).

I picked up the chair, found a place for it among the audience, went to the center of the space and announced: "The next piece is called *Passion*, the dance that follows the prologue in the portrait of Rosa Luxemburg. It has three sections. There will be no music, just the sounds generated by the dance."

The moves of Section One were hard enough to do without the added difficulties of the carpet. I advanced forward to mark a central pathway, rising from bent-over to stretched upward and the reverse, while knotting and twisting, crossing and opening the legs and arms. Stopped for a moment to breathe. Retreated to the starting point. Fell to the floor, gestured there (face-to-face with the well-worn carpet), and lifted to standing. Advance and retreat, advance and retreat. I did my best to make the rhythms audible: scrape, grunt, thump, swish, gasp, stamp, slap, breathe out loud, pound out the gestures. At last a break, a release: I moved forward without backing up, grapevined sideways around and along the edge, crossing and opening the feet, and walked forward.

Circling close to the audience, I could see that the initial shock of the aesthetic had turned into intense excitement for some and writhing discomfort for others.

Section Two was a cooler and more inviting manifestation of passion. The andante tempo made it easier to deal with the ripples, dips, slides, and resistances of the carpet. I tacked back and forth, as if navigating a river, signaling in various ways to those on shore, who sometimes answered with a smile, a wave, or a shift forward or backward on their chairs. The section ended with a turn on the toes that swirled me into a corner.

Sitting there was a person central to the planning of Metamorphosis, a mask-maker with startling red curly hair. I was intrigued by her presentation that afternoon with large metal masks, but couldn't speak with her. She was surrounded by a crowd of friends and admirers and oblivious to strangers. I could tell that she was a mover and shaker and wanted to meet her. Wait until tonight, I thought. After my performance, she'll want to meet me. How fortuitous to be facing where she was sitting, as I began the third and final section of *Passion* with its tumultuous emotions, evocative of a women's consciousness raising session.

Figure 11. “A flying motif.” Passion, Section Three (1971). Photograph by Virginia Blaisdell.

Still on the toes, I pivoted away from Mask-maker and then toward her, away and toward, away and toward, until a drop of the heels propelled accelerating steps backward. In the center, the steps became higher, knees lifting and body lowering, as the body rotated on axis. A vamp set off the interweaving of the five dramatic motifs along a web of pathways that ran between the center and corners.

DESPAIR began with a gesture that could be seen as clinging to oneself to keep from splintering: a balance with the legs forming the number four, one hand up to grip the face and hide one eye, the other arm grasping the torso. A move followed with counter motions that seemed to be tearing the body apart: one leg lunging forward, the other lunging back—body and neck twisted—arms pulling backward. A swing from one side to the other with the legs apart indicated the potential for release, and on the repeat of the gestures, the swing became an arc—a rainbow of hope.

For **TALK**, I flung out to one corner and back to the center with a burst of squat jumps, followed by raps of the heels front and toes back, and twisting tap/steps. (The squat jumps were treacherous, made all the more so by the shifting carpet.)

STRIVE required lunging strides and dragging steps to the opposite corner, arms reaching and retracting. The strides and drags along the resistant carpet diminished into faster limping steps and small jumps. Cornered, I strode backward for another bout in the center.

The gestures of **DESPAIR** reappeared with added difficulties: the balance was threatened by hands and free leg banging, the lunge intensified by rapid contractions and releases of the torso, the swing broken by jumps. Repeated slowly, the gestures merged into one continuous writhing cry that broke off.

With a phrase of **PRANCING** in one spot and step-tapping sideways, I bobbed and twined to the edge, around a corner, and back to the irresistible center. Lightness and springiness in the moves, but always done with awareness of the ground, of the pull and twist of forces we cannot control.

A **FLYING** motif entered. Standing with one foot forward and the other back, the arms circled down, back, up, and over, while the torso undulated. The circles and undulations grew smaller, faster, and higher, and compressed into vibrations with the arms extended like wings, as if flying.

The frustrated attempt to fly ended in **DESPAIR**—a slap of the hands over the face and a descent until the body was folded into a small lump. A flop on to the side, one arm clinging to the waist, the other reaching back, and a skitter around on the hands and knees built enough momentum to generate a slap on the floor and spring to the feet.

A return of the squat jumps, raps, taps, and stamps **TALKED** me backward into a corner and then forward into the center toward Mask-maker, who was leaning forward, elbows on knees, hands clenched at her cheeks.

A return of the **STRIVING** jumps, limps, lunges and drags, hands clenched in fists, backed me into Mask-maker's corner. Turning around, as I lunged to start backward, I almost grazed her red curls with a fist. She didn't pull back.

(From low squat jumps to high prances to deep lunges to hard stamps—the contrasts and repetitions were brutal on my knees, especially on the damn sliding carpet.)

The balance, lunge, and swing of **DESPAIR** returned, varied with percussive mechanical motions to indicate new possibilities. On the repeat of the gestures, the arms, which had been close to the body, opened out into FLYING positions—moments of release—but then closed in again.

I **PRANCED** and twined out to the edge and around the corner where Mask-maker was sitting straight up, hands gripping her thighs.

Another attempt at **FLYING** turned into a thoughtful rather than tempestuous descent with the gestures of **DESPAIR** done like everyday moves.

The squat jump sequence returned to **TALK** me to a corner and back to the center.

More **STRIVING** lunges, drags, limps, and jumps to the opposite corner, arms reaching from high to low, and then the reverse—jumps to lunges, arms reaching from low to high.

The high reaches signaled a change, and when the **DESPAIRING** gestures reappeared with hops in the feet, they turned into joyful moves. On the repeats, the arcs of legs and arms became smaller and faster, until they were just low springing crisscrosses.

CODA! The synthesis of the five motifs was lightning fast: an explosion of squat jumps and spring-taps forward to a corner and backward to another corner. (I felt a twinge in my left knee, but it passed.) The ebullient race continued around the space with step-taps sideways, hands slapping the thighs, clapping from low to high, and then opening out to the audience. As I passed Mask-maker, our eyes met.

Back to the center for the final movements: the balance was tested, as the gesture leg extended forward, the torso leaned back, and the hands covering the eye and gripping the waist lifted and reached high. The lunge backward and down became a kneeling **WINGED VICTORY,** body arched back, arms sweeping out. A push-off to standing launched the arms into a high arcing RAINBOW OF HOPE with the legs apart, followed by a pivot to a walking stance and a **DETERMINED STRIDE FORWARD**. I held that Stride before announcing: "That's the end."

After the applause, a group of people rushed up to me with Mask-maker in the lead. "That was electric! I could feel all your moves. I was dancing with you."

"I saw that."

"We have to talk," she said and stayed to hear the comments of others.

The woman standing next to her remarked: "Thank you for proving passion in art is still possible."

One of the few men in the audience commented, "Your view of passion is complex." Then he asked about the rhythms. "Contagious. I was trying to tap them out."

"Yes, he was," confirmed the woman by his side.

"They seemed to come from music."

"You're right. They come from Beethoven's *Appassionata*."

Two older women, who looked like sisters, were standing a bit apart from the others. They came forward, and one of them spoke in a thick German accent: "Your gestures reminded us of Mary Wigman. We saw her dance in Germany forty years ago and thought those ideas had disappeared forever."

I wanted to learn more about the performances they saw, but all I could do in the rush of the moment was make a deep bow and say, "That is a great compliment." They smiled, and the one who had spoken added: "We expect to hear more about you."

After each person had had a say and moved on, Mask-maker asked, "Would you like to go someplace where we can talk and have a drink?"

"And food," I said. "I haven't had dinner."

"I still have arrangements to make for tomorrow. It will take me a little while."

"I'll wait here. I have to collect my things and cool down."

As Mask-maker hurried away, one of the musical review performers and the lieder singer were saying good-bye to Balletomane. Oh no, I thought, how can I avoid another confrontation?

"How can we avoid each other?" Balletomane spoke my thoughts.

"We seem destined to meet. How are you?" I asked.

"I should have left after the review and songs. Now I'm uncomfortable."

"*Dance Against Comfort!*"

"Indeed ... The last time we met was after your performance on the Green, where I had to stand in wet grass, and tonight I had to move an uncomfortable chair over a bumpy carpet. Why didn't you perform on the stage?"

"It's too small, and most of the audience wouldn't have been able to see my movements on the floor."

"A dancer crawling and rolling on the ground a few feet away from me is hard to watch." He grimaced.

"You would prefer to see sylphs gliding on a stage in front of a painted landscape?"

"Don't put words in my mouth."

We were standing in amongst the chairs, which were still higgledy-piggledy with the carpet bunched up in places where people had shifted their positions. The audience had left except for two women, who were trying to put the chairs back in rows.

"What was that dance you did on the Green?" asked Balletomane.

"*Growing.*"

"You called it a ballet. I hope you're not making the same claim for *Passion.*"

"No—though there is a balletic variation in Section Two."

"Lost in amongst the ungainly shapes."

"Passion demands ungainly shapes, especially in a period of change."

"I expected you to dance at a festival called Metamorphosis."

"I didn't expect to see you here."

"I came for the lieder, Brahms and Debussy."

"Obviously not for the Women's Liberation Rock Band that's playing in the basement right now."

Just then Mask-maker dashed in and picked up a folder of papers. She looked at us and frowned as she dashed out. The contentiousness must have shown in our faces and bodies. Although I wanted to lie on the floor, lift my legs, and test my knee to see if it was okay, we continued to stand and argue as if we were on a talk show with me bringing up issues and Balletomane dismissing them.

"In a period of ferment—" I began.

"Here come the battle cries."

"In a revolutionary period, bodies change. Strict rules of behavior and dress no longer apply."

"Anarchy."

"New fields open up to minorities, such as women and people of color."

Figure 12. "A flying motif." Passion, Section Three (1971).
Photograph by Virginia Blaisdell.

"Communism."

"History has to be rethought to include those who have been left out."

"Revisionism."

"Technology makes it possible to be mobile and communicate and accomplish things in new ways."

"Bravo."

"There's contact with people from all over the world. We can learn many different movement traditions."

"Eclecticism."

We were standing at the back of the hall. The two women lining up the chairs were coming closer, but suddenly decided to quit, maybe because of us. "We can finish tomorrow morning," one of them said on the way out. Their leaving put an end to the talk show, though not to the argument about dance and politics.

"All these political issues can be explored through dance," I said, sitting down on the nearest chair.

There was one at an angle to me, and Balletomane sat down on it before asking: "How much content can dance bear?"

"More than we usually see. It can talk about struggle—and against comfort. Your reaction is proof."

"Negative!"

"Negative is better than passive, sitting back and letting things wash over you."

"No way to do that on the Green or here."

"An offbeat performance space, even a difficult one, is best for me. The event becomes a world in miniature with viewers close to the action. They seem to understand what I'm doing."

"An experimental dancer is protected by hidden status."

"Okay, but oppressed as well." My left knee was aching. "I have to lie down on the floor and see if my knee is okay. Sorry to make you uncomfortable."

"I have no problem with someone doing that, as long as it's not called dance."

I slowly exercised the leg and messaged the knee. All the squat jumps in *Passion* were taking their toll.

"It can be touching to see a choreographer pursuing an idea with great intensity," said Balletomane.

"Slowly, the experimental becomes articulate, but not in the old codified ways."

"Codified form requires technique."

I had to sit up to respond. "An experimental dancer may have the technique to perform the old phrases."

"Beautiful phrases ..."

"But not necessarily true—and wrong for a body undergoing trials and transformations."

"Why do you have to put the body on trial, to question everything we know about moving?"

"A victory for thought, a word that disappears from dance in periods of complacency." I stood up and walked around the chair before sitting down again. "When the codified forms become lifeless, we have to go back to the streets and fields and re-define the gests of dance."

"Gest—each experimenter makes up new words or dredges up old ones, adding to the confusion," he said.

"Gest, meaning both gist (essence), and gesture (an expressive body movement)—the archaic word also related to historic deeds. I've been searching for gests on the borderline between formal dance and everyday motions."

"The borderline between art and reality—I've heard visual artists talk like that."

"Why not dancers?"

"Dance is the least theoretical of the arts, thank goodness."

"Sometimes we have to turn to books."

"Cerebral dance. Bookish dance. Why not just use words and give a lecture?"

I stood up. "The challenge is to realize the new ideas in dance."

"Sometimes you run and skip with abandon, but more often you're twisted or bent over or stamping, a return to the primitive."

"First you accuse me of being bookish, and now primitive. What do you mean by primitive?"

Balletomane stood up and took a few steps. "Crude, awkward, weighty"—

"But meaningful. Better than polished, light, and meaningless."

He turned as if to leave and then faced me again. "You're an idealist."

"Yes, but also a realist."

"Observation against convention."

"A person doesn't move in the old conventions in a period of metamorphosis."

"Did I hear the word metamorphosis?" Mask-maker rushed in, giving Balletomane an excuse to skirt out. "You look like a gesture from your dance. Are you okay? What happened?"

"The person, who was leaving as you came in, is a ballet buff and sometimes writes reviews and articles. We have very different outlooks on dance—and politics."

"What a pity."

"Not unusual for people who love dance to be on opposite sides of the barricades."

"Sorry to be gone so long. I stopped to hear the rock band in the basement."

"Do you want to hear more music?"

"No, I'd rather go somewhere and talk."

It took me a few minutes to change out of my sweaty clothes, and then Mask-maker and I headed for a restaurant with a tiny courtyard in the back, where there was a stabile of rods, flexible joints, and rounded triangles by Alexander Calder. I thought she would like the sculpture, and she did. We sat at a particular table with a good view of it, and I reminisced:

"A few Yale boyfriends and I huddled here during the McCarthy period, glancing over our shoulders to see who was in the restaurant before discussing modern art and literature. In the Fifties, it wasn't 'shoe' to be an intellectual."

"'Shoe.' I haven't heard that word in ages," said Mask-maker with a grin.

"The Yalies did most of the talking, and I listened. It was an important part of my high school education."

As we ate and drank, we discussed how the feminist movement was leading to new opportunities for women artists, who weren't even part of the art history we studied in the 1950s.

"Dance has been a woman's province for a long time," I said, "which is probably why it's at the bottom of the art totem pole."

"I took a modern dance class ages ago. Learning about Isadora and how she danced and lived free of the old rules was a critical step in making me a feminist."

"Me, too. It seems to me that dance is being replaced by sports, martial arts, and body building, things we couldn't do before."

"From what you did tonight, I would say dance has a very important part to play in the new image of women we're forging."

"I wondered if you had any dance training. The way you used the masks to tell the story of Sarah and Hagar was fascinating."

"A focus of my work has been retelling Bible stories from a woman's point of view."

"I'm interested in Eve, in standing her up on her feet."

"That's a dance I have to see!"

We clinked glasses and took a sip of wine. It was challenging to eat in between words, especially when the conversation zoomed in on the relationship between sculpture and dance.

"I make torsos as well as face masks," said Mask-maker, putting a hand to her solar plexus. "Your use of the torso gave me lots of new ideas."

"The torso is difficult to move one part at a time. It wants to be an inexpressive bloc."

"But when you succeed, the gestures are astonishing. The ribs and hips become unfamiliar and new."

"With sculpture, you could emphasize those parts."

Mask-maker put down her utensils, touched her ribs, and then shook her shoulders. I shook mine in response, and we both chuckled.

"Sometimes your upper torso moved apart from the lower one."

"I can imagine your metal shapes shifting right and left, forward and back, and even circling." I demonstrated and almost upset the table.

"Your sides were alive."

"From thinking of one side lengthening, while the other shrinks or folds."

"A major concept in torso sculpture, especially from antiquity."

"You could make side masks."

"I have to think about that," said Mask-maker, stroking her sides.

"I've followed other modern dancers in borrowing another concept from antiquity: the parallel stance, same arm and leg forward." There was enough space by our table for me to stand up and show the parallel and oppositional stances.

"Is the parallel position better for some actions?"

"Yes. It's a pivotal base for fighting with a sword," I assumed a fencing pose, "and for work gestures, such as sawing"—another demonstration. "Its awkwardness can also be exploited for laughs." Before sitting down, I walked a few steps bringing the same arm and leg forward, which makes the body dip from side to side. "I call this the 'zombie' walk."

Mask-maker laughed, and we both agreed the Women's Movement needed more laughs. She pushed further with the discussion of movement. "How does the change in emphasis from the legs to the torso affect moving in time and space?"

"The feet lend themselves readily to meter and locomotion. For the torso, it's better to work with the more irregular rhythms of breath, speech, the emotions."

"In my performances with unwieldy metal masks, I've been experimenting with irregular rhythms, but I have to remain pretty much in one spot. Maybe I could try more walking steps."

"Backwards, sideways ... long strides, short ones ... slow, slower ... zigzags."

"Zigzags, I like that." Mask-maker shifted from side to side, red curls bouncing. We had eaten our fill, and she poured out the last of the wine. "To say what I want to say, I put on masks. You strip them away."

"Both valid. What's the aphorism: 'The means must be asked what the end is.'"

The owner of the restaurant brought the check. We looked around and realized we were the only customers left. We paid and gave the Calder in the courtyard a final glance. As we were leaving, Mask-maker said, "I've been making sketches for a life-size sculpture of Susan B. Anthony. Have you finished your portrait of Rosa Luxemburg?"

"I've composed the two dances you saw, the prologue: *Rich Man Poor Man* and *Passion*—and another dance, called *Growing*. I'm still working on two more for the premiere next month: *Prisoner* and *Last Battle*."

"Send me information about that performance, and I'll try to come." Mask-maker and I parted with a handclasp and a hug. About two weeks later she sent an honorarium with a note:

> Your extraordinary performance stays with me. I find myself hiding one eye and standing with the same arm and leg forward. I'm afraid this isn't much recompense. As it turns out, we can't repay all the money we owe for renting the hall, etc., but at least we can give the performers something. We must continue our discussion ...

Mask-maker didn't attend the premiere of Rosa, but we had many more conversations, and late in 1972, I performed my version of Eve on two programs she organized. For the moment, however, Eve was on the backburner. I had two more Rosa dances to finish.

Chapter Five: Prisoner

Halfway through composing *Last Battle*, which I knew would end the portrait of Rosa, I realized the story wouldn't be complete without a dance about her as a prisoner. It would come after *Growing*, a stark contrast to the evocation of her rise as a political leader, moving outward in ever-widening circles with bigger, higher, faster, more energetic and powerful movements, the audience joining in at the end. Then suddenly—Constriction! Confinement! Isolated in a cell, what happens to a person, especially a revolutionary?

While Rosa was incarcerated for short periods for her participation in the Polish upheavals of 1905, by far her most difficult stays were during World War I. For protesting the war, she was imprisoned for a year—released for a few months—then locked up for another two and a half years and finally released in November 1918. Unable to help the small group opposing the war, unable to participate in the second Russian Revolution, personally ill much of the time, she put her fierce energy, powers of observation, and skills as a thinker and communicator into writing. The naturalist, the philosopher, the lover, and the cultural critic moved into the cell with the political economist, and correspondence reached flood level.

I immediately came up with the idea of confining the dance to a four-step-by-eight-step box.

I
want
the
pen
To be on a par with the bayonet.

The old study had found a new home. Constriction made it more telling. Although Mayakovsky's words were particularly appropriate to Rosa's situation, I didn't say them out loud, as I did when showing the study. Of all the Rosa dances, silence seemed most important for *Prisoner*.

"Weeks pass without my hearing the sound of my own voice,"[1] she wrote in one of her letters. And so I performed the introduction with the words running through my mind to give rhythmic shape to the variety of moves I used to establish the cell.

At the premiere of the dance for an audience, I realized spatial confinement wasn't enough. The movement material had to be restricted, distorted, and tied together by gesture as well as space. The solution was to cross my hands and keep them crossed until the moment of enacting Rosa's release from prison. To execute the range of movements, I had to cross my hands in front rather than behind. The idea of constriction still read, and I extended it by inviting audience members to keep their hands crossed as long as I did.

Once I set up the four-by-eight dimensions of the cell, I turned Rosa's writings on nature, love, art, and politics, and on her battles to keep herself going into dance episodes. Somehow Mozart's *Fantasy in C Minor* (K. 475), which I had played and loved as a piano student, came into my mind for structuring the choreography. The insightful musicologist Alfred Einstein describes the work as representing "a moment of great agitation," which Mozart conveyed through improvising "the most extreme contrast of ideas, the most uninhibited variety of lyric and virtuoso elements, while yet preserving structural logic."[2]

For gestures to realize the episodes, I drew ideas from Rosa's letters, but also turned once again to works of art: Matisse's painting of five nudes in the midst of an ecstatic circle dance, Carpaux's frieze of a sensual dance that decorates the Paris Opera House, Rodin's sculpture on a low pedestal of the Burghers of Calais on their way to sacrifice their lives for their city, and an ancient Greek pediment of soldiers in a battle. Painting, frieze, pedestal, and pediment: all the artworks depict powerful figures confined to small spaces. The artists have handled the constraints of their media so skillfully that the message of the players seems all the stronger for being compressed and constricted.

Prisoner at Brockport State

An especially meaningful performance of *Prisoner* took place at Brockport State University in December 1971. I had finished the dance just in time for the premier of the whole Rosa portrait in May. Aware that Brockport was located near Attica, a federal penitentiary, where a protest by prisoners had turned into a massacre not long before my performance, I knew I had to include *Prisoner* on the potpourri program.

Rather than dance in a gym cut off from student activities, I decided to brave the cafeteria of the University at dinner hour. A couple of students helped move the tables to the periphery so there was a clear space in the middle, bounded by chairs on three sides. The fourth side without chairs or tables was a glass wall with a corridor running perpendicular to it. While dancing, I could see people coming down the corridor, doing a double take, standing and watching through the glass wall, or coming into the cafeteria to join the more formal audience. About sixty people remained for the whole program, sitting in the U-shape arrangement of chairs or at the tables just outside of them. Beyond that, the cafeteria kept serving dinner, and people came and left.

I took a deep breath and persisted in my decision to perform the whole program I had planned. No music, no change of costume, no intermission—I gave a brief verbal introduction to each piece and then danced:

Rich Man, Poor Man
On the Wall ...
I Want the Pen ...
When the Landlord Left ...
Prisoner
Growing

On one side of the space, there was a responsive trio of students, who often applauded and commented. When I nearly bumped into one of them while running laps as *Poor Man*, I heard, "That's me—poor and running."

As I circled close with kicks during *I Want the Pen...*, one of them said: "Now I understand the meaning of a kick."

After stumbling, falling, and getting up as the student in *When the Landlord Left...*, one of them tried to hand me his cup. "Would you like some orange juice? This is a hard way to perform."

For *Prisoner*, I introduced the dance in relation to the tragic Attica incident as well as Rosa's life. "You can participate by crossing your hands (I demonstrated) until the end of the dance."

Head down, I walked to the center of the space. It was essential to pull in, to feel but ignore the audience, to let the inner voices take over and propel me through the sequences.

Pacing

No matter which prison Rosa was in, she was locked up for the night and sometimes for the day as well. *On the toes to defy gravity and backward to feel rather than see, pace off four steps, turn ninety degrees, then eight steps and another turn. Step sideways—crossing and opening the feet—with stamps at the corners.* In a few letters, she describes herself as reacting "like a beast in a cage." *Walk forward, thrusting the crossed hands forward on the fourth and eighth steps. Continue the rounds with low kicks of anger and frustration, lunges, crawls, and finally just ticks of the head to indicate the dimensions of the cell. Finish in a heap.*

Rosa didn't allow herself to stay down long. *Use the crossed hands to rise from the ground. Lift them high, glaring at them, and let them drop.*

At an earlier performance of *Prisoner*, an audience member made several comments before revealing a stint in the military police and prompting me to heighten the sense of fear.

"I saw it again and again—a prisoner frightened by the slightest shadow or sound." Rosa echoed his words: "My poise and cheerfulness can, alas, be disturbed by the slightest of shadows."[3] *Stumble forward, look back sharply in fear, and stumble again before crumpling sideways. Turn and stumble fearfully in the opposite direction. Turn and pace, turn and pace.*

"I have paced (the prison courtyard) to and fro for months now, so that I know every stone and all the weeds that grow in the crevices of the paving."[4] *Switch to rhythmic tap steps and jumps sideways and in half circles, using the feet like investigative tools. End by rising on the toes and slapping the floor, rise and slap, rise and pound the floor.*

"Enough of me and my troubles."[5] *Straighten up and walk with firm steps across the cell and back, lifting the head and making fists. Bow to the walls, releasing the fists, to begin the first interlude, inspired by Matisse's circle dance.*

Gestures from Matisse

Matisse called his painting *La Danse*, and his nudes do indeed dance: a sweeping front attitude, a reaching arabesque, a twisting grapevine step, a hovering bent over gesture, and a rising suspended one. The figures are facing inward, hands joined as in a folk dance, and by their leans and twists, they appear to be circling clockwise. Matisse put them into several different paintings. Small and distant, they circle in the background of an idyllic landscape. Truncated, framed, and hung on a wall, they ornament a still life. Large-scale, vividly colored, and totally absorbed in movement, they fill two large canvases with dance.

Once I started working with the gestures, I realized they could be varied in multiple ways: circling in one direction, then the other—repeating a gesture, such as sweeping a leg over in higher and higher arcs—changing the order, beginning with the arabesque or the twisting grapevine step—running the sequence retrograde—doing the movements over hops and slides—stamping instead of stepping between moves—breaking the phrase apart—fragmenting the gestures.

I also realized, fitting for Rosa as a prisoner, that the variations could evoke a dance of death as well as a dance of life. Interestingly enough, in Curt Sachs's *World History of the Dance*, I found a "Dance of the Dead" from 1493 with skeletons circling in gestures remarkably similar to those in the Matisse painting.[6] Did the artist know the early work? Did he turn a ghoulish mockery of death into an ecstatic celebration of life?

In the cafeteria at Brockport, aware of the silence of the nearest viewers with their hands crossed, I began circling with a sequence that went from a low hovering gesture to a high suspended one. *Step and hover on one leg, the other folded behind, body bent over, giving in for a moment to the pull of downward forces. Step sideways and resist by raising the crossed hands and bent leg sideways. Find the strength to step forward on the toes and lift the hands and bent leg across and higher to the other side—a suspended pose that couldn't be held for long.*

The circling continued, evoking Rosa saying: "We have to take everything as it comes and find beauty in everything. That is what I manage to do."[7] *Step and sweep one leg forward and over, crossed hands sweeping the other way, as if painting contrary rainbows. Step into arabesque—leg reaching back, body lowering, hands reaching forward in a horizon-like pose. Step across, lifting and twisting the body, as the crossed hands arc over like a tree branch.*

Around and around the cell I went with variations of the Matisse gestures. I circled in the hopeful manner of Rosa's letter from a prison in the countryside on a day in May: "It is so lovely here now (*big sweep of the leg*). Everything is green and burgeoning (*step into reaching arabesque).* The cherry tree with its reddish leaves is already in flower (*step, twist, and raise torso and arms*), and the black alder will soon blossom (*step and hover on one leg*). The foliage of the horse chestnuts is resplendent (*step and raise leg and crossed hands to the side).* The currant bushes are covered with clusters of yellow stars"[8] (*step and lift leg across and upward).*

I also circled in the angry downcast manner of Rosa writing: "You make too much of my equanimity ... *(Like a cornered fighter, prance in place and punch out the crossing, side, and hovering gestures on a hop. Hammer the floor with the toes. Then circle the twisting, sweeping, and reaching gestures with taps, stamps, and hops, making them choppy, restless, anxious.*) In an instant my radiant spirits can give way to the profoundest gloom."[9] *(Circle again while breaking the moves: a broken halo with crossed hands, a broken circle of the leg, scrapes of the feet along the floor, a kick back with a bent leg, a broken twist of the torso as the crossed hands jerk from low to middle to high. Snap the body over, snap the knee side, snap the knee across and high, stamp the foot down.)*

To end the Matisse interlude, the circle dance in slow motion around the cell became like a ghost of itself—*extending, twisting, hovering, opening, crossing, circling the leg and lowering it.*

Thoughts of Suicide and Escape

The section following the ghostly circling was unresolved until the ex-military police officer told me: "Each and every prisoner tries to commit suicide." *(Pivoting on one leg, wheel around, stabbing the floor with the free foot.)*

Did Rosa think of it, as one year turned into two, then three? *(Drop to the knees with a thud, crossed hands overhead.)* If she did, she didn't write about it. *(Grind the wrists together. Pound the back of the head. Punch into the eyes. Bite the hands. Slash the neck. Jab the heart, abdomen, crotch. Double over in pain.)* "It is my way to suffer in silence."[10] *(Lift the hands as if they were weighted down with chains, swivel on the knees, and grind the wrists again. Zigzag down the face and body as if trying to rub them out. Double over.)*

"I felt my position keenly for a moment today (*rise to standing slowly*). The whistle told me my visitor was leaving *(hop off one leg, hammering with the other foot, and jab with the crossed hands up up up: if only these actions could open an escape hole).* If only I too could get away from here, if only I too could get away."[11]

Gestures from Carpaux

The desperate hops gave way to sensual gestures from Carpaux's frieze of figures for the Paris Opera House. They circle an elevated godlike musician with arms raised and a tambourine in one hand. (*Circle slowly almost on axis. Run the crossed hands down the face and body and then back up.)* Unlike the Matisse nudes, who are spaced to execute expansive movements, these dancers are tightly squeezed on a pedestal, twining around each other like lovers. *(Twining the legs, wind backward and forward into a descent to kneeling.)* This was Rosa writing letters to her young lover, Hans Diefenbach, a doctor on the battlefield with the German army. *(Ascend for a reprise of the wish-to-escape hops and stabs upward. Repeat the sensual circling in the opposite direction. Conclude with more resigned hops to usher in a new episode.)*

Rodin's Burghers of Calais

On a trip to Italy with Harris shortly before choreographing Rosa, I saw a full-scale version of the Burghers of Calais. I couldn't resist walking around them, imitating their tilted, twisted, weighed down gestures. Harris knew immediately that the moves would find their way into a dance, and sure enough, while working on *Prisoner*, the Burghers came back to me as a powerful source for enacting Rosa in her cell.

Rodin was commissioned to create a monument to the six leading citizens of Calais, who in 1347, during the Hundred Years' War, donned sackcloth and rope halters and gave themselves to the English as hostages in return for lifting the bloody siege of their city. Rodin insisted on capturing his models while moving, therefore the arrested moments of the Burghers translated readily into dance. The figures are tied together by the same sacrifice, but each one responds individually, which Rodin realized in their stances, but also in having them face different directions. I danced the gestures as a succession of Rosa's moods, executing them slowly to give them weight: move into a gesture, hold the climactic moment, move out and on to the next.

Anguished—*press the crossed hands down on the head, as the body sags;*
Fearful—*tilt sideways and cover cheek and eye with the hands;*
Hopeful—*legs apart, rock and swing the hands from side to side;*
Disconsolate—*cross the legs and spiral torso, arms, and neck into a twisted position;*
Conflicted—*reach the hands forward, as the body pulls back;*
Stalwart—*stand tall, crossed hands making fists.*

Reaching Out and Drawing In

To keep herself stalwart and hopeful, Rosa sat by the window of her cell and wrote. *(Keep the gaze focused on one spot.)* A speck of life minutely observed—a bird, an insect, a plant, a cloud, a poem, a song—became a universe with its own laws and purposes, strong enough to reach out into the consciousness of others and draw them into the consciousness of the writer. I turned from the dramatic Rodin gestures to basic dance moves of reaching out and drawing in, while staying in one spot. *(Stretch a foot along the floor forward and draw it in, to the side and in, to the back and in.)*

She responded to the politics of the times with articles, such as a study of the war that was raging as an imperialist war *(intensify the stretches into leans outward that pull back in)*. She produced a critical dialogue, pitting the ideal of proletarian revolution against the Russian revolution that was taking place *(extend the stretch further with lunges, sometimes pivoting half way around, so the only way to maintain the gaze is over a shoulder or upside down from a backbend).*

What seemed to lift Rosa's spirits the most was her intimate relationship with birds. *(Change to birdlike tapping steps on the toes from feet together to feet apart—one forward and one back—to feet back in.)* She fed them crumbs from her meals, listened to their cries and identified them, talked and sang arias to them. *(Tap the feet out to the sides and in.)* While at the prison in the countryside, she even walked with one of the birds. "I always walk on two sides of the garden along the wall, and the bird keeps step with me by hopping from bush to bush. Isn't this nice?"[12] *(Tap the feet out and in on different diagonals.)* She came to the conclusion that, like King Solomon, she, too, could understand the language of birds.

The war was never far away. An often-quoted section of one of Rosa's letters details her heart-wrenching encounter in a prison courtyard with buffaloes, war booty from the lush green pastures of Rumania. *(With as much effort as possible, lunge and extend the crossed hands forward and return.)*

"Unsparingly exploited, yoked to heavy loads, they are soon worked to death." *(To make the moves more tortuous, turn and lunge lunge lunge sideways, arms pulling across in the opposite direction. Straighten up.)* She stood in front of one of them, who was bleeding from having been flogged unmercifully *(cover the face with the crossed hands).* "The beast looked at me; the tears welled from my own eyes *(shake the head 'no').* Poor wretch, I am as powerless, as dumb, as yourself; I am at one with you in my pain, my weakness, and my longing"[13] (walk a tight circle bending over, drop to the knees, lift the hands and let them fall).

Death of Diefenbach

October 10, 1917 — "I have just received word that Hannes has fallen. For the moment I am unable to write more."[14] *(Lie down on one side and curl up.)*

A month later —"It seems to me like a word that has been silenced in the midst of a sentence, like a suddenly broken-off chord which I still hear. *(Uncurl, rolling on to the back, crossed hands at the crotch. Fold the legs in, open the knees and close them.)* We had a thousand plans for the time after the war. We were going to enjoy life, travel, read good books, marvel at the spring as never before. *(Stretch the arms overhead.)* I cannot comprehend it; is that possible? *(Contract the middle to sit up and whip the arms over to clasp the folded legs.)* Like a flower that has been torn off and trampled upon ... *(Lie down, roll, curl up, and writhe through the same gestures.)* I continue to live in a dream as if he were still here. *(Sit up in a lump, hands at the crotch. Extend the legs, draw them in, open and close the knees.)* I see him alive before me, chat with him in my imagination about everything. *(Extend the legs again. Reach out with the hands and pull the legs in, knees to the chin, hands to the ankles.)* In me he continues to live."[15]

Ascend and Descend Like a Wounded Soldier

From an ancient Greek pediment of soldiers in battle came gestures of ascending, standing, and descending. This was Rosa after the death of Diefenbach *(sit sideways, crossed hands to the floor)*, grieving *(kneel, hands at the crotch)*, willing herself to take courage *(lunge, hands across the face)* and continue to meet whatever life has in store *(stride forward, hands at the crotch)*, no matter what. *(Pivot to strong stance, facing forward, hands across the face.)* Discouragement. *(Pivot again to face the other side and descend.)*

"My petition for release was rejected *(lunge backward)*, to the accompaniment of a detailed description of my incorrigible wickedness *(kneel)*; a request for a brief furlough had no better fate *(sit on the heels).* I shall have to stay here, apparently, till we have conquered the whole world"[16] *(sit sideways and crumple to the floor).*

Struggle to Find Hope

The war ended, but Rosa remained in prison. "My nerves, my nerves. I cannot sleep at all."[17] *(Rise to standing slowly—body part by body part: feet, ankles, knees, hips, waist, ribs, shoulders, head—and stumble across the cell.)* A reprise of Rodin's Burghers embodies Rosa tapping into her underlying strength and fighting spirit. *(Raise the crossed hands to the face and tap the forehead, making the body sag and fold over. Lift the body and walk backwards haltingly across the cell).* She writes about reading Voltaire's Candide *(step sideways, hands to one cheek), enjoying Flemish tales full of emotion (turn and swing the arms in a cradling motion)*, consulting a botanical atlas *(step across and back, twisting and arcing the body and rocking in that posture like a plant in the breeze)*, remembering works by Breughel, Rembrandt, and Titian *(circle in one spot, feet skittering, torso contracting and releasing, knees bending and straightening, crossed hands reaching out and pulling in)*, and finding consolation in the poems of Goethe *(step with feet apart, torso upright, hands in fists).*

After receiving news of the release of other political prisoners, Rosa's impatience grew. *(Pace forward and backward across the cell.)* "My mood is such that the presence of my friends under supervision has become impossible. *(Step sideways along the edge.)* I prefer to renounce every visit until we can meet as free people. *(Cross the feet in front and behind along the diagonal.)* It cannot take long."[18] *(Stumble backward from end to end.)*

Finally the Release from Prison

Twist around, crossing the feet and lifting the crossed hands overhead (an echo of the most tense and knotted gesture in the first section of *Passion*). *Turn the other way, uncrossing the feet, untwisting the body, releasing the raised hands until only the middle fingers are touching. Let the hands drop.*

Take one step outward ... two steps ... three steps, head lifts ... four steps in a different direction ... five steps, looking around ... six steps ... seven ...

I walked around the space cleared for dancing. Some viewers still had their hands crossed, some were hunched over, others were looking intently at the center of the space. Dinner was still being served, but the cafeteria was remarkably quiet. How many people had been watching? I stopped walking.

"That's the end of *Prisoner*." There was no applause. The audience was visibly caught up in the mood of imprisonment. I broke it by announcing that I wanted to end the program on a more hopeful note with a dance called *Growing*. "I'll move in larger and larger circles, until I reach where you are sitting and ask you to join me. I hope you will."

Faces and bodies lifted and lightened, as I went through the ever more expansive motions of *Growing*. At the end of the dance, I went first to the trio to ask: "Will you join me?" They were on their feet and ready to move instantly. One of them whispered, "This is our first politics since we were suspended for protesting Attica."

Another whispered, "I've read about Rosa." I knew something was different about those three, and we all squeezed hands. The fourth person to join was someone I was aware of while I was performing, because he was watching with such intensity. When he stood up I was amazed at how tall he was. He bent down and told me: "I'm a Vietnam Vet against the war."

Quickly, a line of students formed that wove in and out of the chairs and tables of the cafeteria, attracting more and more participants. Not all of them returned to the cleared space, where we formed a circle and

Figure 13. Grieving gesture from Prisoner (1971). Photograph by Virginia Blaisdell.

then stepped into the center, arms rising, and backed out, arms lowering, coiled into a snail and uncoiled, and circled around with three steps forward and two back. Applause turned into a crescendo of clapping and jumping, and when it died down, I announced that there would be a workshop immediately following, open to non-dancers as well as dancers.

"We'll be focusing on *Prisoner*. You'll have an opportunity to try out some of the gestures you've just seen."

A dance student led about twenty of us to a studio. The trio came along near the head of the line. As we walked, one of them shared more of their story. "You're the first person to mention Attica on this campus."

"That's surprising, since it happened only a few miles from here."

He shook his head and continued, "We were suspended for organizing a protest and only allowed to come back on condition that we focus on our studies. We're glad you spoke out."

"The privileges of a visitor."

Walking the corridors and stairs seemed to generate halting comments from the Vietnam Vet: "I identified with the characters in the *Landlord... Pen, Bayonet...* really grabbed me... I was very moved by *Prisoner*."

The dance student directed the conversation to the aesthetics of the performance. "That was amazing!" she exclaimed. "Dance where people really are—in a busy cafeteria—talking about real issues. I looked around. There were students watching who would never come to the theater."

"Why don't you give a follow-up performance?" I suggested.

"I don't know if I would have the courage."

"Is there a dancer or someone else, who could collaborate with you? I've worked with artists, scholars, scientists."

"I'll see who comes to the workshop." The student glanced behind. "So far I see mostly non-dancers. Our department is very technique-oriented. The students only care about how high they can kick and how many turns they can do. My concern for politics makes me an outcast. Dancers aren't interested in politics, and political people aren't interested in dance."

"I'm interested in dance," said one of the trio, "but I'm a painter, not a dancer."

"You could walk, stop, run, fall down, raise a fist," I proposed.

As the dance student talked with the painter, her enthusiasm grew, and by the time we all arrived at the studio, the two had agreed to meet and try out some ideas.

I began the workshop with a warm-up suitable for dancers and non-dancers, then told people: "Spread out so each of you can create a cell of four steps by eight steps. Cross your hands—on your toes—now follow me through the opening descent of *Prisoner*.

"I feel the confinement and frustration already," said one student, sitting in a heap on the floor.

"I feel depressed," said another.

"You've made your point," said a third.

I led the participants through other episodes of *Prisoner*: a modified version of the lyrical Matisse phrase; the sequence of writhing on the floor in frustration; the reaches to the outside world with feet, hands, head, torso; the gestures of Rodin's Burghers, which people seemed to enjoy the most.

Only a few dancers came to the workshop, and some left early. At the end of the session, the political dance student stayed to thank me and tell me how much she had enjoyed the class. I asked her if the students left because the movement material was too easy, not enough of a technical challenge for them.

"It was different, not what they're used to. That's why they left," she said. "After one of our technique classes, I feel as if I've just finished roller skating. I have to adjust to earth again. Whereas your class was part of life—I feel more aware, not cut off."

"I guess the dancers who left prefer roller skating." We both shook our heads and laughed.

About a week after the performance and workshop, I received a mailing from the responsive trio of students with a poem from one, two drawings from another, and a prose piece from the third.

The poem had five stanzas. My favorite was the fourth:

> Heavy, slow, tired, and weak
> Prisoner, dance your soul
> Not quite broke, not yet meek
> But hope of life not whole

The painter sent the following commentary along with the drawings:

> The first drawing shows the part of *Prisoner* when the figure presses the bound hands into all parts of the head and body as if wallowing in the full despair of the situation. The time is darkest; there is a momentary loss of hope.
>
> The second drawing shows the part in the middle of the dance, when the figure falls into a mental calm and seems to create a poetic dance, using the bound arms as an extension of the torso. It occurred to me that this represents the art and eloquence of the letters.

The prose piece was quite unusual, because it was written in the plural—perhaps a response to the performance and workshop, but more likely an identification with the prisoners in Attica, whose plight the student was stopped from protesting:

Sometimes they dream of freedom. Their spirits soar as they envision life without the confines of chains and walls and routines. They can laugh! They can jump! They can move! They are spirit ...

No, the chains at their hands admonish them, they are prisoners. They are not free. They survey the walls around them. They stare at their chains. Are we alive? they wonder. Dropping to their knees, a fear begins to gnaw the edges of their minds. It wrenches at their souls. Their bodies struggle against the thought, thrashing from side to side, turning, twisting, rolling about on the ground.

Then they stop. They do not breathe. They do not think. They only lie curled up, not moving. For these moments, the life is out of them. Slowly, almost imperceptibly, they move. They rise and resume their march again in firm, deliberate steps. They have reconciled their thoughts. They will live to be free again.

When the day comes, their hands are unchained and dangle at their sides. They have almost forgotten what it feels like to be free. But they accept this freedom and gradually become accustomed to it. Trusting it, they rejoin the living.

Chapter Six: Last Battle

Dramatic political events were happening in New Haven, while I was composing *Prisoner* and *Last Battle.* I was reading about Rosa's tragic last days and trying to dance them, but the battles outside my windows were also affecting what I was creating. Bobby Seale and Erica Huggins, national leaders of the Black Panthers, were on trial for conspiracy to commit murder. AIM and the HPA (the inner-city civil rights group) were struggling to stay alive. In a small way, our experiences echoed Rosa's. As the brilliant twentieth century philosopher Michel Foucault argues in his mind-body approach: power is measured not only by its role in big national and international events, but also by its effects on all levels of society down to the trials of one body. Caught in a life or death situation, what motions are available to a person without weapons or machinery?

To structure *Last Battle*, which I then performed in silence, I used *Chopin's Sonata in B-Flat Minor.* Musicologists have long puzzled over the relationship among the four sections, because they follow none of the rules of sonata composition. Schumann concluded that Chopin had "bound together four of his maddest children," while another music critic described the piece as a "linking of four wild horses." For tumultuous political happenings, the rhythms, phrasing, textures, and emotional range of the sonata provided a powerful scenario. As the composer's biographer James Huneker commented: "it is Chopin mounted for action and in the thick of the fight."[1]

I heard the first section as a ballade. Its episodes of agitation, lyricism, and heroism seemed to echo not only Rosa's story, but also the more immediate story of Seale and Huggins. The opening gestures in one arm were the key to the whole section: *a sharp reach up to the chin, out to the side, across the chest, and high over the head—in contrast to arcing smoothly over and down and coiling inward to the heart.*

I saw them as enacting Rosa's warning: "With all our stormy impatience, we must not lose the necessary seriousness and the need for reflection."[2] As in my other dances, division of the terrain was critical to developing the argument. I placed quicker sharper movements across the space and along the edges to signify action and slower sustained ones in the center to signify reflection, used the corners for talking with arms and feet, and the diagonal to parade with gestures of hope.

SECTION ONE

In a corner of my studio, I began Section One of Last Battle, thinking of the local battle—

There was a political murder in New Haven.

Thrust the fingers to the throat like the point of a knife.

The details were unclear.

Whip the head one way and the arm out the other way.

Was the victim a provocateur, an informer?

Slash the arm across the chest and snap the head in opposition.

Several members of the local branch of the Black Panthers were arrested.

Lean sideways and stretch the arm upward.

National leaders Bobby Seale and Erica Huggins were implicated.

Softly arc the arm over and down, head following, knees bending, and coil the hand inward to cradle the heart.

The trials were going on in the courthouse I passed every time I went to my studio.

Slide the hand down center of the torso to the crotch and across the thigh to neutral. Vamp by bouncing, ready for action.

Activists from coast to coast came to join local activists for a rally in support of Seale and Huggins.

From the corner, hop, gallop, and prance across; then lunge, glide, kick, and jump to return.

Tensions in the town were palpable and visible.

Zigzag across and back to a new corner.

Merchants boarded up their windows, anticipating a riot.

Talk with the feet: tap forward and back—in and out—side to side.

The National Guard arrived and ringed the center of the city.

Spring with pauses to a new corner.

Armed soldiers lined the streets in full battle regalia.

Dash the steps across and back, looking this way and that.

Downtown looked like a war zone.

Zigzag again to a new corner.

Rumors circulated that people in surrounding neighborhoods had armed themselves.

Talk with furtive taps, springs, and pauses.

In my studio, I continued to search for movements to process and dance what was happening.

Step haltingly to the center of the space. Circle with a sustained version of the frantic zigzag steps: lift on the toes, extend the legs gradually, strut slowly, elongate the glides and lunges, kneel smoothly. Turn and circle other way. Hop to break the reverie and run out of the center. Parade along the diagonal with hope—ascend from low lunges to hops to glides to prances to a high kick and a big jump!

The New Haven Green seethed with ardent supporters of Seale and Huggins, milling about, carrying signs, waving to friends, hugging, talking, gesticulating.

Zigzag with renewed energy, alternating arm moves with leg moves like a demonstrator trying to weave through the dense crowd.

Speeches by local and visiting leaders focused people's attention!

Thrust both hands to the throat.

Individuals shouted their feelings and opinions!

Whip the arms out to either side.

When singing, everyone felt the power of togetherness!

Slash the arms across the chest.

The police and soldiers were edgy. Anything could set off a clash.

Reach one arm high, the other low; circle the high arm over and under, the low one under and over.

Organizers and marshals of the rally were scattered throughout the crowd in an effort to avert violence.

Cup the breasts with the hands. Lower and separate them to either side.

Who knows what provoked the police to use tear gas.

Zigzag twice more at top speed, arms and legs moving disjointedly, like a frenzied demonstrator on the run.

Thanks to the actions of rally personnel and a decision by the president of Yale not to close off the campus adjacent to the Green, the crowd dispersed without a major catastrophe.

Patter in a corner, toes forward and back, in and out. Spring and pause along the edge. Hop and step slowly to the center.

The inner courtyards of the dormitories became safe havens for out-of-town demonstrators.

Circle the center with a reprise of the sustained leg movements, made more lyrical by an arm floating across the waist and out to the side, across the chest and out, curving over the head and down.

That night, Harris and I heard chanting from one of the courtyards, as we walked along a street that bordered the campus, past a line-up of heavily armed soldiers.

Pause—then hop and run to a corner.

A jury found Seale and Huggins "not guilty."

Parade along the diagonal—hop, slide, prance, lunge, kick, and jump in as large and powerful a manner as possible.

The victory celebration on the Green almost turned into another clash with the police.

Skip and jump joyfully—around and around—lifting the hands and slapping the thighs—skip and jump, skip and jump.

When I danced SECTION ONE as part of the Rosa portrait, I imagined the grave opening gestures as Rosa with no time to recover from her three and a half years in prison for protesting World War I. She immediately assumed a leadership role in the revolutionary Spartakusbund, which she and Karl Liebknecht had founded when they left the German Social Democratic Party, which supported the war.

The frantic crossings of the space embodied her working day and night primarily as a strategist and propagandist for the insurrection of soldiers and workers that had broken out in Germany. They also showed her on the run, staying in a different place each night to escape from the government forces that were out to destroy her.

The foot-talk in a corner evoked the intense daily meetings of the inner core of the Spartakusbund—Rosa planning the next moves with her most valued and trusted friends.

The sustained circling of the center evoked Rosa thinking, writing, and editing impassioned articles of criticism, encouragement, and hope for the revolutionary newspaper, *Rote Fahne* (Red Flag).

The parade of forceful determined gestures along the diagonal was Rosa enacting her belief that the workers' cause would somehow triumph.

My first performance of *Last Battle* was for Harris in my studio, and he didn't like it. This was the first time he reacted to my work in such an unsupportive manner, and I was upset.

"This is my most architectural dance," I said. "Division of the terrain is critical to the whole argument."

Harris was going through hard times. His private architectural practice was virtually at a standstill, and the daily commute to work on projects he didn't respect was taking its toll. He would have liked spending his time writing and illustrating his essays and acting as an advocate architect for AIM and the HPA, if only those pursuits produced an income. I could tell by the way he dragged himself up the stairs to my studio that he was especially preoccupied that day. But I needed to do *Last Battle* for someone other than myself to see if it worked.

One of the problem areas was costume. I was wearing white tights and a black leotard, and Harris kept eying the outfit.

"Too balletic?" I asked. He was silent. "For contrast," I said, "rich vs. poor, white vs. black, turning inward vs. reaching outward." He listened and shrugged. For the premiere of the Rosa portrait, I decided to change to burgundy tights and leotard, which felt better, though better yet, was the burgundy jumpsuit I made for subsequent performances, which suggested a worker's outfit.

Despite Harris's reaction, to my mind, *Last Battle* worked. I didn't revise the choreography for the premiere, and when he saw the dance in the context of the whole portrait, with a burgundy outfit, and an audience on three sides, his response was positive. At the rehearsal in my studio, he found SECTION ONE hard to understand and SECTION TWO, even harder. Both sections truly needed an audience up close to make clear the call to action, as I moved along the edges, and the need for contemplation, when I withdrew to circle the center.

SECTION TWO

The most complex argument. I interpreted Chopin's "Scherzo" as an interweaving of three dance forms: **polonaise**, **mazurka**, and **waltz**. All three are in triple meter (three or multiples of three beats per measure), their rhythms, phrasing, and textures varied to yield a wide range of expression.

The **polonaise** was performed in the courts of Europe in the eighteenth and nineteenth centuries as a processional dance. It originated from a warrior's triumphal march, but because of Chopin's music and Poland's embattled history, it came to be associated as much with defeat as with victory. I placed the militant **polonaise** moves along opposite edges of the space.

The **mazurka** is a lively Polish folk dance with changing accents and unexpected pauses, which allowed Chopin to be inventive like a poet or a jazz musician. I put the bounding **mazurka** steps along the diagonals.

The **waltz** revolutionized dance in the nineteenth century by breaking from the highly structured court forms like the minuet and opening the floor to any couple that could circle the space, spinning along face-to-face in a repetitive three-step pattern. I used the **waltz** for a lyrical circling of the center.

Much of SECTION TWO moved backward, evoking the cultural critic Walter Benjamin's angel of history, flying backward into the future, watching the debris of the past piling up in its wake.[3] In dance, progressing backward can be seen as feeling one's way, guided by the kinesthetic rather than the visual sense, as if approaching uncertain situations, in which moving backward or forward is less critical than daring to move at all—an embodiment of the counter-culture struggles of AIM and the HPA in New Haven and of Rosa's last battles.

AIM projects were moving up and down like the cadences of a **polonaise.**

From a corner, move backward along one side of the space.

The original **newsletter** grew into a small **newspaper** with a reputation for uncovering and reporting news ignored by the official media.

Step high on the toes, step low and kick—high and low—high and low—hand sweeping outward from the body, as if throwing a newspaper.

No doubt the paper's impact on local affairs played a role in the starting of a more commercial, alternative newspaper.

Halt and turn on the toes.

Aiming at a wider circulation, plans called for more coverage of the arts and entertainment and a more inclusive viewpoint on politics.

Kneel down, arm whipping overhead and down.

AIM writers and photographers were contacted to work on the new venture.

Rise and continue backward—step step hop, step step hop.

The **press** had developed into a small business.

Halt and lean forward like the figure on a ship's prow.

It served alternative political and arts groups in the area by printing their informational materials at low rates.

Circle the forward leg higher and higher and drop it down to the back, arm echoing.

The income was enough to support a few activists.

Tap the toes forward and back, as if calculating.

The **children's school** was folding.

Still moving along the same side, take lunging steps backward.

But its non-traditional curriculum and teaching methods had stimulated public school authorities to set up an alternative high school program.

Turn slowly.

They wanted to hire the children's school faculty to teach.

Walk forward to reach the corner.

The AIM **coffeehouse** was vandalized!

Step backwards furtively along the same side of the space.

Neighbors say a car pulled up with its lights off after the place closed.

Spin around and take lunging steps backward.

Three men climbed out with baseball bats and pipes and smashed the plate glass windows.

Stab the floor with the toes forward and back, arc the leg high from the back and smash it down to the front.

They snuck back to the car and drove off.

Step almost in place, crossing the legs.

It was too dark for the neighbors to see the license number.

Kneel.

Off-duty police, they suspected, from the jackets and the way they moved.

Rise and turn.

The large panes of glass were replaced with small panes, the rest of the openings were bricked up, and the coffeehouse reopened.

Step high and kick low to reach the corner, hand moving across the body and out, as if recounting the incident.

For a short time, two inner-city neighborhoods gathered enough clout with local politicians to have a say in the spending of government funds for **neighborhood projects**.

Back out of the corner and start down the diagonal in hopeful mazurka fashion: hop high and sweep the other leg back into arabesque, hands slapping the thighs before reaching outward—gallop and turn in the air, arms flying.

The **Fair Haven neighborhood** established a community center that housed a health care program, classes in various subjects (including dance, which I taught with another AIM member), social events, and a political campaign to stop companies from polluting the rivers that form two of its boundaries.

Repeat the aerial steps back to the corner, then set out once more along the diagonal.

The **Hill neighborhood** set up a job-training program, organized crews to clean up vacant lots, and drew up plans to improve living conditions. Harris participated as the advocate architect.

More hopping arabesques backward and another gallop and turn in the air led to emphatic stamping and striking the heels together, moves characteristic of the mazurka.

Funding never came through, so the plans for housing, stores, schools, daycare, health care, arts and recreation facilities were never realized.

A brief surge forward—step hop hop, step hop hop—turn and complete the diagonal with broken, decelerating toe-heel steps, arms dangling.

The opposition to art in AIM surfaced when Liz Henderson, the chief defender of the arts on the newspaper staff, was out of the country.

Return to the call-to-action **polonaise** *gestures along a new side of the space.*

Harris had a ferocious argument with one of the editors about the rejection of two articles on the arts with no explanation.

Insert springing **mazurka** *steps into the polonaise to travel backward like a ranting warrior.*

The editor said that the paper had to fill its few pages with more important news on economic and political issues.

Step high and kick low, grunting and gasping.

"No room for even one article on the arts?" asked Harris in exasperation.

Lunge forward, circle a leg higher and higher, and strike the foot down.

The editor personally had little interest in the arts. Harris pointed out that many of those in the New People's Group joined not just to seek an end to war, discrimination, and economic inequality, but also to seek a way of becoming musicians, painters, and poets.

Turn, setting off hops and kicks forward.

The editor maintained that the arts are individualistic, elitist, and irrelevant to politics.

Gallop and turn in the air, arm whipping overhead.

"Art is central to politics!" insisted Harris. The editor shrugged and laughed. Harris stood up with fists raised and challenged him to a fight.

Hop and kick backwards, arms slashing.

Friends intervened, and stopped the argument. Unfortunately a constructive dialogue about the left's hostility to art never took place.

Kneel and rise slowly.

Liz had returned when a potpourri program took place at the Exit Coffeehouse as part of a Strike Day for Gender Equality. An AIM member, who gave up dance for the martial arts, turned a demonstration of wringing, feinting, and striking into a verbal assault on dance: "You waste your time studying dance. It doesn't build strength. It's nothing but an obstacle to personal and political growth. The martial arts are powerful. You learn to defend yourself." Looking directly at me, hands on hips, she lifted her chin and concluded: "Dance is nothing but selfishness and narcissism."

Continue the polonaise-mazurka backward along the edge with fierce down-up-down stamps, heel strikes, high springs in arabesque, and twisted lunges.

"It's my turn next," I countered.

Hands on hips, turn and take measured steps forward to reach the corner.

Liz rushed over to me and whispered: "Don't say another word. Put your anger into your dancing."

No dwelling in the corner. Back into the center, walking and halting ...

Section Two Continued with a despairing waltz around the center, a sustained and rounded version of gestures that stabbed and lashed along the edge and down the diagonal. The movements *(repeats of a low gliding step, arm drifting inward, and a sinking step with the lift of a bent leg, arm drifting outward)* embodied what was happening to the HPA *(a slow kneel to emphasize the pull of downward forces)*. Since the inner city riots, caused by urban renewal, the group had been under siege *(a rise with torso curving sideways, then leg swings forward and back like the tolling of a bell)*. Any demonstration, any sign of protest had resulted in arrests *(down-up-down steps suddenly broke into strides out of the center, as if to return to battle—impossible!)* Fred Harris, the leader of the HPA, was arrested, tried, and sent to prison for possession of drugs, which he claimed were planted by police *(steps backward and a pivot to face the center of the space).*

Fred was already a leader in junior high school. He was an excellent student, insightful, good-looking, a persuasive talker, popular with both black and white students, and a favorite with teachers and administrators. We became friends when we discovered we liked dancing together in the gym during lunch hour to the music of Bill Haley, Chubby Checker, Chuck Berry, and other rock 'n' roll musicians of the day. He taught me the Lindy, the Skate, the Fish, and got a big kick out of the ballerina doing street dances. He also helped me recruit guys to participate in my ballets, and along the way, he learned some ballet and folk dance steps.

We had less contact in high school, and then I went off to college, and we didn't see each other again until a meeting of the Independent Political Action Committee (IPAC), out of which AIM and the HPA grew. After the initial surprise—"Fred?!" "Joan?!"—we reminisced about the old dancing days and talked about the new political struggles. I introduced him to Harris, and they immediately struck up a friendship. By the end of that meeting, we knew we would be working together as allies in what was happening in New Haven.

Fred gathered audiences for AIM Mobile Theatre events and came to a few of my solo performances. He and Harris worked together on plans to improve the Hill neighborhood, where HPA headquarters was located and members lived. His arrest along with other key members of the organization and the legal battles that ensued virtually destroyed the group. While Harris and I anguished over Fred's imprisonment, his one letter to us from prison was upbeat, reminding me of how Rosa Luxemburg wrote to her friends on the outside.

Back to SECTION TWO. The focus was downward, the timing sustained, as I moved through inward-turning arcs and loops of the legs and arms in the center of the space. Harris described those moves as "staring at death." In writing about them and the rest of the section, a Brecht poem about an imprisoned organizer (revised to fit the new context) seemed to embody the situation of Fred and the HPA and how I realized them in dance.[4]

There in the prison cell sat an organizer
    Lift leg and arm from the back
Not organizing on the street
    Arc them through the air and lower them to the front
Not speaking at a meeting
    Lift the other arm and leg higher from the back
Not leading a demonstration
    Loop them in the air, before lowering them to the front
Not working three jobs to feed four dependents
    Arc higher still
Not painting in stolen moments
    Loop leg and arm
Not drinking and dancing at a jazz club with friends
    Loop them again before lowering
But sitting in a cell with wounds all over
    Repeat the back-to-front arcs from high to low

Since the prisoner was an organizer.

Turn and kneel on one knee

Identified as harmful to self and others

Rise and circle the other way gliding and sinking

Addict!

Swing a leg backward and forward

Malcontent!

Waltz backward

Troublemaker!

Turn and stride out of the center

Organizer!

Halt!

Take that body off the streets, isolate it, shove it into a cell

Back into the center again and repeat the staring-at-death arcs and loops

And tell those that listened, worked alongside, gained self-respect, learned they can make a difference

Turn, setting off almost mechanical kneeling and rising, kneeling and rising

That they are marked people.

Swing a leg, waltz, run, step cross-legged backward and forward in another attempt to leave the center, and this time the effort succeeds.

The HPA organized and demonstrated for many things:

Return to the militant **polonaise** *along the edge, but in a disrupted form.*

for schools with enough books for all the children and functioning bathrooms—

Take high steps, low steps, and kick, then stop at a kneel

for an end to redevelopment that destroyed neighborhoods for poor people—

Start again and stop at a lean forward

for changes in the operating procedures of the Welfare Department—

Start and stop after each twisting lunge backward

for low-cost, do-it-yourself housing projects with businesses to create jobs, so people could get off welfare—

Turn with an arm whipping overhead

And for solidarity with all working people, who were in favor of the same things.

March to the corner.

Fred Harris ran for office saying: "Poor people, working people need representation, a voice in where and how we live, Community-Run-Communities!

Return to the bounding **mazurka** *down the diagonal, but with gaps*

"We're the majority, but we act like a minority.

Phrases broken off—gestures lost

"We have to hit the streets and make demands, or we'll always stay behind."
Toe-heel forward to the corner
And for thinking, asking questions, speaking out, leading—
Slide and lunge backward to the center
Fred was arrested, tried, sentenced, and thrown into a cell—
Waltz forward to the corner and swing a leg forward and back
Isolated as a menace to self and society.
Step backward and pivot to face the dead center.

And why is it that whoever speaks in favor of schools that teach—
Reprise the inward spiraling arcs and loops in **waltz** *time*
Of jobs that give self-respect—
Arc a leg from back to front, arms reaching out to the sides
Of community-run-communities—
Arc higher, loop, and lower the other leg, arms lifting overhead—
And whoever indicates the ability to organize others, who question and recognize the necessity of change—
Arc higher still and loop and loop, arms crossing and lowering with the leg
Ends up not a leader, but a prisoner—
Turn slowly
Buried in a cell, if not under the earth.
Crouch on one knee, cross the hands and lower the head.

When I danced SECTION TWO as Rosa, I thought of the **polonaise** along the edges as her actions in the doomed insurrection *(step high, sink low, kick forward, whip a leg around and down)* that had broken out among scattered groups of soldiers, who returned from the First World War in defeat *(kneel)* to find their towns and homes destroyed and jobs nonexistent *(rise and lunge backwards).* Joined by groups of workers, they formed themselves into Councils *(reach an arm out)*, and the Spartakusbund helped them organize demonstrations *(circle the hand overhead)*, public meetings *(punch down)*, and strikes *(reach the arm out again).*

The **mazurka** along the diagonal I saw as Rosa fiercely defending the revolutionary challenge: [Those] "who are shaking in their shoes for their property *(spring in the air, slapping the thighs)*, their privileges *(sweep a leg back, extending the arms like weapons)*, and their profits *(slide and turn in the air)* fabricate myths about anarchy and terror *(stamp tap stamp)* and pile them on the shoulders of those without property, privileges, or profits *(slide backward, contracting the body)*, in order to unleash their own anarchy and terror *(step and hop, turning)*, to stifle protest *(step hop, slashing an arm across)*, to drown revolt in chaos *(toe heel forward with changing accents)*, and to perpetuate their own dictatorship of capital forever and ever *(hands at waist, elbows out in defiance).*"[5]

For the waltz circling the center, I could imagine Rosa thinking about the plight of the defeated soldiers, best expressed in an anti-war poem by Brecht.[6]

The town, how can I find it? *(rise on the toes)*
Following swarms of bombers *(brush one leg back, as the body leans forward)*

I come home *(glide backwards)*
Where does it lie? *(lift an arm overhead)*
Where huge mountains of smoke arise *(curve the body sideways)*
There in the flames *(turn on one leg, other leg back, heel thumping)*
Is the town *(glide into a slow swing of a leg forward and back)*
How shall it receive me? *(step backward—up-down-down, up-down-down—and turn slowly, lowering the arm)*

For the inward spiraling arcs of the legs alternately, I could picture Rosa facing the daunting problems of the insurgents.

"We suffer unceasing troubles (arc), constant insecurity of existence *(arc higher)*, daily arrests *(arc higher)*, and the threat of death to all *(arc lower)* who are taken into custody" *(arc, turn, and kneel)*.[7]

The break out of the center with a leg swing and waltz steps for the brief reappearance of the polonaise and mazurka were moments of hope, when Rosa could write: "Despite everything, the work progresses, great meetings take place, handbills are written and printed, and the newspaper appears almost every day *(call-to-action gestures along the edge and down the diagonal)*, albeit amidst sighs and groans"[8] *(limping steps to the corner)*.

The push and pull between periphery and center made me think of the fatally loose alliance between the Workers' and Soldiers' Councils and their inability to formulate a clear program *(slide backward)*. Rosa and the other leaders were able neither to drive the movement forward *(waltz forward)* nor to negotiate its rapid end *(lunge backward)*.

The final staring-at-death arcs in the center: the government, which began to see crushing the rebellion as compensation for losing the war, took advantage of stalemate or disengagement *(arc of a leg from back to front)* to mount successful counter-actions *(other leg arcs)*, which included the arrest and murder of Rosa *(last arc, turn, and crouch down)*.

SECTION THREE

Even at the unfortunate preview of *Last Battle* for Harris, he had a positive reaction to Section Three, the *Dance of Death*, composed to Chopin's famous *Funeral March*. By the time I was creating it, I was deeply into the portrait of Rosa, no longer dancing about local events, but only about her last battle. The "Funeral March" with its relentless four-beat measures of booming chords, interrupted by a floating unearthly trio, lent itself well to a *Dance of Death*.

The Genovés gestures, from which I built my study honoring those who were killed at the Kent State anti-Vietnam War demonstration, seemed to echo viscerally Rosa's last hours. I alternated the desperate gestures with falling to the ground in different ways. *(Crumple down—crawl forward and raise a fist. Pull into a lump—scramble up to legs apart, body sagging.)* The moves were restricted to the center of the space. *(Fall—rise to a lunge and reach forward. Drop with a thud—stand and protect the head with the arms.)* This was Rosa shut off from the revolutionary struggle on the streets *(Sink down—lift to kneeling, fist raised. Collapse—heave up and clutch the abdomen.)*, engaged in a futile battle for her life. *(Crash down—rise to full height and stretch the arms up.)*

In mid-January 1919, Rosa was arrested by a section of troops, recruited by the post-war government to quell the uprising of workers and soldiers and restore law and order by any means. *(Circling the center, lunge and turn reaching forward for help.)* She was brought to a hotel lobby and tortured by the soldiers. *(Lunge and turn shielding the head from blows. Lunge and turn stretching high toward freedom.)*

"I shall never forget how they knocked the poor woman down and dragged her around," reported one of the maids.[9] *(Lunge and turn clutching the wounded middle. Lunge and turn on the knees, fist raised.) Half dead, she was dragged out and thrust into a waiting car. (Lunge and turn tilting sideways. Lunge and collapse, fist in the air.)*

The commanding officer immediately shot her in the head. Fearing that news of her assassination would give impetus to the foundering insurrection, her body was thrown into a canal, and a story was concocted that she was carried off to an unknown fate by an angry mob. The real story soon began to emerge, but Rosa's body remained in the canal, undiscovered, for four months.[10]

One music critic described the trio, a lyrical interruption of Chopin's relentless "Funeral March," as a "gaze into the beatific regions of a beyond."[11] *(From the collapsed position, use the fist and arm like a jack to rise from kneeling to squatting to bent over to upright.)*

The tormented gestures of the *Dance of Death* reappeared as floating weightless ones that swiveled from side to side and turned in one spot. I imagined Rosa released from the daily struggles of the abortive revolution, swiveling and floating, sinking and rising in the canal with the currents, at one with the plants and animals that fascinated her from the time she studied botany and zoology at Zürich University.

"Yesterday I was reading about the reasons for the disappearance of song birds," wrote Rosa in a letter from prison.[12] *(Swiveling left and right, knees bending and straightening, raise the arms in a cradling position until they rest on the head like a caryotid, a column in human form.)*

"The spread of scientific forestry, horticulture, and agriculture have cut them off from their nesting places and their food supply." *(Pivoting around and still swiveling, lower the cradling arms and open them to the sides, palms forward, head tilting sideways, in a universal gesture of vulnerability.)*

"More and more, with modern methods, we are doing away with hollow trees, wastelands, brushwood, fallen leaves." *(Pivot the other way and let one arm zigzag upward in response to the swiveling, until it rests on the head in a posture of weariness.)*

"I was not thinking so much about the loss of pleasure for human beings, but I was so much distressed at the idea of the stealthy and inexorable destruction of these defenseless creatures, that the tears came into my eyes." *(Change direction again, lowering the arm from resting on the head to hugging the chest. Float the other arm out to the side, and let the head sink sideways like a wounded warrior.)*

"I suppose I must be out of sorts to feel everything so deeply." *(Maintain the dying warrior pose and swivel downward, pulled by the extended arm, until the fingers touch the floor. Drop the other arm and let both hands dangle.)*

"Sometimes, however, it seems to me that I am not really a human being at all, but like a bird or plant in human form." *(Shift the weight to one side, rise and lift one arm to the side. Then use it like a sickle—swish across to tap the other arm and swish back out, across and out, across and out.)*

"I feel so much more at home even in a scrap of garden ... and still more in the meadows when the grass is humming with bees—than at one of our party congresses." *(Pick up on the sickle motion with one leg crossing the other leg and out to the side, across and side, across and side. With the legs and arms fully crossed, stop swiveling.)*

"Do not suspect me of treason to the cause! I really hope to die at my post, in a street fight or in prison."

(Turn around in one spot on the toes with tapping steps—once, twice—uncrossing the legs and arms. Extend the body, lifting the arms to the sides, and then reach as high as possible!)

The tormented gestures occurred for the last time as a descent in slow motion. One gesture dissolved into another with subtle shifts of the weight, angularities softened and smoothed over by the sustained timing. If I had spoken while moving, I would have shared these words of Rosa, which resonated in her own time and still resonate today.

"Revolution has no time to lose, it marches on ... toward its great tasks."[13] *(From the extreme position—body stretched up, arms reaching high—contract the torso by degrees, arms descending to clutch the head—)*

"Freedom is always and exclusively freedom for the one who thinks differently."[14] *(Double the body over gradually, arms crossing and lowering to hug the abdomen—)*

"To be human means throwing one's life on to the scales of destiny."[15] *(Rise only to sag, legs and arms opening to either side and head crunching sideways—)*

"The world is so beautiful in spite of all the misery."[16] *(Lunge, reaching arms forward little by little—)*

"People think the struggle has been abandoned, but it has only gone down into the depths."[17] *(Sink slowly to one knee with fist raised—)*

"A victory will blossom from this defeat."[18] *(Collapse over the crushed knees, lowering the fist to the ground.)*

SECTION FOUR

From that fallen position, I wanted to resurrect Rosa and show that her spirit is still moving among us. When I first improvised to the Finale of Chopin's *Sonata No. 2 in B-Flat Minor*, all I did was walk as if blown by the wind. It's unique in piano music, composed of triplets (three-note clusters) from beginning to end, played by the right and left hand in unison, an octave apart. The sound rushes smoothly and relentlessly upward and downward over the keyboard. Critics have described it as "disquieting," "enigmatic," "filled with half-repressed meanings," and "winds sweeping over graves." Chopin's biographer, James Huneker, came to the conclusion that "it bridges the vast, silent gulfs between human souls with its humming eloquence."[19] I handled it as a release for the audience and me from the tensions and torments of the previous sections and a way back to the happenings in our midst.

The pause between Sections One and Two indicated how I could realize this release. One day after rehearsing Section One, I became conscious of how I always paused to recover before beginning Section Two—walked out of the corner and back, took deep breaths, stretched, and shook out the kinks. It struck me that with a little shaping, the moves of Section Four could look like a recapping of *Last Battle's* gestures in a pedestrian manner, as if processing the events that had just happened. It felt right when I tried it and led to my composing the whole finale by stripping away the drama from the movements in the tormented Section Three, the militant Section Two, and the frantic Section One, and performing them with the weight and timing of everyday gestures.

In the center of the space, I imagined myself as Rosa down on her knees in the middle of her study. *Check out the floor (she was fastidious)—sit back on the heels and put fist to chin, thinking—stroke down one arm with the other—*

push off to standing. Walk a little circle, arms folding in and rising to rest on the head—stop and take a deep breath. Reach up to stretch and let the arms fall. Walk around again, scratching head and shoulder. Bend over sideways to touch a spot on the floor and straighten up, flicking the fingers. Circle again, rub an elbow, and stop.

With an abrupt turn, leave the center of the space and start walking along the edge. This was Rosa with hands on hips and a slap of the thighs, looking at what was on the shelves along one wall. *Take a few steps, waving a hand overhead—drop the hand to the opposite shoulder. Step and look right and left. Stop, hands to one hip. Turn and step backward—turn and go forward again, hands to both hips. Jab a heel and kick in response to a memory. Step to arrive at a corner of the space.*

*Dash across the diagonal—backward, forward, backward, forward—*like Rosa heading for a corner window, smiling at the words suddenly running in her head: "North and South and West are splitting, realms are bursting, empires trembling, and I'm thinking of [the opera] *Figaro*."[20]

My thoughts turned to Rosa writing to a longtime on-off lover. *From the corner, back up to the center and circle backward with slow steps, hand drifting out to the side and in to the crotch, out to the side and in to the chest, out to the side and in to rest on the head.*

"I was happiest of all with that part of your letter where you wrote that we can still arrange our personal life, our own little room, our own furniture, a library of our own." The letter continued with Rosa's dream of "quiet and regular work, long walks, an opera from time to time, perhaps even a little baby." (Bring the hand down over eyes, nose, mouth, torso, and continue the reverie with a foot tracing inside circles on the ground.) "Will this never be permitted?" she asked.[21]

The reverie in the center broke. *Kneel down, knead the foot, stand up, and look to a new corner. Walk towards it, hands to the hips, to the thighs with a slap, to the hips, and stop.* I fancied Rosa walking to a self-portrait in oils on a wall, which she painted for Diefenbach. *Scratch the middle of the back and tilt the head to one side and the other.*

The self-portrait was titled Ein Klumpen von Lumpen, a clump of lumps.[22] *With a little skip, turn, run into the center, and circle forward with slow steps, raise an arm and lean the head against it. Bring the hand down one side of the face to under the chin—pivot, bringing the other hand up to the chin: prayer hands—circle backward, lowering the hands and running them across the thighs.*

Imagining Rosa with the self-irony and sense of humor to see herself as a clump of lumps, made it possible for me to create a dance portrait. *Leave the center and head for a corner with strong firm steps, arrive and reach up with one arm, twist the head to look over it, turn head and body away from the arm, and let it drop behind.*

It was daunting to dance a legendary political leader, economist, journalist, philosopher, and naturalist, who died fighting in an abortive workers' revolution. *From the corner, walk forward toward the center of the space, fingers to the chin—walk toward the audience at the edge, fingers down the torso and across a thigh—toward the center, other arm up, face rubbing against it—toward the edge, arm down.* But what is Rosa's life worth, if an ordinary person, a dancer, cannot try to understand her struggles and keep her ideals alive? *I found a place among the audience, sat down, and raised a fist to my chin.*

Interestingly enough, after we moved to Kansas and Harris was teaching architecture at the University of Kansas, the dance he wanted me to do for his students to show the expressive potential of different spatial configurations was *Last Battle*. Seated in the round in a large meeting room, I told the students to view the dance in terms of the division of the terrain: center, periphery, diagonals, corners, lines, circles. An older student responded in writing:

> 'Last Battle' gave me a greater sense of architecture through time than through space. The first movement seemed primitive, the second more formal with elaborations and refinements, the third introspective and somewhat tortured, the fourth a release into vernacular, everyday life.
>
> These were my on-the-spot reactions. Later I thought about how the use of space probably did contribute to these reactions—that is, the use of diagonals, squares, and circles. (Interesting that 'square' means formal in other contexts, too, and that angular, tangential, jagged have less peaceful, more electric emotional meanings for us.)
>
> As the dance related to history: the second movement reminded me of the Baroque period, when fundamental patterns were well set and elaborations could be made. The third movement seemed more like the 'age of anxiety,' the birth of the 'modern' movement, the industrial revolution. The fourth may be a prophecy—a period when we accept the vernacular in art and architecture and begin to see value in the way things prosaically evolve. (The meek shall inherit the earth?)

Janet Hamburg, the director of the dance program at the University of Kansas, was in the audience with the architecture students. She was a good critic of my work and often made helpful suggestions over the many years we worked together as colleagues, friends, comrades, and confidantes. She loved *Last Battle*, hugged me at the end of the performance.

"The unusual phrasing along the side in an early section..." she said.

"Probably the eleven measure phrase," I said.

"And along the diagonal?"

"Twenty one measures." She nodded and smiled.

Like Janet, dancers often responded positively to *Last Battle*, commenting on the gestures, textures, and phrasing, as well as the emotional impact.

Figure 14. Architecture students at the University of Kansas learning a gesture from Last Battle (1980). Photograph by Suzanne Burdick.

Chapter Seven: Clear a Space and I'll Dance Rosa

Premiere of Rosa (May 15, 1971)

With the completion of *Prisoner*, the dance portrait of *Rosa* was ready for an audience. I gave the premiere as a benefit for Catherine Roraback, a local lawyer, who defended Erica Huggins in her trial with Bobby Seale for conspiracy. For more than twenty years, she had taken on political cases that no one else was willing to handle, leaving little time for cases that paid. When legal issues arose for AIM, we took advantage of her pro bono services. Unable to attend the performance, she sent me the following note:

I wish I could see the dance on Sunday evening—or rather Saturday evening. All days seem to have merged into one these last few weeks of the trial, and I do not seem to get to anything that I really want to see. Maybe some day when the world quiets down I will get a chance to do some of these things.

Anyway, need I say that the thought of your doing a dance concert for my benefit is, even in my weak financial condition, far more exciting to me than any tangible results there may be. Even with all the friends in town, it is easy to get lonely during these cases, and to be remembered by you and the others during this period is just plain nice.

The benefit performance took place in a Yale dining hall with oak paneled walls hung with portraits of distinguished alumni, a carved stone fireplace, a wide-planked wooden floor, heavy wooden tables pushed to one end, and sturdy wooden chairs arranged in the three-quarter round. During rehearsal, I wondered if it would be possible to bring Rosa to life in such a non-revolutionary setting. Yes. She had attended just such a university before graduating to the streets, meeting halls, newspaper offices, and prisons of the world.

Clear Me a Space and I'll Dance about Rosa Luxemburg!

Prologue: Rich Man, Poor Man
Passion
Growing
Prisoner
Last Battle

I was proud of having choreographed and performed a full evening portrait of Rosa. Wrote in my journal: "The dance is so right! It was thrilling!" Many friends came up and congratulated me. Liz and Harry Henderson, who had just returned from a long stay in Poland, gave me a bottle of Polish vodka to celebrate the performance (and my birthday, which was a few days before).

There was also negative commentary. One AIM member launched a tirade that hit me like a series of blows.

"Your dance has nothing to do with Rosa, who was a brilliant economist and political leader. You used to do dances that were short and humorous. They had props and music. The subjects were understandable and so were the gestures. Now more than an hour of solo dancing—Too much ballet—How can we see politics, a revolutionary, the class struggle in such private and personal dancing? The form of your dances should be popular. There are rock songs and movies that reach large audiences with a political message. At least if you worked with a group, if you performed in factories and prisons." My attacker rushed out of the room before I could respond.

However, an activist from AIM's Young People's Group came to my defense. "That person is wrong. I want to do what you're doing."

Still reeling, I took a deep breath and focused on my young supporter.

"What you're doing is what art is all about—the lonely struggle."

"Sometimes it's too lonely."

"Lonely work is the only real work. You can be a whole person. Though I hear you're doing good work with people of all ages at the Fair Haven Community Center."

A leftist from the 1930s, who also worked at the Community Center, entered the exchange.

"The ideal of the whole person is antiquated. We live in a fractured society."

"I refuse to adapt myself to a fractured society," said the young activist. "We have to defend our human essence. That's what Joan's portrait of Rosa is all about."

"The aesthetic makes things too easy. I agree with the commentator, who said: 'art is winged irresponsibility.'"

"I think those who oppose art are irresponsible — irresponsible to humanity."

The 1930s leftist looked away. "I gave up painting for the political struggle."

"Do you have any regrets?" asked the young activist.

"It was a depression. Painting is a luxury."

"Painting is a necessity. How can we call ourselves good political fighters if we don't stand for the self-realization of people?"

The old leftist shook his head. "Sometimes the group has to come first."

I entered the discussion. "Has a group ever existed for the realization of each individual in it?"

There was a pause, before the old leftist said: "That would be a new kind of collective."

As I sat down on one of the sturdy chairs to rest, a Yale instructor, who occasionally wrote on theater and dance for local papers and took pride in being up on the latest trends, came and sat down on an adjacent chair. "I saw a collaborative dance group perform at a civil rights benefit in New York. The work was more radical than yours. Not form and content, a dated concept—the 'medium is the message' for those dancers."

"They were performing for the civil rights struggle. Did their art relate to the it?"

"Subject was unimportant, another dated concept."

"There's always a subject, a message, consciously designed or not."

"The group plays with surface and process, and that's enough for me. They seem to choose non-referential movements and put them together by improvisation. The result is lighter and easier to watch than your dances—not as rich in movement material—but I could imagine myself doing the motions."

"I saw that kind of performance, and it encouraged me to do my own thing."

He seemed to ignore my comment and went on with his own thoughts. "A lot of how people moved and related to each other was determined by objects, such as empty cardboard boxes. The space was cluttered with objects that became obstacles or playthings."

"Did anyone get inside a box like a homeless person? Was the group commenting on our trash-filled society?"

"Non-referential, Joan! Don't interpret! The dance went on for too long. It seemed to be more fun to do than to watch. Eventually it fell apart. The dancers ended up laughing and so did the audience."

"The group was dancing for civil rights activists, who can't be content to titillate an audience with new gimmicks. They know the message as well as the medium has to be changed, and they're being jailed and killed for trying!"

"Why are you getting so emotional? Lighten up. Dance isn't politics and vice versa."

"But dance can make people think about political issues in new ways."

"The group was identifying with the civil rights struggle by doing a benefit." The Yale instructor stood up and walked away.

Liz Henderson and Harris approached, clearly in the midst of an animated conversation. "I think you should write an article about your portrait of Rosa for our newspaper," said Liz.

I stood up, still upset by the previous conversation. "I already wrote one that was rejected."

"That was when I was in Poland. There was no one on the staff to fight for the arts. This one will be accepted." Liz was true to her word. I wrote the article, and the paper printed it the following week.[2]

Figure 15. Passion, Section Three (1971). Photograph by Virginia Blaisdell.

DANCER CLEARS SPACE FOR THOUGHTS

By Joan Stone, Political Dancer

Editorial note:

In the past few years, Joan Stone has danced for regional audiences about the costs of urban renewal and the pressures on people to define themselves by the things they buy "Downtown." A new work, *CLEAR ME A SPACE AND I'LL DANCE ABOUT ROSA LUXEMBURG*, was enthusiastically received at a recent benefit performance. Stone will perform it again on Thursday evening at nine at the Exit Coffeehouse.

A few days after the premiere of *CLEAR ME A SPACE AND I'LL DANCE ABOUT ROSA LUXEMBURG*, Liz Henderson, who is on the staff of this paper, handed me a list of questions that the performance had generated:

- *Why dance about Rosa Luxemburg?*

- *What does it mean to link your dancing so closely with politics?*

- *Some of your earlier dances were direct propaganda pieces, for example, "When the landlord left" was used in the fight against urban renewal. ROSA is not political in this sense. How then?*

- *What kind of audience do you want to dance for?*

- *How can dance affect an audience?*

- *Can you talk about the meaning of involving the audience within a totally choreographed piece, as you do in* Growing?

- *Sometimes you do formal dance steps, at other times ordinary gestures. How do you explain such a dance vocabulary?*

- *Sensuality, strength, weakness, frustration, anger, peevishness, militancy, grace, distortion, control, loss of control, passion—how do you get these qualities across?*

- *Why do you dance solo?*

- *Why no music?*

- *Why no theatrical devices, such as lighting or costumes?*

- *Why do you call your works "dances against comfort"?*

A member of the audience at the same performance sent me the following interpretation:

CLEAR ME A SPACE AND I'LL DANCE ABOUT ROSA LUXEMBURG is variations on the theme of reaching out.

Passion is the adolescent: the dance twisted upon itself. It is incapable of reaching out. It stretches upward but this never means outward. The dance ends with the determination to reach out.

Growing is also young. The dance starts from a point in time and space and expands outward into both. It ends by including people. It is a study in reaching out physically.

Prisoner carries the struggle into the world of the mind, of ideas. It echoes the twisted motif of *Passion* but is even more confined. Unlike *Passion*, there are now specific reaching gestures, but they are utterly boxed in.

Last Battle has broken out of the box. The dance indeed reaches out, but the gestures and movements meet no response. They fall into a void. The dance falls back upon itself with a sense of doom. It is doomed. It dies, but it dies reaching out.

We are left thinking about what we've seen.

To me, Liz Henderson's list of questions and the audience member's interpretation add up to the best reviews a dancer could receive. What could be better than people leaving a performance thinking about a revolutionary, asking questions about the relationship between politics and dance, pondering the choices made by one dancer, trying to assess the exchange between dancer and audience, mulling over the range of human strengths and weaknesses, making observations on the gesture of reaching out.

Recently I went to the ballet in New York—a dazzling performance—light, color, sound, bravura technique—everything lovely, perfect, under control.

When I left the theater, the street looked even worse than usual. A siren blared. An ambulance pulled up to a hospital. A stretcher was wheeled to the emergency entrance. The ambulance screamed off on another call.

I was too numb to care. No questions. I had just been bombarded with answers. The theater couldn't be wrong. It must be the street—it must be life that's wrong ... Or else, that performance was a lie!

Demonstration by Yale maintenance workers

It was commencement day at Yale in the center of New Haven. I was riding the bus to go and rehearse *ROSA* for the upcoming performance at the Exit. As the bus approached the commencement location, it slowed down and stopped. The street was blocked by a demonstration.

A large passenger, who had been occupying two seats at the back, rumbled forward to peer out the windows and pronounced: "If Yale paid the workers decent wages, they wouldn't be on strike. Such a rich university—so much money—and they pay the workers nothing. See what happens when the workers go on strike. The campus looks like a garbage dump. I say 'bravo' to the workers!"

The police cleared the street so the traffic could move. I knew about the demonstration, but hadn't planned to go because of the need to rehearse. After the passenger's unexpected, on-the-mark outcry, I signaled for the bus to stop, got off, and joined the raggle-taggle group of workers and their supporters.

The Yale maintenance workers had been on strike over a new contract for a number of weeks. The dining halls had been closed, and 'the campus looked like a garbage dump'—quite an embarrassment for Yale at commencement time. The demonstrators had placed themselves so the whole parade of administrators, distinguished guests, faculty, and students had to go past them. The police lined themselves up as a human barrier, and the commencement participants did their best to ignore the printed signs, shouts, and bodies of the demonstrators.

Co-workers from AIM greeted me. I also recognized and said hello to one of the police officers and one of the maintenance workers, who were former high school classmates. They were still good friends and now found themselves pitted against each other. A scuffle broke out some distance from where I was standing. It was hard to tell what was happening, but the word spread that several people had been arrested. "For driving without a vehicle," quipped my friend, Harry Henderson, one of several Yale faculty members and students, who were among the demonstrators.

We stood outside the commencement until it ended, and the demonstration continued afterward, but I left and headed for the Exit Coffeehouse. Where was the huge poster announcing the performance of *ROSA*? It was such visible advertising, and there were so many people around for the weekend. No doubt the church took it down along with all other signs of the Exit's existence. This presentation was likely to be my last there. The supportive minister was moving to a new congregation, and according to Exit Player's director, the refuge would soon close its doors for good. He was in the process of converting a second floor office a few blocks away into a Gallery and Space for exhibits and performances.

ROSA at the Exit (June 17, 1971)

A booking agent from New York came to the Exit performance at the invitation of Bob Cook, the AIM candidate for Congress in 1966 and 1968. He had been the central figure in our political group for more than five years and a supporter of my dance projects since the first in the basement of the arts center, when he gave me a red rose. He was instrumental in having school and neighborhood groups invite me to perform and threw himself into playing the guitar and acting in the Mobile Theatre Anti-war Collage. In addition to teaching sociology at Yale, he had begun touring on the college circuit as a speaker on alternate politics and had persuaded his booking agent to consider representing me.

The performance was not one I would have chosen for the agent to see. The audience was small and varied and sitting at tables scattered along the walls of the dark cavernous space. There were a few Exit regulars, a few university students, a few friends from AIM, and a few community people. It was difficult to bring the groupings together for the participatory ending of *Growing*, and they never seemed to join together as viewers of the whole Rosa portrait.

I realized that my left knee, which gave way with a sharp pain during *Passion*, was still aching—something was definitely wrong with that knee, and it was getting worse. Preoccupied with the injury and the shortcomings of the performance, I joined Harris, Bob, and the agent at a table when the applause died down.

The agent was very straightforward. "For the most part, I handle speakers who have made a name for themselves by appearing on national television, by writing a book that receives a lot of media attention, or by running for national office like Bob. My best-selling speaker is a recognized expert on UFOs and how to fend off rapists. I can book that speaker anywhere. These are subjects that interest people.

"I just took on a new speaker, who became well-known by doing carpet ads on national television. She presents the opposite political position from you and Bob. She'll lecture on topics such as 'Gender is No Problem,' 'Knowing Your Place on the Gender Scale,' and 'Happiness Is Being a Homemaker.'

"I'm the agent for two dance groups that represent two different ethnicities. They do programs of short dances in between musical numbers. There are singers and musicians as well as dancers. They give the audience action, music, storytelling, colorful costumes, and lighting—lots of entertainment! In the lobby, before and after the show and during intermission, people can see a display of crafts and buy artifacts and recordings.

"Dance like yours ..." the agent shook his head. "A revolutionary is not an appealing subject to most people."

The agent shook his head again. "And the way you dance—you're working at a terrible disadvantage off the stage without music, costumes, and lighting. I can't imagine how your act could be sold. But maybe you could do it yourself. In many colleges now, the students control the money for cultural activities, and they decide what to bring to the campus. The students in some places haven't been responsive to my roster—that's one of the reasons I took on Bob. They may be interested in your dancing.

"Assemble all the materials you have—reviews, photographs, letters, programs, press releases, a list of your performances—and come to my office in New York. I'll show you my brochures and tell you how to go about being your own agent."

Among the materials I assembled was a review that was written just after the *ROSA* performance at the Exit. The reporter from the New Haven Register had come to Yale for the premiere, as well as to the Exit, and had interviewed me in my studio. His reaction to the portrait was much more positive and empathetic than the New York agent's.

Dance Review in the New Haven Register, June 20, 1971

By Edward King

If I were slim and sixteen again, I would roam the earth as a free spirit. And move ... from city to city with a lithe step. I would talk to people in small groups, articulately and earnestly. And in the countryside, I would bob and weave and soar into the night.

I would be a dancer, expressing my thoughts and feelings in the movement of my art. Such a dancer is Joan Stone, who recently made appearances at Yale's Branford College and at The Exit.

Joan is not an ordinary dancer in any sense. She dispenses with what she calls the 'magic and ritual' of dance—the costumes, the props, the lighting, the staging, the music—and exercises pure movement.

Although trained in the classic forms of dance, she has, for the most part, thrown them away and uses what she calls 'gut gestures' to express ... the potentialities of the human form in movement with a social consciousness.

The tools of Joan's dance are simple space and time. In her most recent performance called *CLEAR ME A SPACE AND I'LL DANCE ABOUT ROSA LUXEMBURG,* she uses these basic tools to great advantage.

Not on a stage but in a space cleared amongst the audience, Joan simply begins, and in a hush broken only by her grunts, she does her piece.

Audiences are sometimes startled to see this pure human expression of feeling without the background commercialism, but they are soon fascinated and involved.

Rosa Luxemburg was a revolutionary figure—a leader of the abortive German Marxist revolution of 1918-1919. The dance about her is broken up into five sequences.

The prologue, called *Rich Man, Poor Man*, sketches the two main figures in the struggle for which

Rosa Luxemburg lived and died. It is mainly talky and introductory. Breaking a cardinal rule of dance, Joan does sometimes talk during her performance.

The first sequence called *Passion* opens with a burst of energetic emotion, evolves to a sinewy sensuousness and ends with a heaviness expressing Rosa Luxemburg's feeling: 'The world is so beautiful in spite of all the misery.'

The second sequence called *Growing* is generally gay and bounding, and is followed by Prisoner, which tends to be stark and stagy. The final sequence *Last Battle* is pure 'guerrilla' dancing—shrill, militant, startling. It fulfills Rosa Luxemburg's relentless prophecy: 'Revolution has no time to lose, it marches on—over victories and defeats—toward its great tasks' ...

What Stone is doing is as old and natural as the flight of a bird, a mother cradling her child, a worker with a scythe in the fields. She expresses it all simply, purely, articulately and artistically.

That's what I wish I could do—if I were slim and sixteen again.

Making a brochure

Harris was impressed by the stack of materials I pulled together, and so was the agent, when I spread them out on a desk in his New York office. "The speakers on my roster don't have dossiers as good as this. I have to solicit letters of praise and have photographs taken. They have far fewer reviews, but they have the one that counts, the one that attracts national attention."

The agent showed Harris and me one of his brochures and explained the logic of having several pieces of paper of different sizes and weights. "If the papers slide out on a desk or fall to the floor, there's a good chance something might catch the reader's attention." The agent indicated options for the placement of different kinds of information and emphasized the need to be very clear about the programs offered and the arrangements expected from sponsors.

We then discussed what would be an appropriate honorarium for a performance followed by a discussion and preceded or followed by a workshop plus travel expenses. "It mustn't be too low, or you won't be taken seriously," said the agent. The fee decided upon—$300-400—made him shake his head. "None of my speakers could work for so little, but doing everything yourself ..."

For the next several weeks, I stewed and brooded and fumed while sifting through the materials, choosing the letters, reviews, and photographs. I went to the press run by AIM members to learn prices on graphics, printing, and paper. I was full of doubts and saw only obstacles, personal and social, to continuing on. Harris tended to cajole and encourage, but sometimes he became exasperated at my self-doubt. Suffering from insomnia, headaches, and allergies—exhausted, head splitting, nose running and in a rage, I sat down and wrote the autobiography, cover letter, and other necessary information in one burst. When I showed the result to Harris, he said: "This is good—this is really good! I'll help you assemble a mock-brochure, and we'll deliver all the materials to the press."

While waiting for the press to produce the brochure, I went to the studio. My body was stiff and aching from doing tasks associated with the brochure instead of warming up, composing, and rehearsing. I had to get myself in shape for an upcoming performance as part of a Sunday afternoon "arts salon." It was organized by Mask-maker as a follow-up to *Metamorphosis*, for people interested in continuing the activities of that arts festival. The salon took place outdoors on the lawn of a country home. *Downtown* was the wrong choice for the setting. The items critical to the argument, particularly the pearls, belt, and wallet, were lost in the grass. Why didn't I do *Growing*, which wasn't as urban and indoor? A little demon said, "Confront this audience with the issue of compulsive buying."

About the response, I wrote in my journal: "Some people didn't want to face the content of the dance—too close to home." Dissatisfaction with what and how I performed in an outdoor setting added impetus to my growing urge to compose dance sketches about nature.

The press did a skillful job on the graphics and printing of the brochure. Harris and I returned to New York to show the agent a sample and take advantage of his offer to use the office addressograph system. I put a stuffed envelope on the desk. The agent pulled out the brochure, and the reply memo fell to the floor. Laughing, he picked it up, glanced at it, and turned to the black and white main document, putting aside for the moment the blue cover letter and red comment sheet. "It's so obvious," he said, "but I never thought of printing the negative or using paper of different colors."

The main document's black cover with white printing received a careful examination:

at the top, *Clear a Space and I'll Dance*—

in the middle, Joan Stone, next to a photographic cut-out of me leaning forward with head thrust back and hands clutching the forehead—

at the bottom, **Performance Discussion Participation**.

The agent opened the main document and read the AUTOBIOGRAPHY; the information about Program A, *I'VE ALWAYS LIVED IN THE CITY*, and Program B, *CLEAR ME A SPACE AND I'LL DANCE ABOUT ROSA LUXEMBURG*; and the copy about DISCUSSION, PARTICIPATION, ARRANGEMENTS. He flipped the brochure over and looked at the photographic cut-outs of me in four dramatic gestures adjacent to a newspaper review. Tossing the main document aside, he perused the long narrow red sheet of COMMENTS before unfolding the light blue cover letter and reading it thoroughly:

> To those in charge of cultural activities:
>
> Going to a dance performance usually means sitting in a darkened auditorium watching people in costumes and make-up dancing to music on a specially lit stage with curtains or a set and props. My performances are a very different experience.
>
> I dance in a space cleared amongst the audience without music, costumes, special lighting, etc. I'm interested in a direct confrontation between dancer and audience and in the potential of dance as an art form in and of itself.
>
> I've composed dances, complex in gesture and structure, about some of the troubling issues of our time. I've performed for all different kinds of people in all different kinds of spaces. Audiences

> are initially surprised to see dance so close up and stripped of music and theatre, but they are soon intrigued and enthusiastic. And when I ask people to join me in a dance called "Growing," hardly anyone says no. Participation and discussion follow naturally from this kind of performance.
>
> I'm now accepting invitations at colleges and universities interested in such a presentation of dance through performance, discussion, and participation.

"I didn't think you could do it. Congratulations!" said the agent, as he reached out for a handshake. "I myself am going to put the envelopes through the addressograph system." After expressing our thanks, Harris and I left with envelopes ready to be stuffed and mailed out to more than three hundred colleges and universities nearest to New Haven.

The first response to the mailing came from a small local religious college: an invitation to teach a class. "Well, now you know the brochure arrived," said Harris. "Don't you remember that college asked me to teach last year without a brochure?"

I stormed around the apartment before telephoning and telling the student: "My impact as a dancer comes from performing. Teaching alone is insufficient." The student was dubious about a performance before the class.

"Those are my terms," I insisted. "We hoped you would come and teach," said the student with disappointment in her voice. There was no discussion of an honorarium. I felt depressed and drew Harris into my mood.

The next day two memos arrived, and the day after two more, each requesting a performance. Once the momentary excitement was over, I had to confront the next problems: mustering the courage to telephone, having the patience to call and call again and to send out supplementary mailings, developing the skills necessary to turn an inquiry into a commitment. After a few successes, I even tried cold calling to colleges within a particular area with the idea of arranging a tour. No tour, but one invitation resulted.

Within a month, I had lined up eight engagements, and more were pending. I shared the results with a member of AIM, who worked for an advertising agency in New York City. "An impressive response," he said, "it indicates there are people out there interested in what you're doing."

Although the honorarium per engagement was low by the agent's standards, my earnings, plus a small amount of savings along with living rent-free in a house owned by my parents, made it possible for Harris to give up his unsatisfying architectural job in Westport. For the time being, he could concentrate on writing and illustrating his first book. I worked with him on the manuscript, and he went to most of my presentations within driving distance.

Prisoner and other dances at Essex County College, Newark, New Jersey (November 4, 1971)

The first performance that resulted from the brochure took place in Newark in a dilapidated office building that had been converted into a community college. The elevator rattled up to the seventh floor. A student directed Harris and me to a long narrow lounge with doors in all the wrong places. There was a group shooting pool at one end and a group rolling dice at the other. In between people were perched and sprawled on a motley array of furniture—eating, drinking, sleeping, hanging around—as loud rock music blasted from a mounted wall speaker.

The person in charge of student activities, who invited me, appeared and explained that the students laughed a poet out of the room the week before. With that warning in our heads, Harris and I moved all the furniture to the periphery, using the displacement of people as an opportunity to arouse their curiosity about the dancing. Harris found a broom and swept, I did a cursory warm-up, and interest grew as the lounge took on the look of a performance space.

"Is it possible to turn off the music?" I asked.

"Sure," said a student. He tilted the speaker, ripped the wires off the back, and there was silence.

From the center of the space, I announced that I was going to do a program of *Dances Against Comfort.* "There won't be any music. Some of the dances have words. But the meaning is in the gestures. The first dance is called *Rich Man, Poor Man.*"

I strode down the spine of the space as *Rich Man*, seeing that nearly every seat was occupied. Ran back and forth as *Poor Man*, trying not to trip and stumble over feet and furniture protruding on each side of the narrow space. At the end of the piece, there was solid applause. Some people left, but others seemed to come and take their places.

I performed *On the Wall, I Want the Pen..., Calf to Swallow.* The audience kept changing, but there was very little disturbance—occasionally feet shuffling, furniture scraping, whispering to inform newcomers about what was happening. I introduced *When the Landlord Left...* by telling the story of **Inner-city Dweller's** battle with urban renewal. The audience clapped after each character. *Newspapers* was a real give-and-take, as I wove back and forth, bowing to those on either side of the space, getting someone to hold a paper as a flag, sitting down next to a guy and wrapping a paper around us, circling very close to people while sailing a paper over their heads.

Because the space was too small for *Growing*, I decided to end on a serious note with *Prisoner.* "If you would like to participate, cross your hands."

In the center of the space, I walked, kicked, lunged, and crawled to establish the four-step-by-eight-step cell —
paced to and fro like a caged animal —
danced a lyrical phrase in spite of confinement —
gave into the yearning for obliteration —
pulled up from the depths by twining like a weed —
circled in the gestures of medieval martyrs —
reached out with the feet, hands, head, torso—in vain —
writhed on the floor in frustration —

rose from the floor with difficulty —
paced forward, backward, sideways —
pivoted to uncross the feet and hands —
stepped ... paused ... stepped ... paused ...
walked away from the cell —
walked haltingly along the periphery, reestablishing contact with the audience.

From the time I crossed my hands and rose on my toes to the end of the piece, there was silence, which lasted a few seconds before applause broke out. A number of people came and shook hands with me. "Just standing up and dancing," said one person, "that takes guts." As Harris and I left, the students were pushing the furniture back to the accustomed places, and the games were beginning again at either end of the lounge.

ROSA at University of New Hampshire, Durham, New Hampshire (December 2, 1971)

After a five hour drive to the University of New Hampshire, I enjoyed moving around the high-ceilinged, wood-paneled ballroom, getting the kinks out of my body for an evening performance of *ROSA*. The floor was springy. Harris figured out that it actually had springs in the gap between the sub-floor and the hardwood surface. Dancing on it was like dancing on a drum.

With the audience forming a boundary on three sides in the resonant space, I concentrated on articulating all the different sound textures and rhythms of *Rich Man Poor Man, Passion, Growing, Prisoner*, and *Last Battle.*

During the intermission after *Growing*, I was resting by lying on the floor with my legs elevated on a chair. One student after another approached with a question or a comment:

"Who was Rosa?"

"Where do you begin to make a dance?"

"This portrait is as vivid as a portrait in paint or words."

"What is the relationship between gesture and word?"

"Let Joan rest," pleaded Harris. "Raise these issues at the discussion after the performance." And the students obliged.

Harris and I stayed overnight in a unique hotel, a glass tower nestled in the pines. Run by the university program in hotel administration as part of a regional convention center for a consortium of universities, the food and service were superb for both the late night supper and breakfast the next morning. The large number of guests in the dining room attested to the hotel's well-deserved popularity.

After breakfast, I taught two classes, one for dancers and one for non-dancers. Many of those who came for the first class stayed for the second. The dance faculty member introduced me by talking about how the early modern dancers began as revolutionaries and then became established and conservative. She considered that an "Outrageous betrayal. How did it happen? Why did it happen?"

I started by asking the students if they were struck by any gestures in the portrait of Rosa that they would like to explore in their own bodies. Once one person had an idea, it jarred other people's memories. I made a list on the blackboard and used it to structure the class. Because the participants were open and responsive, I could explore group versions of the gestures: dividing the class in half and having the two lines come toward each other from opposite sides of the room and back away; come toward each other, thread through, turn around, and thread through again; form inner and outer circles that moved counter to each other. A student remarked: "Even the class is choreographed."

Although not in the contract, I also conducted a session for theater students. "We've been asking our teacher to work on ways of putting gestures and words together," an acting student explained at the performance the night before. "We've experimented on our own and in class, but we haven't gotten anywhere. Would you come and show us your approach, if I can persuade the teacher to agree to it?"

Just as the second dance class was ending, the acting student appeared: "I've arranged it."

Harris and I went with the student to the university theater. The class had already gathered on the stage, which was empty except for a table and chairs in an upstage corner. The teacher, who was sitting with his feet up on the table reading a newspaper, didn't greet us. I performed *Rich Man Poor Man, I Want the Pen...*, and *On the Wall*, and took the students through some of the gestures with and without words.

We were in the midst of the dramatic descent that is central to *On the Wall*, when the teacher abruptly announced: "Time is up."

The students applauded and surrounded me.

"This is the first clue we've had about different kinds of gestures and how to make them speak."

"Gestures can contradict words."

"Gestures can add meaning to words."

"Words can dance."

"I wish we could do more."

"We have to go to our next class. Come back!"

Harris crossed the stage to join me. The acting teacher followed with a rolled newspaper in his hand. "Which should come first, the gesture or the word?" he asked, tapping me on the head with the newspaper.

"The gesture," I said.

"Wrong. Both should happen simultaneously."

"I'm a dancer—" I was about to launch a defense when Harris interrupted:

"We have to leave. A severe storm is predicted."

The teacher returned to the table with no acknowledgment of our departure. Harris was fuming. "Did you see? Back turned to you and the class the whole time—flipping the pages of the newspaper to make as much noise as possible—and then, quizzing you and tapping you on the head with the paper to emphasize each word."

"I should be bothered by that kind of behavior, but I was too excited by the enthusiastic reactions of the students." As we left the theater, another thought occurred to me: I suppose I'm used to that treatment as a small woman.

ROSA at Goddard College, Plainfield, Vermont (January 19, 1972)

Two months later, at the next performance of *CLEAR A SPACE AND I'LL DANCE ROSA*, I met a different kind of acting teacher: a playwright in residence at Goddard. The playwright and the technical director of the theater invited Harris and me to supper in their apartment. They cooked and then we ate and talked in the kitchen. Harris usually contributed to the discussions of my dances, but I don't remember him saying anything this time.

Playwright: There you were in the space when the audience arrived, walking around with a sweater on your shoulders. And then you performed in everyday clothes, and it was everyday and anything but everyday.

Tech director: Everything can be found in the everyday.

Playwright: Not everything. There are lots of dancers just running around saying nothing these days. Joan does all kinds of dancing to set off the everyday.

Tech director: The last section of *Last Battle* was my favorite: pure everyday—

Playwright: which came at the very end of the portrait to bring us all back to the everyday.

Dancer: The dance teacher at Goddard offered to show me how to wring much more emotion out of my dances.

Tech director: That would be unbearable. *Prisoner* was almost too much for me.

Dancer: I work to figure out gesture, space, and time. Once those are right, the emotion follows.

Playwright: Not quite. You know a great deal about Rosa. That was revealed in the discussion period. Doesn't that knowledge affect your performance?

Dancer: Yes. I'm always a dancer and myself when I perform the portrait, but I have to think of quotes from Rosa, look at art works, or read poetry of the period to get my mind in the right place.

Playwright: I knew it. The truth of the moment! That's where our ideas come together.

Tech director: For *Last Battle*, were you inspired by Kollwitz's *No More War* poster?

Dancer: Not directly, though I can see why you would make that connection. I've seen the poster many times and love it. One hand thrust high, the other pressing the heart—that powerful expression of protest must have made its way into my body.

Playwright: Your gestures called up image after image for me.

Tech director: For me, too.

Dancer: Actors, painters, and poets tend to be more responsive to my work than dancers.

Playwright: You pose a hard challenge for most dancers. They don't question the stage. Their primary concern is technique. And they've run away from meaning.

Tech director: Who was the person that got down on one knee and put his hands over his heart at the end of your dance? It looked like a scene from a play.

Dancer: He's eighty-three years old, a retired factory worker, who never met Rosa, but was a member of the Spartakusbund and knew people who fought in the insurrection.

Tech director: I've never seen that person at any of our productions.

Dancer: He lives in Montpelier and had to come by taxi, but arrived before anyone else. I was still warming up when a voice said: "There was an announcement in the paper. I could not miss a dance about Rosa Luxemburg. I never thought to see such a dance again."

Playwright: If he were the only person in the room, you would have had a whole audience. At the end of Growing, limping and wheezing, he cried out: "This is the spirit of the revolution!"

Dancer: Of course, I had to end Last Battle sitting next to him.

Tech director: And after all the applause came the kneeling scene.

Dancer: He whispered: "You must forgive an old romantic. In my country, when one is moved by a performer, one offers the heart."

ROSA at Keuka College, Keuka Park, New York (February 3, 1972)

One of the easier *Rosa* performances for me to arrange took place at Keuka College. The name on the reply memo belonged to the dance professor, who turned out to be a graduate of Bennington, and we connected immediately. She came and met me at the Elmira Corning airport and invited me to stay at her home. As we were driving to the campus, snow was beginning to fall, and by the time of the performance, it had turned into a driving snowstorm. Nevertheless more than a hundred people appeared at "The Barn," an old barn made into a big open recreation space with a wooden floor. They were with me from the first moves, and the emotion grew. *Growing* ended in wild jumping and shouting. As I wrote in my journal: "People 'grooved' on dance, not music, but dance! The performance ended with a standing ovation."

Many people stayed to talk. One person commented: "Your dancing reminds me of Bartok's music."

I responded by saying, "Bartok has had a deep influence on me. I played his pieces as a piano student and still love to listen and dance to recordings of his music."

The drama teacher wanted to discuss my aesthetic: non-proscenium, audience very involved. She said she was "skeptical, but enthralled."

One of her students piped up: "there's a difference between a performer and an artist. A performer on stage is distant. An artist communicates by being right up near the audience." An undeveloped argument, but she wasn't skeptical.

Several people were deeply moved by *Prisoner*. All who gathered around me wanted to know more, to read about Rosa. My notes conclude: BEAUTIFUL PERFORMANCE!

The two workshops I taught the next day were also successful. One was open to all who wanted to come, and they threw themselves into the warm-up and *Rosa* gestures with great enthusiasm. In the session for dance majors, we had a fruitful exchange of ideas when the students showed me their studies, which impressed me. They were clearly struggling to find their own voices, the sign of a good composition teacher in my book.

I was supposed to fly home after the workshops, but blizzard conditions kept me at Keuka for another night. The dance teacher's husband was a large animal veterinarian and a hunter. He made a cozy fire in their fireplace and cooked venison steaks for us, which were tender, to my surprise, and delicious!

I danced *Rosa* sixteen times between 1971 and 1978. Most of the performances took place in the first few years. By 1978, I had composed many new works, from which presenters could choose. A few still asked for *Rosa*, and I was always happy to oblige. Once Harris and I moved to Kansas, I never danced the whole *Rosa* portrait again, though I did perform *Growing, Prisoner*, and *Last Battle* as separate pieces. The moment for dancing a revolutionary had passed. AIM had splintered with many of the members moving away to pursue teaching, union organizing, farming, the law, the arts, etc. But I'm getting ahead of my story. Back to the activist days, when I was dancing *Rosa* and creating Edgewood Park Before the Olympic Rowing Course—to save the park!

Figure 16. Passion, Section Three (1971). Photograph by Virginia Blaisdell.

Chapter Eight: Before the Olympic Rowing Course

Following the premiere of the *Rosa* portrait, I stopped performing for a few months to work at being my own agent. That involved preparing for the engagements, which resulted from sending out the brochure: telephoning, mailing supplemental materials, writing press releases, designing programs, making travel arrangements. These activities took all my time except for warming up and walking along the seashore or in Edgewood Park, thinking about how to dance nature. At that time, Harris was working as director of the Connecticut Arts Commission's Environmental Awareness Project and as a guest lecturer in Urban Design at Yale. He had seen plans for a proposal to turn Edgewood Park into an Olympic Rowing Course.

"What will it look like?" I asked him on one of our walks in the lower park along the West River.

"A straight highway of water wide enough to meet Olympic standards," he answered.

"How wide?"

"It will take over the whole park."

"That wide? And you said straight." We both looked around. "The park is full of curves."

"A natural oasis in the city—that was the idea."

"What will happen to the meandering river?" I asked.

"It will be flooded."

We stopped at the stand of marsh grasses, where we always stopped. "So these marshes—the beautiful swamp grasses—will be destroyed?"

"Yes. And also the old bridge." In the arch under the bridge was another favorite stopping place, which brought out our romantic impulses.

"There are vines and graffiti and cracks, signs of neglect, but the bridge is important to the design of the park."

"The arch is too narrow and low," said Harris. "The whole bridge is an obstacle to the rowing course."

We continued walking. "Go on with the description: a wide straight highway of water—what else?"

"High chain link fences to keep the public out except for certain hours and activities. And there will be fees."

"High chain link fences like a prison?" What a contrast to the varied open environment we were enjoying.

"I did see token landscaping on the plans."

"High fencing, token landscaping, designated hours and fees—no more people and animals and plants moving as the spirit and seasons move them."

The rowing course idea came from a Yale graduate, who was the president of an international airline and a rowing fanatic. In an effort to convince the city administration into turning a public park into a restricted athletic facility (primarily for the Yale crew), he took the important local politicians to meals at the most expensive restaurant in town. As part of his pitch, he hinted that, through his connections in high places, federal aid might be available for this special project, which was unlikely to be available for fixing up a rundown urban park.

The history of Edgewood Park began in 1889, when the city of New Haven turned over sixty acres of property to the new Park Commission for development. Sixty more acres came from three private donors, one of whom lived on a farm called "Edgewood"—hence the name of the park. It still adheres to the basic layout designed by Frederick Law Olmsted, Jr. in 1910. Early visitors could stroll through a rose garden, view a lily pond, and shoot bows and arrows in an archery field. They could roam trails, groves, and glens and take a carriage drive along a bridle path more than three miles long. In hot weather, they could drink from a spring of pure cold water, which was later made into a fountain.

I first went to the park with my mother, father, and brother. It was only a short walk from our inner-city flat, and we found it a welcome oasis in all seasons. Until a few years after World War II, there were still flower gardens and the fountain. Swans as well as ducks inhabited the pond in the lower park, and a boat and shed existed for a river-keeper. I remember a kiddy area in the upper park with sandboxes, rocking boats, and child-size seesaws, swings, and a slide. About a city block away, there was an area for older children with larger seesaws, swings for individuals and groups of four, a pole with cords for swinging, and a big slide.

By the time Harris and I walked, the park was very neglected except for a new skating rink near the north (Whalley Avenue) entrance. There were no cultivated plants. The grass, bushes, and trees received minimal attention. Far fewer ducks lived on the pond. Most of the playground structures were gone, and what remained was broken. Nevertheless we loved to stroll from one end of the park to the other, especially along the curvy river road, which was closed to traffic except for emergencies. The park was still a place where we could escape from the traffic of the city and spend a few hours under the trees, in the grassy open spaces, and along the river. Since childhood, it had been a retreat where I could observe, think, and dream, and it still was. The threat of a rowing course compelled me to create a record of Edgewood Park in dance before it disappeared.

Harris and I had recently seen an exhibition of Vincent van Gogh's art at the Brooklyn Museum, which led me to ask: why can't a dancer make sketches like a painter, using the body as tool and sketchbook? We went twice and would have gone more times, if the car drive from New Haven had been easier. Because of the bumper-to-bumper traffic, it took us hours to reach our destination. However, weariness turned to exhilaration from the first glimpse of a self-portrait. The museum was so crowded it was a challenge to view all the drawings and paintings. We moved from room to room, checking out what was where, returning to rooms when the crowd thinned out for a moment.

I couldn't refrain from imitating a drawing of peasants by sliding a foot, leaning forward, and turning my head. Two viewers passing by had a very different reaction: "What an ugly drawing," one of them said. The other agreed: "Critics of the time were right. Look at the clumsy lines compared with the elegant lines of Manet."

Harris became disgusted with the attack and pulled me across the room to examine a painting of a hut that looked as if it rose from the mud and would soon sink down again.

Reproductions can record Vincent's images, but not the intensity of the colors, the thickness of the paint, or the way the brush strokes dance. I looked and absorbed until my eyes and body refused to absorb anymore—enough to bring the images in books to life—enough to compel vivid new ways of seeing Edgewood Park: the river, grasses, mud, trees, and the strollers, as subjects not just for a painter, but also for a dancer.

I was determined to create a landscape of moving sketches, to explore what a person brought up in the inner city could say about nature in our time—a person whose experiences of nature took place at public beaches and in a public park, albeit a large one.

Thirty-four little dances, each one different—that was the challenge! Beethoven's *Diabelli Variations*, which has a folksy waltz for its theme and ends with a variation marked "tempo of a minuet," acted as a goad and structuring device for the composition process. I interpreted the theme and thirty-three variations as a dancing landscape for solo piano.

From October 1971 to the premiere of *Edgewood Park Before the Olympic Rowing Course* in July 1972, I gave sixteen performances, each requiring a different program. During that same period, in between performances, the dance sketches of the park were emerging. My journal notes for October and November indicate I was so busy being my own agent that I was composing mostly in my mind: nature studies (trees, flowers, grasses, fly, worm)—people: pregnant woman, jogger—gestures from van Gogh, Hokusai, Giacometti, Bruegel—movement ideas from Doris Humphrey, Pina Bausch, Curt Sachs's World History of the Dance. At home, I sometimes listened to the Diabelli Variations and improvised.

One of my performances, at Greater Hartford Community College, resulted in an unexpected connection to my work on Edgewood Park.

"An old factory building as a setting for dance — magical!" said an audience member at the end of the program, which began with short pieces (*Rich Man Poor Man, On the Wall, I Want the Pen..., Donna, Donna*), followed by *When the Landlord Left..., Newspapers*, and *Growing*.

"Concrete walls, exposed pipes, faded seats from an old movie theater—magical!" For me, the band practice room that doubled as a small theater was one of those spaces that provoke nightmares. The audience and I entered through a large dark recess, useless for performing or viewing because of an extra-wide column straight ahead and the underside of bleachers rising up on either side. I had to go past the column to reach the platform for performing, which projected from a corner of the room. I felt as if I was dancing in a shallow pit. The audience had to go past the column, turn to either side, and ascend the risers to their seats.

As I was leaving with the music teacher, he looked around the room and banged his fist on the column. "This room wasn't meant for dancing, but it's the best we have. I hoped more students would come. They have no exposure to dance, which is why I invited you." He paused and thought a moment. "Do you know the testament Beethoven wrote when he learned he was going deaf?" I shook my head no. "I'll send you a copy. Your performance reminded me of what it says about making art in the face of insurmountable difficulties." Decades later, I still have the copy of the *Heiligenstadt Testament* he sent.

I had read about Beethoven for the dance *Passion*, but had never seen the *Testament*, which was written in 1802 when he was thirty-two. It addresses his growing deafness and the sad changes he anticipates in his life. Nevertheless, he continued to compose one piece of music after another. Writing in the third person, he says: "in spite of all obstacles which nature has thrown his way, [he] has still done everything in his power to be received into the ranks of worthy artists..." What better example of struggle against the odds, which was central to the art and politics of the 1960s and '70s! Beethoven composed Diabelli in 1823, when he was deaf, and yet it's a happy piece—thirty-four episodes in the comedy of life—that's what I hoped to realize in Edgewood Park.

My 1971 engagements ended with two more performances after Greater Hartford, one of which was the whole *Rosa* portrayal in early December. After that I could finally concentrate on *Edgewood Park*. When I worked at home, Harris said fire came out of the rooms! However, I wasn't convinced I was making progress and therefore kept a record. The composing wasn't orderly, as the entries indicate. Two of the first are about library trips, where I was reading about van Gogh, Hokusai, Hiroshige—trying out gestures in the aisles between banks of books:

- A circle of figures with a prominent hand motif flattened into a lineup, fearful and defiant. The change to moving sideways proved to be a good way of executing the phrase.
- For two figures running in the rain, I came up with a stylized run in one spot.
- Hokusai's *Sparrow Dance* was another experiment. It made me laugh to do his rows of imaginative bird movements in the aisle with the books for an audience, though I had to be careful of banging my legs and arms when making wing gestures.

References to a sore knee recur in my journal, especially during the process of composing *Edgewood Park*: *may never do certain steps again—can't believe it—only 32—thought I would go on physically as a youth for many more years... no more winged feet? have to move more slowly and carefully...* The knee had started to bother me more than a year earlier while making the dance *Passion*, which had multiple squat jumps in the third section. Fortunately it held up for the park showings, but two months later, the left medial meniscus tore during a performance at Westbrook Junior College in Maine. The injury didn't stop me from dancing at two events before the surgery, and I resumed composing and performing soon after.

Back to December 1971, when the knee was sore, but workable. The journal record shows a busy time for choreographing.

December 27

Var. VIII undulations—Var. IX peasant motifs—Var. X bicycling—Var. XI conversations

Worked on all the above—have outlines but not clear on details—so many fragments!

December 28

Work yesterday on Var. VIII, X, XI—banal—can't make satire out of *Edgewood Park*—can't laugh at people out bicycling or jogging—what's laughable is the Rowing Course!

December 29

Diabelli is definitely *Edgewood Park*: a collection of characters inspired to be and do all sorts of things by their environment

Worked today on 8 characters from a Greek vase—introduction, theme of whole piece?

Also worked on joggers—had a good laugh for myself

Giacometti's "dog" for Var. VIII seems a likely possibility

December 30

Giacometti's dog didn't work—instead sequence of swaying, rocking, bending branches for Var. VIII ... Grass, branches, trees will recur throughout Diabelli—most dominant features of *Edgewood Park*

The frequent entries continue from January to July, though many of them deal with longer works, which were emerging along with the park variations. It was as if I were making paintings as well as sketches. No wonder I thought a dance about Vincent van Gogh was beginning to take shape. A note in my journal for early February reads: "to evoke gray and brown, yellows, red and green, blue... using Vincent's paintings for images, various music for time structures." Sometimes I wasn't sure if I was composing Vincent or *Edgewood Park*. Two of the longer pieces were included on my mixed programs, before the park sketches were ready for an audience. In the end, I made both dances: first *Edgewood Park* before the *Olympic Rowing Course* and then *Gestures from Vincent van Gogh*.

With the Vietnam War and Urban Renewal still raging, I danced my anti-war and anti-urban renewal pieces whenever and wherever I could. It was a crazy period of choreographing and performing! Although my notes indicate that I had made twenty-one sketches of the park by February, I showed only nine of them to Harris in early March. His comment was, "More!" Thirty-one were finished by May, but the dance wasn't ready for an audience until a few days before the premiere performances on July 7, 8, and 9. By a stroke of fortune, those days turned out to be just prior to the public hearing on the Rowing Course, scheduled for July 10. Therefore my article, which appeared in *Modern Times* on July 1, became all the more important for bringing out an audience.

Duck The Park Rowing Course!

by Joan Stone

Edgewood Park may become an Olympic Rowing Course because Lee High School needs athletic facilities. Maybe that sentence makes as little sense to you as it does to me. How did Edgewood Park, an Olympic Rowing Course, and Lee High School's athletic facilities get linked together? Was such a mixture concocted at Mory's [an exclusive Yale eating establishment] or the clubhouse at the Yale Golf Course? Wherever this bit of political maneuvering took place, we people of New Haven will lose a great deal if we lose Edgewood Park.

We'll lose a place for walking, riding a bike, throwing a ball, feeding the ducks, jogging, going sled riding in the winter, escaping the heat in the summer, enjoying the trees and bushes and weeds in different seasons.

We'll lose a place to go when we're feeling depressed, a place to go when we're feeling happy, a place to go and flop down on the grass and dream.

I'll be performing a dance-in-progress called Edgewood Park before the Olympic Rowing Course on July 7 and 8 at 8 p.m. and July 9 at 6:30 p.m. in the Coogan Skating Rink at the Whalley Avenue end of the Park (indoors in case of rain). There's no charge for admission.

> The Exit Experimental Theatre Company, an offshoot of the defunct Exit Coffeehouse, has secured the cooperation of the New Haven Parks Department and the New Haven Foundation and is presenting experimental productions in the Park on weekends. Here is another example of how Edgewood Park can be used by and for the people of New Haven.
>
> It seems to me that superb athletic facilities could be provided for Lee High School on the land cleared for Route 34. As for the Olympic Rowing Course, DUCK IT!

I wanted to perform in the outdoor skating rink with the sky and trees and birds visible, but the flooring was built for flooding to make ice, not for dancing, and lighting was problematic. So I had to perform in the warming hut, which had a good size open space that worked well for the piece. While *Diabelli Variations*, as its title announces, is a theme and variations, my dance is better described as a prelude and thirty-three sketches. I pictured myself walking through the park with Harris, enacting observations and experiences present and past.

EDGEWOOD PARK BEFORE THE OLYMPIC ROWING COURSE

Prelude

The Preview began with an invitation for everyone and everything to join the dance—*a big arcing reach of one arm forward, up, and back, and buoyant steps forward.*

— Next came *gallops and long strides* to embody the freedom of movement possible in the park, which would disappear with the rowing course.

— The noble trees were honored with *low courtly steps backward, feeling the ground, arms rising and lowering like branches.*

— A bird flying overhead became *running steps to take off into the air, arms and legs flying.*

— Imagining intense conversations with Harris led to *walking along in an irregular pattern rocking forward, lifting a leg to the back—and rocking backward, lifting a leg to the front—turning and rocking backward and forward—turning and rocking...*

— The river's currents were enacted in *walking sidestrokes, the torso pulling one way, limbs resisting, until the release of the leading arm in a big circular sweep. Or perhaps the oppositional pulls and releases signified the political battle over the park.*

— To dance the marsh grasses in a breeze, *running steps backward on the toes, arms rising and lowering, head nodding.*

The Preview ended with a *fleeting reprise of each image in reverse order, circling the perimeter of the space*—welcome to Edgewood Park!

Sketch 1—On the road

Actions I had done since childhood shaped this sketch. While zigzagging through space, *kick* imaginary stones, *lunge* as if smelling a flower, *jump* over invisible obstacles, and *draw circles with a foot* in illusory dirt.

Sketch 2—Clouds

Clouds overhead prompted me to undulate along with them. *(Undulate sideways along a curving path, up on the toes and down, body waving from side to side, slowing into deeper, more billowing undulations for big clouds and speeding up into jerky little waves for wispy ones.)*

Sketch 3 — Pregnant woman

A pregnant woman caught my eye, and I imitated her with nine inward circles that grew larger. *From the crotch, move a hand outward and upward and then inward and downward along the center of the torso.* Walking in the park seemed to summon all of nature into the pregnancy and birth. *End with a push of the hands to the ground and back up to arms in a cradling position.*

Sketch 4 — Sun and Moon

What gave me the idea for the sun moves was a sundial in the upper park that fascinated me as a child. *Beam one arm out from the body and back in and strike a foot on the ground like six ticks of a clock. Then switch to the other arm and foot for the other six ticks.* My brother showed me how to tell time by the shadows on the dial. *Repeat the twelve ticks, extending the beams by sliding away from the center and reaching out—then returning and crossing the center to reach out in the opposite direction.*

Once I danced the sun, I also had to dance the moon. *Raise the arms sideways into a sliver moon shape, open them slowly to full moon shape, and close them to a sliver on the other side. Drop arms and body over to mark a disappearance.* Harris and I occasionally made a night visit to the park. Since the river road was closed, we had to walk along the dark surrounding streets, which made us especially aware of the changing phases of the moon. *Repeat the moon gestures, while circling the space in steps up on the toes and down.*

Sketch 5—Pondering a problem

When dealing with a problem, walking in the park often led to a solution. *Treading the same path in one direction and then back, hands clasped under the chin, accelerate the footsteps from one every other measure to one per measure, to two, to three, and then just a clattering of heels and a crash down of the arms with a loud exhale!*

Sketch 6—Catching and throwing

Any grassy clearing in Edgewood Park was better than a neighborhood backyard for a softball game—no windows to break, no clotheslines to tear down, no trash cans to knock over, no angry shouting neighbors. I played with friends from the neighborhood and my Girl Scout Troop. We never had nine players on a side; we were lucky to have six: a pitcher, a catcher, two infielders, and two outfielders. By the time Harris and I walked, those just-for-fun pickup games were a thing of the past, but my memories of them continued. For the dance sketch, I focused on the gestures of catching and throwing.

It started with outfield moves—*run to the far edges of the space and reach high to catch—lunge to throw.* Next came infield moves—*run and scoop to catch—spin and twist to throw.* Then staying in one spot like a pitcher—*from hands cupped, lean back and thrust body and arm forward to throw—straighten up to catch. Finally, fall to the ground, crawl and roll to catch and throw from a lopsided prone position.*

Sketch 7 — Milkweed seeds

I learned about the plants in Edgewood Park and elsewhere from my mother, who grew up on a farm. She always picked an autumn bouquet of milkweed pods and bitter sweet, and I continued the tradition. The moment when the pod explodes—*burst in the air, arms and legs flying*—and the seeds are released—*light running steps this way and that*—was particularly fascinating to me as a dancer—*another burst and then walk with the legs fanning out from back to front.* With its dense center and feathery periphery—*running steps to alight and loop a leg higher and higher*, the milkweed seed is built for floating and alighting—*running steps to alight and sweep a leg and both arms around from front to back, setting off little hops to keep circling.*

Sketch 8—Marsh grasses

The marsh grasses danced to the fluky rhythms of the wind, and I danced with them, experiencing the oneness of nature. The arms led the way with the body and head following. *Lift, nod, lift, nod, lift to high—then bend over and down haltingly—lift and swivel around.* Audible breathing accompanied the moves: inhaling on the upward ones and exhaling on the downward ones. *Lift the arms high and bend sideways, forward, back, other side. Sweep down, over, and down—and lift haltingly to high.* In a stormy wind, the grasses ricocheted and slashed. *Ricochet down: hit hand to other hand to thigh, driving the leg back and off the ground. Lift the arms and slash them down in zigzags, ending with them wrapped around the torso in a bow.*

Sketch 9—Weeds

Although the gestures came from an illustration of dancing peasants, when I tried them in the park, they seemed to move remarkably like the weeds surrounding me. *Tap the feet ta-ta tum, ta tum—lift legs and arms up-up-up—tip and twist the body—fling high and wrap the arms—swing the legs—turn the head every which way.* Audience members laughed, because the dancing weeds were as bold and determined as the people, who try to stop them.

Sketch 10—Bicycler

One day I showed Harris a sketch of a bicycler, which I was intending to discard as too silly and cute. He pointed out the underlying idea—the hands had become the feet—which he found very interesting. I consciously developed that idea, and the bicycler without a bicycle emerged. *Staying in one spot, pedal in the arms faster and faster and faster, coasting occasionally, until the climactic finish—let the arms flap and shake out the legs.*

Sketch 11—Mudflats

An area adjacent to the river was known as the mudflats, because it was always muddy. *Tap-tap-tap the ground before springing over an illusory muddy spot.* The flood-gates for controlling the flow had been broken for years, so every time it rained the area flooded. *Brush a leg back and front, extend it, spring and land one foot at a time.* Harris and I moved along cautiously—*bend over and use the hands to test for mud*—and carefully—*walk on the toes, opening the legs wide to straddle a squishy area.*

At an earlier time, despite or maybe because of the difficulties—*curve tiptoe steps around to avoid the sink-in spots*, the mudflats was a favorite place for playing kickball, soccer, and volleyball—*take long careful strides*, though they all should have been called mud-ball—*stop and rock, trying not to fall in any direction.* In a drizzle or after a storm—*squat down low in order to leap high enough to clear a big puddle,* we ended up splattered with mud from head to toe! *Brush a foot across—step stamp, legs wide—and jump!*

Sketch 12—Resting

In the summer, my mother and I brought an old bedspread and rested on a lawn in the upper park—*sink down to all fours and roll to a sitting position, legs crossed.* Harris and I preferred the hillside down to the duck pond —*clasp the hands behind the head and lie back.* After finding a few moves on my own—*roll on to the side, head resting on an extended arm, and curl the legs in*, I found a treasure-trove of gestures—*roll to prone, bend the knees to lift the feet, then cross and re-cross them*—in Hokusai's delightful drawings—*roll on to the other side, sit up, and hug the knees*—of *Fat People*—*rub the sleepy eyes and roll to all fours.* Though I would have been a better model for one of his *Thin Types*—*stand up slowly, raising the hands to a prayer position sideways, and rest the head on the hands*, who also sought rest in the park.

Sketch 13—Caught in the rain

Who has not been caught in the rain without rain gear, when going for a long walk? From Hokusai's illustrations came gestures for how we scurry along, trying to protect ourselves. And I altered a haiku by Issa as a basis for describing my sketch.

Running
Lift one leg front, the other back
front, back
front, back
while alternating

to the downpour's beat
crossed arms on the chest and on top of the head
chest, head
chest, head

a dancer
stop—open the arms to feel for raindrops
and skip away ...

Sketch 14—Branches

As I was composing *Branches*, I kept looking at Giacometti's sculpture *Seven Figures and a Head*, inspired by seeing trees as "personages immobilized in their wanderings"—*plant the feet like roots, one forward one back, to allow pivoting in the four cardinal directions.* I remembered the branches of the maple tree that overhung the little porch, where I made my first dances with the tree watching—*twist the body from one side to the other, as the branch-like arms rise higher and higher, sweeping from open to crossed and bobbing from crossed to open.* I thought of Harris the architect's love of wood from working in his father's lumberyard to studying the history of wood construction to designing wooden structures—*arms high and open like the arches of a cathedral, lower them with sweeps from open to crossed to open to crossed, body twisting. End in a trunk-like stature, breathing while rising up on the feet and sinking down.*

Sketch 15—Jogger

Harris jogged in the neighborhood and probably would have run in the park, if I had joined him. I preferred walking and dancing, but liked to observe the joggers for their varied postures. Like the bicycler, the dancing jogger ran in one place. *Arms and legs pumping, run leaning forward—change to upright like a duck—lean back as if running backward—negotiate a curve—take long slow strides and shorter faster ones—race to the imaginary finish line—stumble and raise a fist!* Viewers laughed in recognition.

Sketches 16 and 17—River

The West River extends north and south far beyond the park, so we could walk along only part of it, but enough to enjoy its changes from season to season. Cooling to the senses in summer, beautiful reflections of vividly colored leaves in autumn, fascinating effects of ice and snow in winter, and welcome return of reflections of green leaves and grasses in spring.

Beethoven linked Variations XVI and XVII, and I followed his lead by giving two sketches to the river. The textures, rhythms, and phrasing of the music helped me find gestures. Trills like rippling water were danced in quick little steps on the toes (*bourrées*), moving sideways on a curving river-like path. The broken octaves and other patterns of sixteenth notes that bobbed up and down like waves and currents became *tilting steps back and falling steps forward.* Single notes or simple chords in a steady rhythmic pattern were realized in *low gliding steps sideways* like the ongoing flow of the river.

Sometimes the foot patterns were coupled with arm and hand gestures to enhance the enactment. *Bourrée sideways, looping an arm upward and downward. Tilt back and fall forward in one spot, occasionally raising the arms like a wave and crashing them down. Glide the feet sideways, body bending over, fingers trembling out and in over the ground.*

Sketch 18—Feeding the ducks or the Sower

The river's main attraction for families was the duck pond. We never went without stale bread for the ducks. As a child, I was frustrated when my throws didn't go far enough to reach the ducks and ended up food for the water rats. The experiences of childhood were always there when I danced this sketch, but it was Vincent's *Sower* that gave me the pivotal gestures: r*eaching inward into an imaginary sack—created by cradling an arm and throwing outward with the right or left hand—from short throws to longer to longest ones.*

Vincent's figure is in a walking stance, and I combined the throws with walking in different rhythmic patterns, as if I were moving along the shoreline scattering bits of bread for the ducks or walking up and down a row sowing seeds. When I performed the outward and inward moves in slow motion, it struck me that the inward curve was a reaping gesture: sowing and reaping, planting and harvesting, living and dying.

Sketch 19—Bird dance

Having grown up longing to dance the Swan Queen in *Swan Lake Ballet*, the Bluebird Pas de Deux from *Sleeping Beauty*, and the *Dying Swan*, it was inevitable for me to make a bird dance, when I became a choreographer. Edgewood Park inspired my first one. I didn't choose ducks or swans, but red-winged blackbirds. *Fly and perch as if traversing a stand of marsh grasses.* The brown streaked female with a splash of orange on her shoulders looks like a large sparrow, which set off the idea of using gestures from Hokusai's *Sparrow Dance. Alternately step, spring, and stop—hands raised to the shoulders, arms bent to extending outward—body tipping, tilting, or bending over—legs lifting front, side, or back.* She was harder to spot than the larger male with his striking black coat and red epaulettes. He stood out as he flew and perched in the marsh grasses.

Sketch 20—Tree

Somewhere in the writings of Boris Pasternak, he quotes a Russian proverb: "Storms destroy trees, but they only bend grasses." I saw that proverb played out in Edgewood Park when a hurricane came through. Trees suffered irreparable damage: branches down, trunks cracked in two. The grasses, on the other hand, bedded down and when the water receded, they righted themselves and started waving again. Worse than a hurricane, the rowing course would destroy both trees and grasses.

Diabelli Variation XX, which shaped my tree sketch, differs from any other variation in being very slow, sustained, and quiet (p to pp) throughout. *Plant the feet like roots—one front and one back—and place the arms in a branch-like pose—one arm bent at the elbow, the other straight.* Most of the thirty-two measures contain only two simple chords, each held for three beats. *Raise the arms with gentle twists of the body—knees bending and straightening, until the hands are reaching high.* The musical effect is mysterious and almost motionless, which made me think of a tree trunk, growing internally ring by ring. *Tremble and then snap the body forward and down from the waist, as if struck by a storm or the wrecking crew for the rowing course!*

Sketch 21—Fervid exchange

By a bench near the river, Harris and I saw a couple having a fervid exchange. She was striding this way and that—and he was gesturing in response. It reminded me of one of our exchanges. In *Variation XXI*, Beethoven alternates between eight measures of 4/4 time (4 beats to a measure), good for striding—and eight measures of 3/4 time (3 beats to a measure), good for gesturing.

I immediately came up with spatial configurations for the striding: *from a central spot, stride out and back in irregular spokes and circle around.* The gesturing response was more of a challenge. I was studying an early nineteenth century dance treatise by Carlo Blasis, in which the positions are gentler, more rounded, less athletic than the ballet that followed. He says arabesques—*straight leg lifted to the back*—and attitudes—*bent leg lifted to the back, front, or side*—can be varied in unlimited ways by shifting the torso and changing the positions of the arms—*one forward, one back—both forward—one low, one high—both overhead.* Mirroring his illustrations made familiar ballet moves speak in new ways. I showed Harris the forceful striding, answered by the light, talking Blasis arabesques and attitudes, performed in one spot. A fervid exchange, we both agreed.

Sketches 22 and 23—A fly

I was sitting on a bench in the upper park. A fly alighted on my thigh and started gesturing.

From all 4s, scratch the head with one hand, then the other—scratch and scratch.

I flicked it away.

It buzzed around my head, landed, and danced on my other thigh.

Draw the hands together and scratch one arm with the other, change arms—repeat.

I brushed it away again. It flew off, but soon came back and did new moves on my arm.

Hands lifted, rub them together and rub the cheeks—rub and rub—hands and cheeks. Lower the hands to the ground and rock back and forth.

We glared at each other, before I lifted my arm.

Away went the fly with a buzz, only to return two seconds later and jig on my other arm. *Scratch one leg with the other, change legs—repeat. Bring the feet together, lift them, and cross and uncross them multiple times.*

After moving up and down the arm, it stopped to show more of its vocabulary.

Scratch the back as if scratching under the wings, one hand, the other—keep scratching. Flick a cheek and then the other, as if brushing away tears. Raise the hands into a prayer pose. Pause...

A full-out performance followed, which I watched, fascinated.

Run through the whole routine in a scrambled order and slower.

Next thing I knew, I was down on my knees, imitating what I had observed, amazed at how similar a fly's gestures are to human ones.

Perform the moves slower and slower with no repeats.

The fly flew away.

Finale: from the prayer position, lower the hands, head, and body. Roll on to the back and lift bent arms and legs into the air.

Mission accomplished for fly and dancer!

Sketch 24—Leaf

The leaves of autumn—red, yellow, orange, with glimpses of green—were a feast for the eyes. I waited for when they fluttered down and danced along the ground and in the air. *Use the arms and legs like spines and tips of a leaf and waltzing steps for locomotion.* Responding to the wind, they became my partners in a waltz. *Sweep in large curves and smaller ones—skim along the ground, tapping the toes.* They came towards me, brushed past me, followed me, surged ahead of me. *Move a few steps forward and backward and sideways in zigzags, sometimes swirling in one spot.* They danced with me until the wind died down. *Sweep—skim—swirl—slow down—stop.*

Sketch 25—Faces

As I observed an animated group seated around a blanket with refreshments in the middle, it brought back memories of picnicking with my mother and brother. It also called to mind illustrations by Hokusai of men relaxing and laughing with their whole bodies as well as their faces. I started out with his gestures and soon had a sketch, which went through a range of emotions, expressed in face, body, and sound. My first version was a sitting one, but I came up with a standing one for better visibility in the skating hut.

Hiding—*cover the face with one arm*

Laughing—*lift a bent leg and both arms to one side and then the other, while laughing out loud*

Preening—*rest one hand on the chest, lift the chin, and make preening sounds*

Annoyed—*brush the arms to one side, as if brushing away a fly, and say, "go away"*

Angry—*cross the arms and stamp the feet ta-ta-ta tum*

Thinking—*assume the famous think pose, chin resting on a fist, and walk a little circle*

Growling—*lean forward and make noisy growls in different directions*

Crying—*crumple the face and wipe away the tears, body sagging with the sounds of crying*

The sketch developed by reversing the emotions—from Crying to Hiding—and scrambling them. Some members of the audience couldn't resist mimicking.

Sketch 26—Worm

Having no bones, a worm can undulate along a surface in ways that humans cannot. However, it was irresistible to try. My first attempt came in a duet for a choreography class. I danced a worm and my partner, a bird. The worm-dancer moved mostly along the ground as fast as she could—*from all fours, hump the middle of the body like a camel, slide the hands forward to flatten into the prone position, and then draw the knees up and under, so the body humps again.* Sometimes she tried to fend off the bird's torments by curling in on herself—*roll on to the side and curl in and out, arms over the head.* Once the bird even succeeded in lifting the worm into the air, and yet she found a way to escape. The worms in Edgewood Park were not so fortunate. I usually saw one caught firmly in a bird's beak rather than making its way over the ground or a leaf.

Beethoven's Variation XXVI with its triplets that move up and down the keyboard like waves gave me the impetus to expand the worm story. The new sketch started with the slithering and curling moves on the floor from the old study. The next challenge was to push off the hands and undulate to standing. Once upright with the hands together overhead, the worm-dancer inched along close to the audience, performing an old jazz dance, called snakehips. *The name describes the motions—as the hips slither left and right, the feet slither right and left.* Every so often she stopped to face an audience member and wriggle the body down and back up.

Sketch 27—Playing tag or water rat

When I made this sketch, I thought it was about playing tag, something my neighborhood friends and I often did on the lawn in the upper park or, even better, in the mudflats where there were trees and benches. *From the center of the space, run forward and stoop—run sideways and make feinting movements like "catch-me-if-you-can"—run a diamond shape, hopping and jumping to mark the corners—run a circle and then dart this way and that in one spot—caught! Raise a hand.*

To write about the dance, I had to reconstruct it, and realized it could have been performed as the actions of a water rat. That creature upset me as a child, because it could move much faster than the ducks and would dart out and steal the pieces of bread I threw. Tag or water rat or something else... the provocative ambiguity of gesture!

Sketch 28—Circle dances

My fascination with the circle dance began with a break-through study at Sarah Lawrence. It continued with the circles that grow larger in *Growing* and the constricted ones in *Prisoner.* The Edgewood Park dances furthered my exploration in new ways. For Sketch 28, I composed a small tense circle of KEEP OUT gestures and a more expansive circle of COME IN gestures. In the context of the struggle to save the park, the circles could be interpreted as NO-to-the-rowing-course and YES-to-Edgewood-Park.

For the NO-circle, the gestures came largely from an illustration by Hokusai of figures in a circle, their hands in prominent positions that seemed to be fending off ominous forces. *Press the flexed hands to one side—slap the thighs—thrust the flexed hands to the other side.* The changing hand moves were the key to reading the dance. *Circle the hands from down to striking upward—crash them downward.* Walking steps and pivots kept the poses moving. *Slap the hands together and cover the face, elbows out.* To complete the circle, the sequence was repeated faster and then in slow motion. *Bring the elbows in and make fists.* NO to the rowing course!

For the YES-circle, the gestures and my feelings in performing them changed dramatically. *Scoop the hands down as if digging in the dirt.* They came from a loose interpretation of the figures seated around a table in van Gogh's "Potato Eaters." *Clasp the hands under the chin as if praying—reach one hand across the chest and then the other to an imaginary person on each side.* Their motions seemed to be transferred from the fields, where they worked under the sun, to the table, where they sat sharing a meal by the light of a single overhead lamp. *Scoop down before raising the hands high and opening them to the sides, palms up. Reach both hands to one side, swing down, and reach them to the other side.* Once again, walking steps and pivots kept the gestures moving, and the sequence was repeated to complete the circle. *Swing down and turn on the toes, hands lifting in a V to the sky.* YES to Edgewood Park!

Sketch 29—More grasses

Enacting the marsh grasses always connected me to earth and sky. Unlike Sketch 10, which stayed in one place, this study moved along in a line from one end of the space to the other like the grasses along the river. As a child, I liked to walk in amongst them looking for turtles, until three boys drowned in quicksand near the riverbank south of the park. After that I stepped more cautiously and stayed a little more distant, but close enough to absorb the motions that emerged in this sketch.

In spring, there were new shoots—*move the feet along the ground like roots feeling their way and bend the whole body sideways, to the back, and to the other side*

Slender blades of grass with feathery tops soon appeared, very responsive to the wind—*move along, lifting one arm and waving it from side to side slowly and then faster—switch to the other arm and arc forward and backward, hand quivering*

The weightier cattails were most prominent in autumn when their caps turned brown—*swing down, raising both arms and lean from side to side—swing down and up again to lean backward and forward*

The sketch ended with a circle of the body down, up, over, and down, and a rise to begin the cycle of growing and dying again.

Sketch 30—Old man walking

One day Harris and I saw an old man on the river road. T*ake uneven steps, hands behind the back, body tilting forward.* He was moving so haltingly, we wondered how he had arrived at the park. *Stop and turn the head a little.* Where did he live? Where had he entered? (*Move again, hands behind the thighs as if pushing the legs forward.* How far could he go? *Stop and scratch a thigh.* Maybe it was the threat of high chain link fences for the proposed rowing course that made me think of van Gogh's "Prisoners," circling close together in a small space with the high walls of the prison behind them. *Take a few steps, hands on hips, head up.* Their gestures were remarkably similar to the minimal motions of the old man, though he was free to come and go as he pleased. *Lurch forward, straighten up—pause—trudge on.* Would his walks continue, if the rowing course were built?

FINALE

Harris teased that I should end the dance by sitting on a bench and moving just my head from one side to the other as if watching a crew race. We both knew I couldn't do that. The dance had to end in a majestic way to signal hope that the park would survive. For the FINALE, I assembled sequences from the previous sketches into three longer pieces and called them NATURE, THINKING, and DANCE.

Sketch 31—NATURE

Beethoven's Variation XXXI is in 9/8 time (9 beats to a measure, each 8th note equaling one beat). The 9 beats are realized not just in 8th and 16th notes, but also in clusters of 32nd and 64th notes, which sweep over the keyboard like breezes building up and dying down. The musical pattern propelled the interweaving of grasses *waving, nodding, ricocheting—weeds kicking, tapping, tilting, twisting—a bird taking off into the air—a tree growing slowly upward and outward—branches crossing and opening—a leaf twirling and skimming along the ground—clouds undulating.* I wanted to capture the experience of walking through the park, embodying the natural elements as I saw and felt them.

Sketch 32—THINKING

I thought of calling this part of the finale PEOPLE, but when I performed it for myself, it felt like THINKING in gestures. That title was also convincing to Harris. He said I had turned an inward process into dance. Learning the moves, extracted from various sketches, was a challenge, because the rhythms, phrasing, and spatial pattern were irregular. Though eventually the dance took on its own kinesthetic logic.

Hands behind the back, step backward—
Stop and cover the face with the hands—
A fist under the chin, move sideways—
Swing the arms across the front and back of the torso—
Sit on the ground and breathe—
Rise while rubbing a calf muscle and rubbing the neck—
Look up—
Go forward: step hop, step hop, run run run run—
Fan the face with a hand—

Sequences in the same vein followed, before the ending—*fall to all-fours and roll to sitting cross-legged, a closed hand resting at the chin*—a variation on Rodin's sculpture, *The Thinker.*

Sketch 33—DANCE

There is a slow transition from *Variation XXXII to XXXIII*, which I used to stand up slowly and walk to the starting point for the last sketch, *DANCE.* To Beethoven's majestic minuet, the return to previous images became a day in the life along the river.

Figure 17. Gesture from Edgewood Park . . . with a child watching (1972).
Photograph by Virginia Blaisdell.

SUN RISING—*walk slowly forward along the spine of the space, lifting one arm out and up, the other arm out and up, and then beaming them from in to out and down*

RIVER FLOWING—*travel sideways on a curving pathway with walking sidestrokes*

WIND BLOWING—*sweep halfway around the space with low running steps*

PERSON STROLLING—*look around before moving across the space by rocking and turning, rocking and turning—change to circling with gallops and reaches to one side, then the other—sit on the ground for a moment*

SOWER SOWING—*stand up and stride along the diagonal reaching inward and throwing outward*

SEEDS FLOATING—*lift and arc an arm over, fingers fluttering, while looping through space with quick little running steps*

ROOTS STRUGGLING—*descend and worm the body along the ground, pulling in and stretching out*

TREE GROWING—*ascend slowly from kneeling to feet planted, arms and body rising with gentle twists*

RIVER RIPPLING—*tip the body over and glide the feet sideways along a curving pathway, fingers of the hands rippling out and in—keep gliding and loop the arms out, up, and down like waves*

DUCK SWIMMING—*bob and spring forward along the diagonal, body bent over from the hips like a table top, arms flapping at the sides*

GRASSES WAVING—*skim across the space and back on the toes, raising and lowering one arm, the other arm, then both arms*

CLOUDS UNDULATING—*move sideways up on the toes and down, undulating the torso and arms*

SUN SETTING—*from the front of the space, walk backward along the spine, raising one arm out and up, the other out and up, and then slowly open and lower both arms—bend the knees and end with a deep bow.*

July 7—About fifty people appeared for the premiere performance. As I wrote in my notes, "premieres are always difficult, though I was more 'on top' of this dance than usual—made few technical mistakes." I performed without verbal clues, which made the work puzzling for some audience members. Other troubling issues came up in the discussion at the end:

"Is this new dance political?"

"What about adding music or poetry."

"Why not include sequences about the fight to save the park—create a foil for the lyricism of the vignettes."

On the other hand, one friend found the piece my most accessible, but thought I challenged the audience too much by daring them to figure out what I was doing without words. Another friend commented:

"I was drawn into the dance immediately and let it pour over me. I felt the vulnerability of the creatures represented."

July 8—The audience was larger for the second performance. I used words to introduce some of the more abstract sketches and received a much friendlier response from viewers, which helped me to dance better. Some people said they felt they could get along without words—they found the movement statements very clear. But most liked the verbal clues. There were several children present at each performance, who seemed to prefer the dancing to the talking. A photographer recorded one little girl, who was watching with great attentiveness. Suddenly her mother decided it was time to leave and dragged the child out, crying that she wanted to stay.

The question-and-answer period focused on my aesthetic, on how I create dances, on what goes through my head when I perform. The question of politics and art came up again. I tried to articulate how dance can be political without being agit-prop (agitation and propaganda), a difficult subject. The program ended with a look toward the future from a different artist and art form. A promising young poet, inspired by the surrealist voice of André Breton and the political voice of Nicanor Parra, read fifteen minutes of her poetry.

July 9—The third performance was on a Sunday afternoon, and even more people came than the night before. I talked between the sketches again, and most audience members looked like they were enjoying themselves. The nature sketches went particularly well in honor of the presence of Faith Whitney, the woman whose picture was on the wall of the Hill Parents Association. In addition to her civil rights and anti-war activism, she was also a staunch defender of the environment. I could hear her laughing or sighing or whispering whenever my moves took me near her. A person, who had seen me dance three years before, remarked: "How you've grown—concepts so profound and moving." A poet in the audience said: "You're the only dancer who can move me, make me weep without music. You did it again today." From another viewer came a wonderful comment: "During the nature vignettes, I felt like a person watching; during the people vignettes. I felt like a tree observing."

The Sunday afternoon program was followed by a jazz concert put together by local musicians for the benefit of the Angela Davis Bookstore in New Haven.

Public hearing, July 10—Many people who had come to my performances appeared for the public hearing on the fate of the park. City officials had booked a small room, but had to open a large chamber to accommodate the crowd. Most of those present were against the rowing course. The aldermen, looking around and seeing their constituents, must have had second thoughts about the proposed change. However, what saved the park was the emergency road and bridge, which proved to be too difficult and expensive to replace. And so, the rowing course died, and Edgewood Park survived!

The park sketches accomplished what I hoped they would. They gave me a connection to nature as well as gestures, rhythms, phrases, and spatial concepts for composing many future works. The dance itself, Edgewood Park Before the Olympic Rowing Course, was truly site and time specific. Although I continued to perform it in different versions, it could never have the art-and-politics impact of those park presentations.

Chapter Nine: The Dance Goes On ...

The dances I made after Edgewood Park embodied social issues, but none had as close a connection to activist politics as the early dances. By the time Harris and I moved to Kansas in 1978, I had created five new portraits, using material from the previous works and developing new gestural ideas.

Eve and the Serpent (1972)

First came *Eve and the Serpent*, a dialogue between a contemporary Eve and Karl Marx. In between dance sequences, I spoke a passage by Marx from *The Eighteenth Brumaire of Louis Bonaparte,* contrasting the overwhelming successes of the bourgeoisie with the futile efforts of the proletariat. Marx's gestural language drew me to the passage, especially the last image of the proletariat, when "the situation has been created, which makes all turning back impossible, and the conditions themselves cry out: "Here is the rose! Here dance!"

My aim was to stand Eve on her feet and forge a link between women and workers in their struggle for liberation. But the movements I came up with couldn't match the weight and scope of the words, and I abandoned the piece after two showings.

Gestures from Vincent van Gogh (1973)

Next came *Gestures from Vincent van Gogh*, a dance-in-silence that played well for audiences and for me. Vincent's letters, several commentaries on his art, and his brother Theo's collection, which I saw at the Brooklyn Museum, helped to shape the choreography. After many reworkings, I arrived at the final organization of the piece in eleven sections, each titled with a symbol and a color.

The gestures came from Vincent's drawings and paintings and also from the works of artists, who influenced him, especially Hokusai and Millet. I also developed movement ideas from the *Edgewood Park* sketches and earlier pieces.

Central to my structuring of the dance were three paintings that dealt with Vincent's changing vision of the community and the individual:

The Potato Eaters—a gathering of five figures, who appear to be painted with the earth they've been digging. They're seated around a table in a small room, men and women with individual faces and shapes, joined together by their work, the sharing of a meal, and the light of a single overhead lamp.

The Sunflowers—Looking at Vincent's painting of yellow sunflowers, glorious and varied, gathered in a vase with his name on it, I interpreted the work as depicting his dream of community. While always acknowledging the importance of the committed individual artist, he also dreamed of a gathering of artists in his yellow

Figure 18. Flying gesture from Edgewood Park . . . (1972). Photograph by Virginia Blaisdell.

"house of light," each different but united in pursuit of art—sharing ideas and expenses—living together in a harmony of differences.

The All Night Café (which I could visit at Yale Art Gallery) is a stark contrast to *The Potato Eaters* and *The Sunflowers*: a big empty room—tables up against blood red walls—a few scattered figures either sleeping or drinking—a green billiard table in the middle with the owner in a white suit, standing next to it on vigil—four harshly glowing ceiling lamps dispersing the light. It's Vincent's dream of community shattered.

The dance was linked to my experiences in AIM. Our story was much less dramatic, but at the core was the issue of the community and the individual. We came together with similar political convictions, fought together, and then went our separate ways, when the revolutionary moment passed.

The three central paintings weren't enough for a dance. I had to build up to each of them with place becoming a critical ingredient.

The browns, blacks and grays of the Netherlands:
Brown of the Sower
Black of Roots
Gray of Peasant Women (which contained two circles representing *The Potato Eaters*)
The brief stay in Paris, where Vincent saw the Impressionists, and his palette began to change:
Struggle from Darkness to Light
The move south to Arles, where he discovered light:
White of Orchards in Bloom
That was the first half of the dance.

In the second half came the colors, at first inspired by the light and vegetation of Arles:
Green of Grass and Trees
Yellow of the Sunflowers—the climax of the dance
Orange of Fire—Like Icarus, Vincent went too close to the sun, and it became a fiery furnace.
Red of Blood—my version of the shattering of his dream of community and his own breakdown, depicted in *The Night Café* and *Portrait with Severed Ear.*

Vincent's mental condition required him to move to St. Remy Asylum. Although he was no longer free to roam the countryside, he painted with vigor whenever he could.
Violet of the Fields at Dusk
Blue of a Starry Night

I came to see and perform the dance as Vincent's spiritual journey from the *Brown of the Sower* to the *Yellow of the Sunflowers* to the *Red of Blood* to the *Blue of a Starry Night.* In tracing Vincent's pathway, I was also forging my own as a dance artist.

Three Steps Back, Two Forward OR Three Steps Forward, Two Back (1974), Woman Dance (March 1978), Lady on the Move (April 1978), Figure on the Ship's Prow (1979)—changing titles for the same basic dance

The third portrait was about a woman torn between the call of motherhood and the call of career. I composed the piece partly as a way of grappling with that tug-of-war. Three other married women in AIM were facing the same choice, and we met a few times to discuss our dilemma. One eventually had a child, while the others, like me, decided their careers were enough for them to handle.

The dance also addressed the larger issue of women taking control of our own bodies. It was the time of the seminal feminist reader, *Our Bodies, Ourselves* (1973), which revolutionized our consciousness. A forerunner in the liberation of our bodies was the modern dance pioneer, Isadora Duncan (1877-1927). She stripped away underlayers and overskirts, corset, and binding shoes and performed barefoot, wearing simple Greek and other draped tunics. She also tried to balance being a dancer and the mother of two children, often leaving them to the care of servants, until they died tragically in a car accident. After that, she devoted herself to setting up schools for other people's children to learn dance. I took many of the moves for the choreography from drawings of her by Abraham Walkowitz. For a performance in 1976, I even used words from her writings.

Gestures from paintings, drawings, and sculptures of nudes by Ingres, Manet, Renoir, Degas, Michelangelo contributed to the movement vocabulary. From Greek art, I explored the continuum from the closed-in pose of the Venus of Modesty (*right arm across breasts, hand on heart—left arm down, hand at crotch*) to the open flying pose of the Nike of Samothrace, often called the Winged Victory (*arms up and spread wide like wings*). I wanted to explore the many facets of the dancing body: natural, athletic, erotic, emotional, political.

The difficulties of creating a convincing whole are indicated by the changing title and organization of the piece. At first, I called it *Three Steps Back, Two Forward OR Three Steps Forward, Two Back* (1974) and performed it in two long undivided parts, moving toward the back of the space and then toward the front. Not convinced of that version, I next performed it as *Woman Dance* (March 1978) in two parts, divided into eleven sections with working titles not announced to the audience. A note in my journal says: "try jazzier title, new division in three parts for next performance." Acting on that note, I came up with *Lady on the Move: Stepping Out, Getting Down to Basics, Dancing the Blues Away* (April 1978), but not enough of the movement vocabulary lent itself to a jazz version.

Harris and I couldn't afford a child until we moved to Kansas (July, 1978). By that time, I was thirty-nine and wanted to form a dance group, which I did, once I made a connection to the University of Kansas Dance Program. For the final try at this dance, I had distanced myself enough from the personal issue to call it *Figure on the Ship's Prow* (1979). (An inner voice may have been saying good-by to New England.) My inspiration was the women, who adorned the whaling ships going into the most dangerous waters. Many of them were sculpted wearing dresses with lace and ruffles, a symbol of the clash between domesticity and adventure. From the broader view, any time women assert themselves, demand more opportunities, more recognition, equal rights, they become figures on the ship's prow.

The last version of the dance was in eleven sections, divided into three parts: Unveiling—hesitating, spiraling, groping, protecting, unveiling

Pushing Off—drifting and resisting, weeping, reaching and remembering

Trying to Fly—hurrying, trying to fly, twisting and going on

My notes on the performances, no matter what the title or organization, indicate audience members had strong reactions:

"I saw the struggle with the woman's role and the struggle to transcend that role."

"Like Beethoven's last sonata in thoughtfulness, sparseness, combination of song and speech—a tense, emotional experience."

"I felt terribly uncomfortable."

"Were you talking about yourself or about women past, present, and future?"

One fellow responded with a delightful story about his sister: "One day she came into the living room naked and was faced with unexpected company. First she covered her crotch, then her breasts, then she put one hand over each vital part like Aphrodite herself and ran out of the room!"

I made my dance in 1973-74, when the Women's Movement was on the rise. It waned in the 1980s and even more in the 1990s, when a counter movement started to gain momentum, centered on denying a woman the legal right to a safe abortion. As I write in 2019, we're speaking out and marching again for control of our bodies, our reproductive rights, our lives. The women's struggle continues... We try to fly, twist and go on ... dance two steps forward, one step back, two steps forward...

Aunt Sam's Dying for a Laugh (1975), Diamond (1976), Aunt Sam and the Diamond (1980)

As the Bicentennial of 1976 approached, I came up with the idea of making a portrait of Aunt Sam. Everyone's heard of Uncle Sam, but what about Aunt Sam? I assembled an assortment of comic sketches and called the piece *Aunt Sam's Dying for a Laugh* (1975). I portrayed her speaking and dancing about class, work, sports, show business, love—giving voice to the unknown silent majority.

Another idea I had for the Bicentennial was a dance honoring the great American sport of baseball, and soon after making *Aunt Sam*, I composed *Diamond* (1976). I grew up an avid Brooklyn Dodgers fan like most people in my low-income neighborhood, while Harris grew up rooting for the Yankees in his well-to-do neighborhood. Unlike *Aunt Sam*, the Dodgers were famous, but I saw them as the proletariat of baseball, as women are the proletariat by gender.

From the first performances, *Aunt Sam's Dying for a Laugh* and *Diamond* were greeted with smiles, laughs, positive feedback—viewers enjoyed themselves. Both pieces covered different facets of the same territory, and I danced *Diamond* as the *Aunt Sam* character from its premiere. But it wasn't until the first performance in Kansas that I thought of changing the title to *Aunt Sam and the Diamond* (1980).

These lines from *The Boys of Summer* by Roger Kahn (1972), which I spoke while performing, go to the heart of the dance: "The Brooklyn Dodgers were awesomely good and yet defeated. Their skill lifted everyone's spirit, their defeat joined them with everyone's existence. A national team with a nation in thrall—irresistible—but unable to beat the Yankees."

I played *Aunt Sam* as a pitcher, batter, and base runner and used the baseball diamond for the spatial configuration. She began with a warmup titled *Reaching for the Stars*, also known as *Diamonds in the Sky*. On the periphery of the space, she executed stretches, leans, kicks, body swings, arm circles, lunges, spins—with pauses to wave to the crowd.

Moving to a more central spot/mound for the *Tricky Moves* of pitching, she pawed and kicked the mound—fondled an imaginary ball—stepped back while moving an arm back and kicking the forward leg up—lunged forward on that leg and threw over from different angles, back leg rising with the throws. She shook her head 'no' and 'yes' to signals from the catcher—bent down to field a grounder—jumped high to save a hit—backed up and threw forward again and again—until she triumphed over the batters and raised both fists in the air.

Anything for a Hit was in Aunt Sam's head as she walked to the periphery to take her turn at batting. After a few practice swings, she headed for home plate, a critical point of the diamond, where pitcher and batter engage in a psychological duel. To dig in and claim the plate, she did the heal and toe taps of the Mexican Hat Dance and the slides and jumps of the Bunny Hop. On to different stances, to looks from pitcher to catcher and catcher to pitcher, to watching a pitch sail over her head. She swung and missed, had to duck to avoid being hit, dug in again, put her hands up and back and took a mighty swing. Yes, it was a hit!

The last section was called *You Can't Keep a Good Soul Down*. To run the bases, Aunt Sam tap-danced, imitating parts of routines by Gene Kelly, Fred Astaire, and other musical comedy dancers—took moves from ballet and modern—did the Lindy Hop and other street forms—vamped while waiting at a base—fell and slid a few times, body and arms stretched to touch the bag, got up and brushed herself off—moved between bases like a tight rope walker. In these ways, she made it to third base.

Sometimes she spoke while dancing:

"The Brooklyn Dodgers were awesomely good..." accompanied her moves from home plate to first base. The lines end in defeat, but Aunt Sam managed to reach first base.

"Over there, over there... so beware, say a prayer..." were whispered loudly as she tried to steal a base, which she finally, did to move from first base to second.

"Take me out to the ballgame..." turned out to have just the right rhythm for the tap steps, known as waltz clog (s*tep, shuffle, ball change, etc.)*, good for dancing from second base to third.

At third base, she spoke/sung

"If you bump in to/a 5 foot 2/covered with fur—

Diamond rings (*pointing to the fourth finger of her left hand*)/and all those things,

Bet your life /it isn't her.

Alas, Aunt Sam was stopped at third base. After descending and ascending like a fallen warrior, she tap-danced her way backward past second and first. "Keep on truckin'," she said, as she went past home plate.

In my dance, Aunt Sam had no ball or bat. She was in reality pitching an idea, batting it around, running with it, and hoping to score—if not this time, next time. After works such as *Prisoner* and *Last Battle* from Rosa, *Orange of Fire* and *Red of Blood* from Vincent, *Weeping* and *Trying to Fly* from Figure on the Ship's Prow, it felt good to perform a dance that made people laugh!

Mrs. Live Alone (1977)

My fifth endeavor, *Mrs. Live Alone*, was a play for a dancer, inspired by Tillie Olsen's novella *Tell Me a Riddle*. I wrote a script, using Tillie's words, and culled gestures from various sources, especially the works of Kaethe Kollwitz, to portray the central character. She is an old immigrant woman, who is reviewing her life back to her youth, when she was imprisoned in Siberia for her activism in support of the 1905 Russian Revolution. She has emigrated to the United States, married, and raised seven children, but what has sustained her, deep inside, is the idealism of that activist period: *flame of freedom... light of knowledge... gentle, brave and strong... and every life shall be a song.* That dance has aged with me. At first, I performed it thinking of my grandmother, then my mother, and finally myself.

While I was choreographing and performing the five portraits, Harris was moving away from practicing architecture and more and more toward teaching and writing. After Yale, he was a visiting lecturer at Wheaton College and Hampshire College, which had the side benefit of opportunities for me to perform and teach workshops at both institutions. He finished the handwritten text and drawings for his first book, *Workbook of an Unsuccessful Architect* (1973) and was working on a second book, *Monuments and Main Streets* (1983). When his three-year stint at Hampshire ended, he sent his resume to architecture programs across the country and went on several visits before accepting a tenure track position at the University of Kansas (KU). Although we had questions and doubts about moving to Kansas, we came in 1978 and stayed.

We settled in Lawrence, which was founded by New Englanders as an abolitionist stronghold in the 1850s and has remained true to its progressive origins. We soon learned that we could continue the explorations we began in New Haven and expand them in new ways.

I updated my brochure, sent it out, and toured as a soloist primarily in the Midwest. I also joined the KU dance faculty and, from 1982 to 2010, taught choreography and dance history part-time. With students to draw upon, I began to choreograph group works in collaboration with fiber artist Wendy Weiss and musician Martin Olson.

Soon after Harris and I arrived, a native Kansan took us on a drive through the Flint Hills. I immediately fell in love with the prairie, and my first major group piece was *Grass Variations* for five dancers. While the *Edgewood Park* sketches were a good starting point, the tall grasses of Kansas gave me a cornucopia of new motions and a new political cause: Save the Prairie!

Figure 19. Joan Stone, Guerilla Dancer.

Notes

Chapter One: Dances Against Comfort

1. Bertolt Brecht, "Praise of Learning," Selected Poems, trans. H. R. Hays (New York: Grove Press, 1959), 93. Changed slightly to fit the context.
2. "Johnny I Hardly Knew Ye," lyrics by Joseph B. Geoghegan, was first published in England in 1867. It is a much grimmer version of the American Civil War song, "When Johnny Comes Marching Home," sung to the same tune.
3. Wang Ts'an (177-217 A.D.), excerpt from "Poem of Seven Sorrows." The translation I used came from a Peace Calendar (New York: War Resisters League, April 3-10, 1966).
4. The statement of Paul Valéry (1871-1945), "War: a massacre of people ... " was widely circulated during the Vietnam War period and still appears on English and French websites, but none of them give a printed source.
5. Tuli Kupferberg, "Kill for Peace." The Fugs. ESP-Disk, 1966.
6. Statement by President Lyndon B. Johnson, September 25, 1964.
7. Brecht, "When the Leaders Speak of Peace," Selected Poems, 133.
8. John Huggins, U.S.N., "The People We Bombed Couldn't Fight Back." AIM Newsletter, 18 October 1966, 3-4.
9. Bob Dylan, "Blowin' in the Wind." The Free Wheelin' Bob Dylan. L.P. Columbia, 1963.
10. Alice Fletcher, aided by Francis La Flesche, "Peace Song," A Study of Omaha Indian Music. (Cambridge, Mass: Peabody Museum of American Archaeology and Ethnology, 1893), 39.
11. "Down by the Riverside/Ain't Gonna Study More No More" is a spiritual, the tune dating from before the Civil War. The words "ain't gonna study war no more" refer to a passage in the Old Testament: "Nation shall not lift up sword against nation, neither shall they learn war anymore." Many different lyrics have been written for the song, which was widely sung and recorded during the Vietnam War period.
12. Brecht, "Praise of Learning," Selected Poems, 93.
13. Petula Clark, "Downtown." I Know a Place. L.P. Warner Brothers, 1965.
14. Ernst Fischer, "The Power of Objects," quotes from You are what you have ... to You shall be the fairest of them all. Art Against Ideology, trans. Anna Bostock (London: Allen Lane The Penguin Press, 1969), 81.

Chapter Three: If You Don't Jump In ...

1. Shantung Chant, "A man is rich ... " William Hinton, Fanshen: "A Documentary of Revolution in a Chinese Village" (New York: Monthly Review Press, 1967), 46.
2. Juan Genovés. Hombre Solo (Man Alone), 1967. Catalogue, No. 22 (New York: Marlborough-Gerson Gallery, Inc., October-November, 1967.)
3. Brecht, "On the wall ..." Selected Poems, 142.

4. Vladimir Mayakovsky, "Back Home!," The Bedbug and Selected Poetry, trans. Max Hayward and George Reavey (Cleveland: The World Publishing Company, 1968), 187.
5. "Donna Donna," Joan Baez. Music by Sholom Secunda, Yiddish lyrics translated by Arthur Kevess and Teddi Schwartz. Vanguard, 1960.

Chapter Four: Passion

1. J. Peter Nettl, "Rosa Luxemburg." Abr. ed. (New York: Oxford University Press, 1969), 109.
2. Romain Rolland, "Beethoven the Creator," trans. Ernest Newman (New York: Dover Publications, Inc., 1964), 167-168.
3. Harris Stone, "Workbook of an Unsuccessful Architect" (New York: Monthly Review Press, 1973.)

Chapter Five: Prisoner

1. Rosa Luxemburg, "Letters from Prison" [to Sonya Liebknecht]. Trans. Eden and Cedar Paul (Berlin: Publishing House of the Young International, 1923), 32.
2. Alfred Einstein, "Mozart: His Character, His Work." Trans. Arthur Mendel and Nathan Broder (New York: Oxford University Press, 1945), 247-248.
3. Letters to Sonya Liebknecht, 32.
4. Letters to Sonya Liebknecht, 40.
5. Letters to Sonya Liebknecht, 15.
6. Plate 19, "Dance of the Dead," from Hartmann Schedel, Weltchronik, Nurnberg, 1493. Curt Sachs, "World History of the Dance." Trans. Bessie Schönberg (New York: W. W. Norton & Company, 1963).
7. Letters to Sonya Liebknecht, 21.
8. Letters to Sonya Liebknecht, 27.
9. Letters to Sonya Liebknecht, 32.
10. Letters to Sonya Liebknecht, 32.
11. Letters to Sonya Liebknecht, 15.
12. Nettl, 410.
13. Letters to Sonya Liebknecht, 56-58.
14. Rosa Luxemburg Letters to Karl and Luise Kautsky from 1896 to 1918. Editor Luise Kautsky, trans. Louis P. Lochner (New York: Robert M. McBride & Company, 1925), 204.
15. Letters to Karl and Luise Kautsky, 205.
16. Letters to Sonya Liebknecht, 63.
17. Letters to Karl and Luise Kautsky, 220.
18. Nettl, 442.

Chapter Six: Last Battle

1. James Huneker, "Chopin: The Man and His Music" (New York: Dover Publications, Inc., 1966), 167.
2. Nettl, 474.
3. Walter Benjamin, "Theses on the Philosophy of History," IX, Illuminations, trans. Harry Zohn (New York: Schocken Books, 1969), 257-258.
4. Brecht, "Burial of the Agitator in a Zinc Coffin," Selected Poems, 121-123.
5. Assemblage of quotes from Nettl, 455.
6. Brecht, "The Return," Selected Poems, 171.
7. Rosa Luxemburg Letters to Karl and Luise Kautsky, 108. Although the letter to the Kautskys is about the abortive Polish insurrection, the words apply equally to the German situation.
8. Letters to Karl and Luise Kautsky, 108.
9. Nettl, 489.
10. Nettl, 494.
11. Huneker, 168.
12. Letters from Prison to Sonya Liebknecht, 24.
13. Nettl, 485.
14. Nettl, 434.
15. Nettl, 409.
16. Nettl, 409.
17. Nettl, 226.
18. Nettl, 486.
19. Huneker, 169.
20. Letters to Karl and Luise Kautsky, 184.
21. From a letter to Leo Jogiches, with whom Rosa had an on-off relationship from her days of activism in Poland to her final days, when he devoted himself to her personal needs. Nettl, 93.
22. Nettl, 8.

Chapter Seven: Clear a Space and I'll Dance Rosa

1. "Clear Me a Space and I'll Dance" about Rosa Luxemburg was the original title. I stayed with it, until a poet suggested that I shorten it to Clear a Space and I'll Dance Rosa, which I agreed was much better.
2. Modern Times, June 15, 1971.

About Joan Stone

Joan Stone, author of *Guerilla Dancer,* participated in the American Dance Festival 1959 summer season, dedicated to the dance luminary Doris Humphries. She joined the American In¬dependent Movement (AIM) in 1966 where the union of dance and politics created the space for Joan to choreograph dances with members of the community. She both organized and invited citizens to join in the creative process and the performances themselves during the politically charged years between 1967 and 1972. Joan documented her passion for dance and social consciousness in her posthumously published manuscript, Guerilla Dancer, 2026.

Joan joined the dance faculty at the University of Kansas where she served as director of the dance division from fall 1997 through spring 2001, during which the Bachelor of Fine Arts (B.F.A.) in dance was approved. When Joan retired, the University of Kansas honored her with the title Professor Emeritus. Throughout her period living in Lawrence, Joan choreographed solo and group performances, worked with students, and led an improvisational dance group called 4,5,6 Speed-up.

www.ingramcontent.com/pod-product-compliance
Lightning Source LLC
Chambersburg PA
CBHW040741150726
48196CB00061B/1481
9781960462817